7-29 74

THE GREAT CRISIS AND ITS
POLITICAL CONSEQUENCES

THE GREAT CRISIS AND ITS POLITICAL CONSEQUENCES

Economics and Politics
1928 - 1934

by

E. VARGA

HOWARD FERTIG

NEW YORK   1974

Library of Congress Cataloging in Publication Data
Varga, Eugen, 1879-1964.
    The great crisis and its political consequences.
    Translation of Velikiĭ krizis i ego politicheskie
znacheniía.
    Reprint of the 1935 ed. published by Modern Books,
London.
    1. Economic history—1918-   . 2. World
politics—1919-1932.   3. Marx, Karl, 1818-1883. 4.
Communism. I. Title.
HC57.V355   1974   330.9'04   75-80617

Printed in the United States of America
by Noble Offset Printers, Inc.

CONTENTS

FOREWORD

This book is an endeavour to give a brief review of the period between the Sixth and Seventh Congresses of the Communist International. It is *not a history* but an analysis looking towards the future.

Such an effort is beset with particular difficulties. The crisis of the capitalist mode of production, the clash of the two systems, the imperialist antagonisms, the struggle between the bourgeoisie and the proletariat, and so on—all the factors that determine world events at present, act *simultaneously, and in every respect are interlinked* on all sides. Language, however, allows us to describe matters only in time sequence! Hence the alternative of either making constant repetitions or making an analysis, which, though incomplete at first, would be completed in the later chapters. We have chosen the second path. The book should be read and judged *as a whole.* Each separate chapter is not complete in itself.

Although we endeavoured to write *popularly, without vulgarization of course,* the first chapter will present certain difficulties to a reader not well-versed in Marxism. *A clear understanding of the peculiarities of the great economic crisis and of the special nature of the present depression is possible only on the basis of Marx's theory of crises and cycles.* Since this question is of the utmost importance to the outlook for the development of the revolution, we deemed it necessary to give this theoretical chapter at the beginning. The difficulties of this chapter should not deter the reader from reading further. Even without the first chapter the book represents a complete whole.

The analysis is made, not according to countries, but by problems. Consequently, the unevenness of development in various countries has not been reflected sufficiently. However, an exposition according to countries would require too much space and would involve too much repetition.

The book does not pretend to be complete. The problems of the economic struggle of the working class, and the strategic and tactical problems of the Communist Parties have not been dealt with. It would be overweening on our part to venture to express an opinion on this point before the convening of the Congress, which will embrace the collective experience of all Parties.

E. Varga.

Moscow, September 4, 1934.

ADDENDUM

On page 167 after the words ". . . illusions that will also disappear rapidly."

The formation of the united front between the Communists and social democrats in Spain took place in a different way in the joint heroic armed struggle (while the anarcho-syndicalists, as we know, betrayed the Spanish revolution).

After the armed uprising in Spain had been crushed, the Comintern addressed the Second International with a proposal to organise international united front activity against Spanish fascism in defence of the Spanish workers. The Second International rejected the proposal.

The movement among the workers to form the united front was, however, so strong that the *Executive Committee of the Second International, at its session in November in Paris, was unable to maintain its prohibition of the formation of the united front in various countries.* On this question—the most important of all for the fighting proletariat of the whole world—the Second International split. The social-democratic parties which are participating in bourgeois government or are preparing to do so (Great Britain, Denmark, Sweden, Belgium, Holland, etc.) still reject the united front, so as not to compromise themselves in the eyes of the bourgeoisie, nor to lose their " eligibility " for participation in the government. On the other hand, a number of social-democratic parties (France, Spain, Italy, Austria, etc.) found it necessary to issue a declaration of their special standpoint, emphasising the necessity for negotiations between the Second International and the Comintern for the formation of the united front.

It would, of course, be a dangerous illusion to imagine that the social-democratic leaders, in those countries where unity for the struggle has been formed at the present moment, will not try again to disrupt the united front when circumstances permit.

ERRATUM

P. 17 et seq. The sign " m " is used to denote surplus-value. In English " s " is more usually used, as is done in the authorised translation of *Capital*.

INTRODUCTION

Six years have elapsed since the Sixth Congress of the Communist International. Six short years sufficed to change radically the world aspect of capitalism. At that time, stabilization; now, the eve of the second round of revolutions and wars; then, prosperity; now—after four years of an unprecedentedly deep economic crisis—a depression of a special kind, without any prospect of a new prosperity phase. Then, as a result of stabilization, fresh illusions arose among the working class as to the possibility of peaceful advance within the limits of capitalism on the basis of " industrial democracy "; now, the rapidly growing recognition that there is only one way out for the proletariat : the revolutionary overthrow of the rule of the bourgeoisie. Never before has the contradiction between productive forces and production relationships stood out in such stark relief. Never before has there been such a glut of commodities alongside the misery and starvation of the working-class masses. Never before has it been so clear that the capitalist system of society must be overthrown, if mankind is to live as men!

The change that has set in during the last six years is tremendous. How presumptuous and haughty were the spokesmen of capitalism at that time! Dazzled by prosperity, they proclaimed a new and lasting advance of capitalism; they proclaimed that the capitalist system of society remained unshaken. President Calvin Coolidge, the steward of American finance capital, in his last message to Congress, December 4, 1928, at the end of his term of office, declared:

" No Congress of the United States ever assembled, on surveying the state of the Union, has met with a more pleasing prospect than that which appears at the present time. In the domestic field there is tranquility and contentment, harmonious relations between management and wage-earner, freedom from industrial strife, and the highest record of years of prosperity. . . . The great wealth created by our enterprise and industry, and saved by our economy, has had the widest distribution among our own people. . . . The requirements of existence have passed beyond the standard of necessity into the region of luxury. Enlarging production is consumed by an increasing demand at home and an expanding commerce abroad. The country can regard the present with satisfaction and anticipate the future with optimism."

The captains of American industry were no less optimistic. Charles Schwab, president of the Bethlehem Steel Corporation, stated :

I say with confidence that there has been established a foundation upon which there may be built a structure of prosperity far transcending anything we have yet enjoyed.—(" The Iron Age," November 1, 1928.)

Alfred Sloan, president of General Motors, declared [1] :

" My standpoint regarding 1929 is based on the conviction that our general economic and industrial situation is thoroughly sound; therefore I do not see why the general progress should not continue and ensure us an excellent flow of business and still increased prosperity."

[1] *The New York Times*, October 29, 1928.

At the bankers' conference in Cologne in the autumn of 1928, Jacob Goldschmidt, leader of the German finance oligarchy at the time and director-general of the Darmstädter-und Nationalbank (which finally collapsed in 1931), proclaimed the new revival of capitalism in the same proud manner :

" While the end of the capitalist age and the replacement of individualist profit economy by that of state socialism engages the attention of prophetic minds, and the idea that the present economic system of society is doomed and is to be replaced by new economic forms often haunts mankind like a hallucination, the practical management of industry, with its capitalist methods, energetically continues its advance. In spite of capital losses and the adverse atmosphere of a revolutionary period, it has erected an economic machinery upon the ruins of a lost World War, which, though far from ideal, operates for the present quite satisfactorily. Starting with an obsolete technology, it did this within the brief space of less than five years. . . ."

The leaders of Social-Democracy, the lackeys of the bourgeoisie, followed their masters in proclaiming the new rise of capitalism. Hilferding, in his articles and speeches, has supplied a " Marxist " theoretical foundation for this stand ever since 1924.

" Productive forces grew to an extraordinary degree during and after the War. This growth was not uniform : the branches of industry necessary in waging war were most highly developed . . . while industries manufacturing consumers' goods fell behind. This disproportion is one of the causes of the world crisis. But in the long run, after the overcoming of the crisis, *extension of productive capacity signifies an increase in production and a new boom.* [?] Materially widened and qualitatively changed as a result of the war period, capitalist economy appears to be *on the way to organic economy.*" [?] [2]

This glorification of the future of capitalism was linked with the counter-revolutionary theory that the *state,* ruled by coalition governments composed of Social-Democracy and the bourgeois parties, was *above all classes* and was effecting the peaceful transition from " organized capitalism " to socialism through " industrial democracy." In a book of a programmatic nature published by the German General Trade Union Federation in 1928, this theory was expounded as follows.

The development of the capitalist mode of production proceeds from the individual to the collective enterprise, from free trade capitalism to organized capitalism [the expression " monopoly " is carefully avoided]. Consequently, the contradiction between the power of the owners of the means of production and the masses of the population becomes ever greater. Hence a change in the social order must be had. In the period when capitalism was completely unfettered, it seemed that there was no other conceivable alternative for unorganized capitalism than the socialist organization of economy as a whole; it therefore seemed hopeless and purposeless to try to make any change in the despotism of the capitalist system.

" But gradually it became apparent that the structure of capitalism is changeable, and that capitalism can be *bent* before it is *broken.*"

[2] See, for example, *Die Gesellschaft,* No. 2, p. 118.

The force which is to bend capitalism in the direction of industrial democracy is the state. Industrial democracy can be achieved only through political democracy.

" Hence industrial democracy signifies the extension of political democracy through the democratization of economic relations. . . . Complete industrial democracy is identical with collective economy. . . .

" The state is a commonwealth, *i.e.*, it is a public body transcending all individuals and expressing a definite will. The essence of industrial democracy is therefore only achieved when production is no longer controlled by private individuals as private property used for private ends, but is in the hands of an economic commonwealth embodying a collective economic will, where the decisive factor is not the private use of individuals, but the collective use of the whole." [3]

How unutterably out-of-date, how foolish and ridiculous does the chatter of the Coolidges and the Goldschmidts, the Hilferdings and the Naphtalis sound to-day! And on the other hand, how true have the Marxist-Leninist analysis and prognosis made by the Communist International shown themselves to be. The Communist International was not deceived by the temporary improvement in the situation of capitalism; it fully exposed the empty chatter of capitalism's apologists. It revealed the temporary nature and the inner contradictions of capitalist stabilization, and proclaimed that these contradictions would inevitably lead to the end of stabilization in the near future, that stabilization would be followed by a new revolutionary wave!

In the middle of 1928 the Theses of the Sixth Congress of the Communist International stated that a new, third period of post-war capitalism had set in, whose essence was formulated in the Theses as follows:

" For the capitalist world the third period is a period of the rapid development of technique, of increased development of cartels and trusts, and of tendencies towards state capitalism. At the same time it is a period of the most intense development of the contradictions of world capitalism, operating in forms determined by the entire course of the general crisis of capitalism up to now (shrinkage of markets, the Soviet Union, colonial movements, growth of the inherent contradictions of imperialism). This third period, in which the contradiction between the growth of the productive forces and the shrinkage of markets has become particularly accentuated, is inevitably leading to a new phase of wars between the imperialist states, of wars against the Soviet Union, wars of national liberation against imperialism, imperialist interventions, and gigantic class struggles. This period, in which all international antagonisms are growing more acute (antagonisms between the capitalist countries and the Soviet Union, the military occupation of North China —the beginning of the partition of China—and the mutual struggles between the imperialists, etc.), in which the inherent antagonisms in the capitalist countries are coming to a head (the swing to the Left of the working-class masses, intensification of the class struggle), and in which movements develop in the colonial countries (China, India, Egypt and Syria), *inevitably*

---

[3] " *Wirtschaftsdemokratie, ihr Wesen, Wege und Ziele,*" *herausgegeben von Fr. Naphtali im Auftrag des A.D.G.B.*, 1928. [*Industrial Democracy, its Essence, Paths and Goals*, edited by Fr. Naphtali for the German General Trade Union Federation.]

*leads, through a further development of the contradictions of capitalist
stabilization, to a renewed disturbance of capitalist stabilization and to the
extreme aggravation of the general crisis of capitalism."*

The historically brief interval between the Sixth Congress and the
Seventh has furnished *practical* confirmation of the absolute truth of the
Comintern's conception and of the utter emptiness of the Social-Democrats' apologetics. The economic crisis broke out like a devastating hurri-
cane in the middle of 1929; it brought unheard-of misery to the working
masses all over the world and abruptly ended all talk about the strength
and durability of capitalist stabilization.

The cyclic crisis of 1929-33 plays a special role in the history of capitalism.

Ever since the full development of the capitalist mode of production, its
movement has proceeded in cyclic fashion. Each upward swing ended
with a violent explosion of all the contradictions of the capitalist system in
the cyclic crisis of overproduction, which, however, provided a violent
solution for these contradictions to a considerable extent. Thus cycle
followed cycle, crisis followed crisis.

Yet this repetition of cycles and crises does not denote a mechanical
addition of qualitatively equal units. Each cycle and each crisis has its
own concrete historical peculiarities; each cycle and each crisis has its
specific historical place in the history of capitalism. The change in the
nature of the capitalist system itself: the transition from industrial capitalism to imperialism and to the era of the general crisis of capitalism as
a particular stage of imperialism, likewise proceeds cyclically.

What is then the historical place of the crisis which broke out in 1929?

As Comrade Stalin pointed out at the Sixteenth Congress of the Communist Party of the Soviet Union, it is the first *world* crisis after the War,
in the period of the general crisis of capitalism. The place of this crisis in
history also determines its concrete peculiarities. It is undoubtedly a cyclic
crisis of overproduction, but by no means is it a " normal " crisis, a " mere
repetition of previous crises." Its course was greatly influenced by the
general crisis of capitalism (on the basis of which it is running its course),
by the increasingly monopolist character of post-war capitalism, by its
intertwining with the agrarian crisis (which is a part of the general crisis
of capitalism) and by the extraordinarily sharp fall in prices, which represents in part the liquidation of the excessively high price level dating back
to the World War. Other factors were the measures taken by monopoly
capital and its state for the artificial solution of the crisis, which led to considerable delay in the outbreak of the credit crisis and—in the long run—
to the prolongation and deepening of the crisis as a whole.

The final result is that the first world crisis in the era of the general
crisis of capitalism has proved to be much deeper, of longer duration and
in every respect more devastating than any of the previous cyclic crises.
This crisis also reveals some qualitatively new aspects : currency depreciation in almost all the capitalist countries, almost universal non-payment of
foreign debts, and practically complete cessation of capital export. These

are qualitatively new aspects, which were not present in any of the previous crises.

While the crisis reduced capitalist production to below the pre-war level, the development of productive forces in the Soviet Union proceeded at a tremendous pace under the Five-Year Plan. The economic crisis has strikingly demonstrated the superiority of the Soviet system to the capitalist system for all the toilers of the world. The struggle between the two systems has been decided in favour of the Soviet system in the economic, social and cultural fields. This impels the world bourgeoisie still more to seek the use of armed force, to turn the scales of battle between the two systems in its favour. . . .

The crisis has led to a very marked change for the worse in the conditions of the working class and of the toiling peasantry throughout the world, and hence to an extraordinary accentuation of class contradictions. This has had far-reaching political consequences. The influence of Social-Democracy on the working-class masses is rapidly diminishing. Under the pressure of the radicalization of the masses almost all the Social-Democratic parties are experiencing a crisis, manifested in the formation of Left and Right factions, in resignations and splits. While some of the leaders *openly* desert to the camp of the bourgeoisie and even to fascism (MacDonald and Snowden in England, the neo-fascists Marquet and Déat in France, Löbe and Severing in Germany), the revolutionary Social-Democratic workers in ever greater number seek affiliation to the Communist International, in order to close the split in the ranks of the working class and to wage a united struggle against the bourgeoisie. The crisis in the Second International is plain to all. The weakening in the influence of its main social bulwark and the growth in the influence of the Communist Parties more and more compel the bourgeoisie to brush aside parliamentary democracy, which has become a hindrance, and to take refuge in fascism—in open, violent dictatorship.

At the same time the crisis has led to a general economic war of all countries with one another, representing a kind of prelude to war itself. It has resulted in the beginning of the struggle for the violent repartition of the world in the Far East, to " small " wars in South America and Asia, and to a deliberate orientation of economic policy to the coming imperialist war and to a counter-revolutionary war against the Soviet Union. The conquest of Manchuria by Japan and the wars between Paraguay and Bolivia, between Peru and Colombia, between Ibn-Saud and Yemen, and between China and Tibet, are the forerunners of the new world war.

Thus the cyclic crisis has brought about and hastened the end of capitalism's temporary stabilization. It has caused a profound disturbance of the entire capitalist system, initiated a new and higher stage of the general crisis of capitalism and resulted in the maturing of the objective prerequisites for the revolutionary crisis.

" The tremendous strain of the internal class antagonisms in the capitalist countries, as well as of the international antagonisms, testifies to the fact that the objective prerequisites for a revolutionary crisis have matured to such an extent that at the present time the world is *closely* approaching a new round of revolution and wars." [4]

However great the suffering inflicted by the crisis on toiling mankind in the capitalist countries, and however great the role it has played in accelerating the process of the collapse of stabilization, *it would yet be theoretically and politically incorrect to regard the cyclic crisis as the cause of the end of stabilization.*

Theoretically : The Communist International never considered stabilization anything but a transient phenomenon within the enduring general crisis of capitalism, as a trough in the waves of the revolutionary movement. The same inherent causes which—together with the World War—necessarily produced the general crisis of capitalism, also led to the end of stabilization; to the maturing of a new revolutionary crisis.

The cyclic economic crisis, like all cyclic crises, was the necessary result of the most fundamental laws of capitalism. " As long as capitalism exists, cyclic fluctuations are inevitable. They will accompany it in its death throes, just as they accompanied it in its youth and maturity," state the Theses of the Third Congress of the Communist International. Therefore, we can consider the cyclic crisis only as a trigger force, as the *immediate* cause terminating the process of shattering stabilization.

Politically : If the cyclic crisis were *the* cause of the end of stabilization it would follow that, should capitalism succeed in overcoming the cyclic crisis, stabilization would be restored and a new trough in the wave of revolution would follow.

This conception would inevitably lead to opportunism, to denying the further maturing of the revolutionary crisis in the not impossible event of some delay in the outbreak of the next world war.

---

[4] *Theses and Decisions* of the Thirteenth Plenum of the E.C.C.I on " Fascism, The Danger of War and the Tasks of the Communist Parties," p. 5.

CHAPTER I
THE ECONOMIC BASES OF BUSINESS CRISES

T H E major feature of the six years that have elapsed between the Sixth and the Seventh Congresses of the Communist International is the economic crisis, which occupies almost the whole interval. Three periods may be *roughly* distinguished; we shall fix the dividing lines between them somewhat arbitrarily.

(a) From the middle of 1928 to the middle of 1929, when the industrial production of the world was still on the upgrade, but the commodities produced could not be marketed completely, when stocks were accumulating and the crisis was already beginning in some countries.

(b) From the middle of 1929 until approximately the end of 1933—the actual crisis phase in the strict sense of the term, which reached its nadir approximately in the middle of 1932.

(c) From 1934 on—the phase of the " depression of a special kind," which, though differing from the crisis in the dynamics of industrial production, of price formation, etc., nevertheless represents a continuation of the crisis in its social and political effects, and—for the present at least—offers no basis for a further prosperity phase.

We shall deal only with the crisis and the depression; the period between the middle of 1928 and the middle of 1929 not requiring any special analysis. Before proceeding to a *concrete* analysis of the crisis, however, we shall make one or two theoretical observations by way of a preface.

THE APOLOGISTS OF CAPITALISM DENY THE INEVITABILITY OF CRISES

For a hundred years bourgeois political economists have tried in vain to solve this question : Why does every prosperity phase end in a crisis? Just when profit-making seems to be in full swing, why does overproduction, with no market for commodities, suddenly occur?

Bourgeois political economy always poses the problem as follows : the production of every commodity also creates a corresponding purchasing power for the purchase of this commodity. The value of the raw and auxiliary materials is paid to their respective producers. The increase in value arising in the process of manufacture is divided into wages paid the workers and the capitalists' profit. Therefore no new value can be produced without at the same time creating the purchasing power for its sale. Putting it differently : the total purchasing power of society equals the total value of the commodities produced. The anarchy of capitalist production, its lack of planning, may lead to disproportions; too much may be produced of *one* or of *several* kinds of commodities. But in this case, *too little* must have been produced of other commodities, in relation to the purchasing power of society. A simultaneous overproduction of *all* commodities is therefore impossible. The causes of crises are disproportions, which arise *accidentally* but do not follow from the nature of the capitalist system of society. This, in essence, is also the opinion of Kautsky, Hilferding,[5] etc. Hence, it follows that capitalist " planned economy," " organized " state capitalism is required to prevent the outbreak of crises.

In other words progressively increasing capitalist production would be possible without any crises, provided disproportions were avoided.

More than half a century ago Marx disclosed with perfect clarity the reasons why the periodic recurrence of crises is inevitable under capitalism. The ideologists of capitalism rejected this explanation, however. The bourgeois economists and the revisionist wing of the Social-Democrats did so openly. The Centrists: Kautsky, Hilferding, Bauer, etc.—whom Rosa Luxemburg mordantly called the "Apostles of Harmony"—did lip-service to Marx, called themselves Marxists, and still do so to the present day, but they distorted and falsified the theory of Marx to such an extent that nothing was left of its revolutionary content.

The reason for their rejection is that Marx's theory of crises is indissolubly connected with his theory of the historically transient nature of capitalism and the inevitability of its revolutionary collapse through the struggle of the proletariat. Marx's theory of revolutionary collapse—the correctness of which has been proved in practice by the Russian Revolution and by the building of socialism in the Soviet Union—is unacceptable to the various champions of capitalism.

" I believe I am . . . in full agreement with the theory of Karl Marx, *to whom a theory of collapse is always wrongly ascribed.* Precisely the second volume of *Capital* shows how *progressively increasing production* is possible within the capitalist system. I have often thought that *it is not such a bad thing that this second volume is so little read, since under certain circumstances a pæan to capitalism might be construed out of it.*"

This is how Hilferding expressed himself before an intimate, purely bourgeois circle at the Vienna Conference of the Union for Social Policy.[6] No wonder that the minutes at this point read : " Laughter and applause; cries of ' Hear, hear.' " However, he who denies Marx's theory of revolutionary collapse must needs either deny his theory of crisis or falsify it in an opportunist fashion.

THE THEORY OF CRISES AND THE REVOLUTIONARY COLLAPSE OF CAPITALISM

Marx was the first to make clear the course of the process of capitalist reproduction and circulation. The value of all capitalistically produced commodities consists of three factors : *constant capital* : *c* (machinery, raw and auxiliary materials), which *does not increase in value* during the process of production, but transfers its value to the newly produced commodities (machinery, buildings, the " fixed " part of constant capital, transfer only part of their value, corresponding to their depreciation, to the com-

---

[5] In *Finanzkapital* [*Finance Capital*], page 318, Hilferding wrote: " . . . at the same time these formulæ of Marx show that in capitalist production, both simple and progressively increasing reproduction may proceed undisturbed, provided these proportions are maintained."

[6] *Verhandlungen des Vereins für Sozialpolitik in Wien*, 1926 [*Proceedings of the Union for Social Policy in Vienna*, 1926], Leipzig, 1926, pp. 113-14. My italics.—E. V.

modities produced with their aid); *variable capital,* expended for wages: *v,* which increases in value through the exploitation of the workers; and *surplus value* : *m.*

All commodities fall into two main divisions, according to their use value :

Division I : *means of production,* which serve for further production.

Division II : *means of consumption,* which are directly consumed by capitalists and workers.[7]

All the commodities produced in capitalist society during a certain period of time, say, one year, may therefore be represented according to value and use by the following formula (omitting the portion of fixed capital which is not consumed during the given year and is to serve in production during the following year).

$$I \quad 4{,}000 \ c_1 \ + \ 1{,}000 \ v_1 \ + \ 1{,}000 \ m_1$$
$$II \quad 2{,}000 \ c_2 \ + \ 500 \ v_2 \ + \ 500 \ m_2$$

The figures taken by Marx (they may signify millions or billions in money units) are chosen arbitrarily as far as absolute magnitude is concerned. If production is to begin again or be continued on the same basis (" simple reproduction ") in the following interval of time, however, *the proportion between them is strictly determined by the use to which the commodities are put.* This is proved by the following argument :

v_1 and m_1, variable capital and surplus value in Division I, are produced in their *natural form* of means of production; they cannot serve for individual consumption, for which they are destined *socially* as wages and surplus value. They must be exchanged for goods of Division II. c_2, the value of constant capital in Division II, is produced in the natural form of means of consumption, and therefore cannot be used further in Division II as means of production. $v_1 + m_1$ of Division I must therefore exchange places with c_2 of Division II.

If, therefore, production is to be continued on the same scale, the sum of $v_1 + m_1$, viz., *variable capital plus surplus value of Division I,* must equal c_2, *the constant capital of Division II.* Only in this case of an " ideal, normal production," as Marx says, would simple reproduction, without any crises, be abstractly *theoretically* possible.

But this is *only* an abstract theoretical possibility. In actuality, even simple reproduction would also inevitably entail crises for the following reasons :

(a) Fixed capital (machinery, buildings) cannot be renewed in every enterprise, parallel with its depreciations. It must be renewed step by step, after value has been accumulated parallel with wear over a considerable period of time, which must almost inevitably lead to the disturbance of the " ideal, normal production." This particular movement of fixed capi-

---

[7] At this stage of his analysis, Marx, for the sake of simplicity, presupposes a " pure " capitalist society, composed of capitalists and workers only; he temporarily leaves out of account the existence of all pre-capitalist classes, such as toiling peasants and artisans, in order not to complicate the analysis.

tal, as Marx says, forms the " material basis " for the cyclic course of capitalist production.

" This illustration of fixed capital," he writes,[8] " on the basis of an unchanged level of reproduction, is convincing. A disproportion of the production of fixed and circulating capital is one of the favourite arguments of political economists in explaining crises. That such a disproportion can and must arise even when the fixed capital is merely preserved is new to them; that *it can and must arise on the assumption of an ideal, normal production,* of simple reproduction of the already functioning capital of society." [9]

(b) The above formula covers only *the most general* movement of commodities. Even if the general proportion ($v_1 + m_1 = c_2$) is maintained, tremendous disproportions may occur. For instance, too many ships may be produced in Division I or too much cotton goods in Division II. Overproduction in one or several *important* branches of industry leads to unsaleability of goods, to a drop in prices and wholesale bankruptcies, which, in view of the mutual intertwining of credit under capitalism, draw the other branches of industry into the crisis as well.

However, these statements of Marx as to the possibility and the necessity of crises in simple production merely serve to facilitate an understanding of the process of capitalist reproduction by means of an assumption made for the sake of greater simplicity. In reality, capitalist production increases progressively.[10] " *The capitalist process of production is at the same time essentially a process of accumulation,*" says Marx. That means that the bourgeoisie, as a class, never consumes all of the surplus value appropriated by it, but *accumulates* a part of it, which it uses for the further extension of production. Under pain of ruin, every individual capitalist is compelled by competition to convert part of his profits into capital, and to improve his means of production, in order to be able to reduce production costs. This means that :

The total value of social capital increases from year to year.

The organic composition of capital is enhanced : the distribution of capital between constant and variable capital (capital invested in means of production and that paid out in the form of wages) changes in favour of the former.

Within constant capital, there is a shift in favour of fixed capital : that part of capital invested in buildings, machinery, tools and means of transport increases at a more rapid rate than that invested in raw material.

There is a relative diminution of the total profit (tendency of the rate of profit to decline) *as well as of the wage fund,* as compared with the total value of the annual production of goods.

The " consuming power " of capitalist society *viz.,* the sum available for

[8] *Capital*, Vol. II, Chap. XX, pp. 546-47. My italics.—E. V.

[9] Quotations taken from Volumes II and III of the Kerr edition of *Capital* have been corrected in accordance with the German original because of some errors in the English version.

[10] During crises and depressions there are short periods of *simple reproduction*, but for longer periods of time increasing reproduction is the rule.

the purchase of commodities for *individual consumption*: v + (m − a) (wages plus that part of surplus value which is not accumulated but used by the capitalist class for the purpose of satisfying its personal needs) is thus constantly diminishing *in relation* to the development of capitalist production.

The distinction between the "*purchasing power*" and the "*consuming power*" of capitalist society is of the greatest importance for an understanding of crises. *The purchasing power of society is c + v + m; it tends to equal the sum of the value of the products* (without that fixed part of c, which is not used up in one year, but which, although partially depreciated and therefore diminished in value, continues to serve in the production process). Bourgeois economists always refer to this equation when they deny the possibility of *general* overproduction. The consuming power of capitalist society, v + (m − a), is only a small part of purchasing power, and with the progress of accumulation a relatively diminishing one.

This relative diminution of the consuming power of society, which is necessarily connected with the development of capitalism and which is based on the contradiction between social production and private appropriation, *poses the problem of markets in an ever acuter form, making it ever more difficult to dispose of commodities.* For in the final analysis, as Lenin says, *all means of production serve for the production of means of consumption.* The extent to which the available industrial plant can be utilised, and hence in the long run, the sale of means of production as well—the course of business in Division I—depends, at bottom, upon the sales volume of means of consumption. Productive consumption, according to Marx :

" . . . is in so far independent of individual consumption, as it never enters into the same but is nevertheless definitely limited by it, because the production of constant capital never takes place for its own sake, but solely because more of it is needed in those spheres of production whose products pass into individual consumption." [11]

References of bourgeois political economists to the fact that the corresponding purchasing power is produced together with the production of a commodity, that the total value of the products is equal to the purchasing power of society, prove to be meaningless. The limitation of the *consuming power*, its continual and inevitable relative diminution, is what decides the fate of capitalism.

The contradiction between the limited consuming power of society, and the boundless expansion drive of capital, due chiefly to the proletarian condition of the masses, must necessarily *lead to periodically recurring crises of overproduction.*

" The last cause of all real crises always remains the poverty and restriction in consumption of the masses as compared to the impulse of capitalist pro-

[11] *Capital*, Vol. III, Chap. XVIII, p. 359.

duction to develop the productive forces as if only the absolute power of consumption [12] of society were their limit." [13]

The constant relative diminution of consuming power (disregarding the cyclic course of production) compared to the development of the productive forces leads to a chronic accentuation of the contradiction between the productive power and the consuming power of capitalist society, since the individual capitalists, driven by the necessity of winning in the competitive struggle, develop the productive forces without taking the relative diminution of consuming power into consideration. This is *the economic basis for the general crisis of capitalism,* for the chronic idleness of a large part of the productive apparatus, for chronic mass unemployment.

The relative diminution of the consuming power of society does not affect capitalists and workers alike. At first the working class grows *relatively* impoverished. The value of labour power sinks in conformity with the reduction in the value of the necessities of life required to maintain the working class—a reduction due to the increase in the productivity of labour. The " necessary labour time "—the labour time during which the worker is working for himself—grows shorter and shorter, while the time during which he is working for capital grows longer and longer. The rate of exploitation rises with the rise in the productivity of labour. The proletariat receives a diminishing portion of the *value of the product,* capital getting an increasing portion. This means that v represents a relatively diminishing portion of the consuming power of capitalist society, and $(m - a)$ a relatively increasing one. To put it in popular form : even if the proletariat were to receive the value of its labour power in the form of wages, it could only purchase a continuously diminishing part of the value produced by it with these wages.

Alongside this relative impoverishment of the working class, which goes on continually under capitalism, the *absolute impoverishment of the working class* comes to the fore more and more strikingly in the period of the general crisis of capitalism. In the first place, a large proportion of the workers is chronically unemployed. Secondly, this permanent glut of the labour market enables capital, concentrated in monopolist organisations and dominating the state, to increase the intensity of labour and force down the wages of the employed workers below the value of their labour power. The relative and absolute impoverishment of the masses of the working class, with capital less able to maintain a privileged, corrupt labour aristocracy, together with the wholesale ruin of the toiling peasantry (the causes for which we shall discuss later), reinforce the subjective forces necessary for the overthrow of the rule of the bourgeoisie, for the revolutionary collapse of capitalism.

The Marxist-Leninist theories of periodic crises, of the general crisis of capitalism and of its revolutionary collapse, are thus indissolubly connected. Although Marx's theory of crises is patently correct, the defenders

[12] Marx uses " absolute power of consumption " in the sense of the consuming power of a socialist society freed of the fetters of capitalism.

[13] *Capital,* Vol. III, Chap. XXX, p. 568.

of capitalism—both bourgeois and Social-Democratic—must either reject or distort this theory because acknowledging it entails recognition of the inevitability of capitalism's revolutionary collapse.

ACCUMULATION AS THE CAUSE OF THE CYCLIC COURSE OF CAPITALIST PRODUCTION

Anarchy of production, " lack of plan," is the constant *prerequisite* for economic crises. The contradiction between social production and private appropriation is the *ultimate cause* of crises. This contradiction manifests itself in the constant conflict between the limited dimensions of consumption on a capitalist basis, its continual relative shrinkage, and a production that is always exceeding these limits.

The question now arises : why is there permanent overproduction in capitalism under these circumstances? Why, as Marx says, are there no *" permanent"* crises? Why, until now, have crises, depressions, revivals and prosperity phases followed each other in regular sequence?

The answer to this question is not only of economic but also of revolutionary and political importance. The exceptional depth and acuteness, the unusually long duration of the economic crisis of 1929-33 has caused many comrades to believe—to an even greater extent than during the first post-war crisis—that there is absolutely no way out of this cyclic crisis. At that time Lenin,[14] and now Stalin[15] resolutely opposed this conception, which must inevitably lead to the theory of the *automatic collapse* of capitalism and to opportunist passivity on the part of the proletariat.

The cause of the cyclic course of capitalist production is the accumulation of capital. The accumulation of capital in its *real*[16] form signifies an extension of the purchasing power of capitalist society, an enlargement of the capacity of capitalist markets to absorb commodities. *It is the immediate motive force behind revival and prosperity, but on a higher plane it is also the immediate cause of crises.* Once the process of real accumulation in the prosperity phase has reached a certain stage, *a change of quantity into quality occurs.* The role of accumulation changes abruptly. Hitherto the basis for the boom, it now becomes the immediate cause of the crisis.

Let us explain this in greater detail :

Competition, as we have already explained, compels every capitalist enterprise, " under pain of ruin," to reduce its cost of production. One of the chief means to this end is *increasing the productivity of labour* : enlarging and improving the machinery operated by one worker, " technical progress." In other words, the *real accumulation* of fixed capital, of that part of constant capital (buildings, machinery, apparatus, tools) which successively transfers its value to the product in the repeated turnovers of

[14] Lenin, " *Left-Wing* " *Communism, an Infantile Disorder.*

[15] Stalin, *Report at the Seventeenth Congress of the Communist Party of the Soviet Union.*

[16] We distinguish between " *real* " accumulation, *i.e.*, an increase in the value of social capital in its productive form (buildings, machinery, raw materials, finished products) and *accumulation in the form of loan capital* (deposits in banks and savings banks) which represents only formal, potential accumulation of capital.

circulating constant capital, while it continues to function in its natural form in the production process until its natural or *moral* depreciation.

" . . . this cycle of connected turnovers, comprising a number of years, in which capital is imprisoned by its fixed component, furnishes a material basis for periodic crises, in which business goes through successive periods of lassitude, medium activity, precipitate rush and crisis. The periods in which capital is invested are indeed very different and disperse. *But a crisis is always the starting point of a large new investment,* therefore also—from the point of view of society—more or less of a new material basis for the next turnover cycle." [17]

Only on rare occasions do these elements of fixed capital serve in the production process up to the point of their *natural* wear. The capitalists' efforts to reduce the cost of production, which are dictated by competition, force them to renew their fixed capital, to instal new, more efficient machines in place of the old ones, although the latter are still capable of functioning. The renewal of fixed capital is usually begun in the phase of depression (" a crisis is always the starting point of a large amount of new investments "), is *expanded* in the revival phase, reaches its *climax* in the prosperity phase, and stops almost completely with the outbreak of the crisis.

This peculiar movement of fixed capital forms the material basis for the cyclic course of capitalist production, but is not its cause. It is not actual wear, nor technological progress that determines when fixed capital is to be renewed wholesale; it is the cyclic course of reproduction that decides when the available fixed capital is regarded as morally worn out and is to be renewed on a large scale. The cause of the cyclic movement is accumulation, one form of which is the expansion of fixed capital.

As long as accumulation is in full swing, in the phases of revival and prosperity, it enlarges the *purchasing power* of capitalist society together with the production of commodities in Division I. In these phases, sales present no difficulties, since the capitalists themselves are the principal purchasers of one another's commodities.

" That the development of production (and hence of the inner market) takes place chiefly in the field of the means of production seems paradoxical and doubtless contains a contradiction within itself. This is a real ' production for production,' an expansion of production without a corresponding expansion of consumption. However, this is not the contradiction of a doctrine, but rather of actual life; precisely a contradiction corresponding to the very nature of capitalism and to the rest of the contradictions of this system of social economy." [18]

Accumulation, the expansion of production by increasing the means of production, denotes not only an expansion of purchasing power, but also entails a certain temporary expansion of the consuming power of society. The expansion of production in Division I is accompanied by an increase

---

[17] *Capital,* Vol. II, Chap. VIII, p. 211. My italics.—E. V.

[18] Lenin, *Collected Works,* Russian edition, " The Development of Capitalism in Russia," Vol. III, p. 31.

in the number of workers employed and in the variable capital of this division; the consuming power of the proletariat is raised. The increase in the number of employed workers—provided the rate of exploitation remains the same—is accompanied by a growth in the total surplus value, and consequently in the demand for consumers' goods on the part of the capitalists of Division I. Hence, larger sales and increased production in Division II, an increase in its variable capital, in its surplus value and in consumption by workers and capitalists in that division. At the same time, Division II renews its fixed capital to an increased degree, and gives orders to Division I, thus raising the latter's production still further. Revival mounts to the stage of prosperity. The capitalists can see no reason why this should end in a crisis. . . .

But accumulation is a two-sided dialectical process. As long as the process is going on, its effect is to expand the purchasing power of capitalist society and, within the limits of this society, its consuming power as well. But at the same time the ultimate effect of accumulation is to accentuate the contradiction between the productive and consuming power of capitalist society, since of necessity it reduces the consuming power of capitalist society still further, relatively speaking. This follows from the nature of accumulation. It signifies a higher organic composition of capital, a rise in the productivity of labour through the application of improved and larger machinery, a decrease in v compared to c, the tendency of the rate of profit to sink, and the reduction of the consuming power of society : $v + (m - a)$, relative to the productive power of capitalist society, which grows rapidly just because of real accumulation.

Accumulation thus gives rise to two contradictory processes; on the one hand, expansion of the purchasing power of society and (as a part of the same) of consuming power, as far as the latter's absolute magnitude is concerned; on the other hand, a relative decrease in the consuming power of society compared to its productive power.

Thus, as Marx says, accumulation means continual relative overproduction.

" . . . *that relative overproduction which is in itself identical with accumulation* . . . *takes place in agriculture as well as in all other capitalistically operated branches of production.* . . ." [19]

or elsewhere :

" . . . But the entire process of accumulation consists at first of *surplus production*, which . . . forms an inherent basis for the phenomena manifested in crises." [20]

This is why the revival and prosperity caused by real accumulation cannot last for ever. In the process of social reproduction the means of production serve to produce consumers' goods. As *means of production,* they can serve this purpose alone. (For the capital which produces means of production the object is of course the appropriation of profit.) Therefore,

[19] Marx, *Capital,* Vol. III, Chap. XXXIX, p. 786. My italics.—E. V.

[20] Marx, *Theorien über den Mehrwert* [*Theories of Surplus Value*], Vol. II, Part II, p. 263.

in the final analysis, the production of means of production is limited by the consuming power of capitalist society. The relative decrease in consuming power caused by accumulation must therefore sooner or later put an end to the expansion of production. *The phase of prosperity must lead to a crisis,* which temporarily puts an end to the process of real accumulation.

It is this function of accumulation to diminish consuming power comparatively which caused Marx to identify it expressly as " relative overproduction."

To put it more simply : prosperity continues as long as the process of real accumulation is in full swing, as long as new factories, harbours, railways are built, and old machines are replaced by new ones. But as soon as this process reaches a certain conclusion, after a considerable number of new production plants have been completed, the demand for the commodities of Division I (building materials, machinery, etc.) diminishes, entailing a drop in the demand for consumers' goods as well, since the workers in Division I are becoming unemployed. At the same time, the supply of commodities increases, since the new and the reconstructed factories begin to pour goods into the market. Overproduction already exists, but the open outbreak of the crisis is delayed, since the capitalists (who never believe that a prosperity phase will come to an end) are producing for inventory. But production exceeds consumption to an ever greater extent, until the crisis bursts into the open.[21]

*   *   *   *   *

Glancing back in the light of the foregoing over the course of the industrial cycle in the post-war period, we find the following :

(a) The first post-war crisis of 1920-21 was not a "normal" crisis of overproduction. During the World War, as a result of the tremendous unproductive consumption of the armies and the devastation of large territories, consumption in Europe exceeded production. The tremendous accumulation of fictitious capital (war loans) was accompanied in reality by a " disaccumulation " of capital; at the end of the war, machines were worn out (with the exception of munition plants newly built during the war), stocks of commodities and raw materials were far below normal, the soil was exhausted, houses were out of repair, etc. This devastation of the productive forces led to a general impoverishment and underproduction. " The present crisis in Europe is a crisis of underproduction," the Theses of the Third Congress declare. There was underproduction in the belligerent countries of Europe combined with overproduction in the neutral and overseas countries.

(b) This great demand for means of production in Europe, brought about by the war, made it possible to overcome the first post-war crisis *quickly.* Rapid reconstruction of production plants was begun, largely

---

[21] In this chapter we deliberately treat the problem of crises in a greatly simplified and incomplete manner. The crisis involves the outbreak and the temporary solution of *all* the contradictions of capitalism. We have only emphasized those which are of particular importance for the *present* situation.

financed by American loans, and this formed the economic basis for the revival and the period of prosperity. *But is was precisely this wholesale renewal of fixed capital, coupled with a great increase in the intensity of labour (" rationalization ") which led to an exceptional accentuation of the contradiction between productive power, expanding by leaps, and consuming power, extremely restricted as a result of rationalization.* In other words, this led to a particular accentuation of the problem of markets. The general crisis of capitalism grows deeper. The bourgeoisie is incapable of utilizing the productive forces it has created. Hence, growing, chronic, wholesale unemployment, growing idleness of production plant and the exceptional depth, acuteness and long duration of the industrial crisis.

(c) The surplus of production plant (together with the chronic agrarian crisis) is the principal economic basis for the special character of the present depression. The inner forces of capitalism were sufficient to overcome the lowest point of the crisis and to effect a transition to the phase of depression; but a revival and a prosperity period are impossible without real accumulation on a large scale, *i.e.,* without the renewal and expansion of fixed capital. The surplus of unutilized production plant, which existed even before the crisis, represents a serious hindrance to the investment of capital in new means of production.[22]

Thus the contradiction between the development of productive power and consuming power in capitalist society, which necessarily grows more acute, determines to an ever increasing extent the course of the industrial cycle and forms the economic basis for the accelerated maturing of the revolutionary crisis.

---

[22] In a later chapter we shall deal in greater detail with the special character of the depression.

CHAPTER II
THE GREAT CRISIS OF 1929-33

E A C H cyclic crisis occupies a particular place in the history of capitalism. Each crisis possesses its own features which differ from those of all previous crises.[1] Therefore the outline of the *general foundations* of the cyclic course of the process of capitalist production given in the previous chapter is by no means sufficient for an understanding of the great crisis of 1929-33 in its manifold concrete aspects. *In making a concrete analysis, it is necessary to omit some of the methodological simplifications* which Marx made in order to render the general causes of the crisis more understandable, and on the other hand to introduce the new circumstances created by the development of capitalism.

(a) In his general analysis Marx starts with the assumption of a " pure " capitalism—a society composed of only two classes—the bourgeoisie and the proletariat. In reality, however, the majority of the world's population, down to the present day, consists of "*Independent producers*"— peasants and artisans. The peasantry is one of the most important purchasers of the commodities of capitalist industry. The produce of peasant agriculture becomes a component part of constant capital in the form of raw material, and serves to feed the workers. Peasant agriculture and capitalist industry are interwoven. And although capital penetrates into agriculture more and more, subjugating the peasantry and exploiting it in the most varied ways, the state of peasant agriculture is, nevertheless, an important factor affecting the course of individual cyclic industrial crises. Good conditions in agriculture mitigate crises; an agrarian crisis like the present one intensifies and accentuates them.

(b) *Marx regards all of capitalist society as " one nation," and the capitalist market as an integral " world market."* At this stage of his analysis he disregards the fact that capitalist society is organized in separate territories divided by state frontiers, as well as the differences between "home" and " foreign " markets. In analysing individual crises, and especially the last crisis, we must pay particular attention to the subdivision of capitalist society into separate states which isolate themselves from each other more and more. This has led to an unprecedented shrinkage of international trade, to the collapse of the " world market " in the old sense of the word, to an exceptionally intense struggle for every sales opening in the world market, to the disintegration of the international system of credit, etc.

(c) The economic theory of Marx in general, and his theory of crises in particular, are based upon industrial capitalism, *upon the capitalism of free competition.* Present-day capitalism, however, is *monopoly* capital-

[1] Marx based his theory of crises on a concrete analysis of all the details of the crises of 1848 and 1858. This is proved by his footnotes in *Capital* and in *Theorien über den Mehrwert* [*Theories of Surplus Value*], his correspondence with Engels and the enormous collection of quotations and figures to be found in the Marx-Engels Institute.

ism—imperialism. The monopolist character of capitalism, which necessarily evolves out of free competition through concentration of capital as a result of accumulation and centralization, limits the consuming power of capitalist society and hence the absorbing capacity of the market in general still further. Monopoly denotes the sale of commodities *above* their price of production (cost price plus average profit). The continuous " normal " shifts in the division between capital and labour, between the bourgeoisie and the proletariat of the *new* value created annually, the increase in m at the expense of v—shifts which are occasioned by the rise in the productivity of labour—are supplemented by a new element in the development of capitalism : monopoly profit, the *artificial* rise of the share of monopoly capital in the total profit at the expense of the income of the smaller capitalists and the " independent producers " still operating. At the same time, within the bourgeoisie, there is a shift in favour of the narrow inner circle of the finance oligarchy. The consuming power of capitalist society and hence, in the final analysis, the absorbing capacity of the entire capitalist market are still further limited by the rise of monopolies.

The reasoning of bourgeois economists that solely the absolute magnitude of the newly produced value determines consuming power (with distribution between the bourgeoisie and the proletariat and, within the bourgeoisie, between the finance oligarchy, the middle and petty bourgeoisie, of no significance) is incorrect, as we have explained above. All of v, the total income of the proletariat, is consumed individually, expended for the commodities of Division II. Only a part of the total m, the income of the bourgeoisie, is consumed individually, while another portion is accumulated. An increasingly large part of m, of the total income of the bourgeoisie, is taken by the narrow circle of the finance oligarchy, and a relatively smaller part—notwithstanding the insane luxury indulged in by these topmost monopolist exploiters—is spent on commodities of Division II.

Monopoly capital, as an employer, is in a particularly strong position against the working class. This enables it to force wages down below the value of labour power, directly by wage cuts and indirectly by means of increases in the monopoly prices of those commodities which are consumed by the workers.

Monopoly profit does not arise exclusively from the *sale* of commodities controlled by the monopolies at prices higher than their cost of production, but also from the *purchase of raw materials and other goods at monopoly prices which are lower than the cost of production.* In purchasing agricultural products from the peasants and industrial goods from the artisans, home workers and small capitalists, monopoly capital appropriates part of the value by purchasing at prices which in many cases do not leave the independent producers even a wage worker's income. This reduces the consuming power of these groups still further.

With the development of the monopolist character of capitalist society, the latter's consuming power diminishes more and more, relatively speaking, and since *in the final analysis* the magnitude of consuming power also determines the magnitude of *purchasing power,* the contradiction between the production and marketing possibilities grows greater and greater and the problem of markets more and more insoluble.

Monopoly capital, however, restricts the *purchasing power* of capitalist society, not only indirectly through the restriction of consuming power, but directly as well. Sales at monopoly prices are possible only when the supply of monopolist commodities to the market is restricted. To ensure this, the development of production must be retarded and the construction of new production plant in the monopolist branches of industry must be adapted to the sales artificially limited by high prices.

Hence a new contradiction arises in monopoly capital. The endeavour to restrict the supply of commodities in order to maintain high prices tends to prevent the expansion of production. On the other hand, the drive to *lower the cost of production prompts the erection of new, technically more perfect plants, necessarily entailing expansion of production capacity.* (We must never forget that monopoly does not eliminate competition, that sharp competition exists with the outsiders in a given branch of industry, as well as competition among monopolies whose goods may serve as a substitute for each other, and among the various monopolies for the " consumer's dollar," *i.e.,* for their commodity's share as use value in the total consumption of society.)

The net result is that cyclic crises *under monopoly capitalism are much deeper and more acute than under free competition capitalism.* The thesis advanced by Hilferding in his *Finance Capital, viz.,* that crises grow milder in the period of imperialism is absolutely untrue. *This thesis* is based on Hilferding's false fundamental concept : that crises are caused solely by the involved nature of the market and the resulting disproportions. He fails to see that the fundamental cause of crisis lies in the contradiction between social production and private appropriation, as expressed in the contradiction between productive power and consuming power, which must lead to *periodic overproduction of all commodities.* He mechanically differentiates between the consuming power of society and the proportionality of the various branches of industry.

" ' The consuming power of society and the proportionality of the various branches of industry ' are by no means separate, independent, disconnected factors," according to Lenin. " On the contrary, a certain status of consumption is one of the elements of proportionality." [2]

Since Hilferding assumes that competition dies out and the market becomes " easier to survey " with the development of the monopolist nature of capitalism, he concludes that crises grow weaker,[3] whereas they

[2] Lenin, *Collected Works,* Russian edition, Vol. II, p. 400.

[3] In his programmatic article, *Problems of the Time,* in the first number of *Gesellschaft* (1924), Hilferding wrote :

" .   .   .   A transition takes place from free competition capitalism to organised capitalism. Parallel with it there develops conscious order and management of industry which endeavours, on a capitalist basis, to overcome the inherent anarchy of free competition capitalism. If this tendency could assert itself without hindrance . . . crises, or at least their effects upon the workers would be mitigated . . . employment becomes more steady, unemployment grows less menacing and its consequences are mitigated by insurance. . . ."

must grow more and more acute under monopoly capitalism according to the correct Marxist-Leninist theory. The concrete analysis of individual crises in the era of imperialism fully confirms this.

(d) Marx developed his theory of crises on the basis of a rising capitalism which was expanding at a rapid pace, intensively and extensively. *The great crisis of 1929-33 developed on the basis of the general crisis of capitalism, and this accounted for its special nature.*[4]

Ten years sufficed to prove conclusively the absolute baselessness of this allegedly " Marxist " analysis.

We cannot make an exhaustive analysis of the general crisis at this point.[5] We must limit ourselves to those aspects that are of greatest importance in their effects upon the industrial crisis.

(a) *The blows to the capitalist system of society,* manifested in the existence and flourishing progress of the Soviet Union on a socialist basis, in the existence of Soviet China, in the expansion and intensification of the colonial revolutionary, anti-imperialist movement, and in the maturing of the revolutionary crisis in the capitalist countries, which are bringing closer the beginning of a second round of revolutions, are generating a feeling of general insecurity and are making new capital investments and long-term enterprises rather difficult all over the world.

(b) *The contradiction between productive forces and production relationships in the capitalist world is always of an acute nature.* This manifests itself in the chronic narrowness of the market under capitalism, leading to a sharp fight for every sales opportunity and to such an accentuation of imperialist antagonisms as to bring us close to the second run of wars. Capital's manœuvring possibilities are thus considerably restricted. The chronic narrowness of the market manifests itself economically in the following way :

(1) *The chronic agrarian crisis* permanently reducing the agricultural population's purchasing power for industrial commodities.

(2) *The chronic surplus of capital,* particularly of industrial capital (permanent idleness of large portions of the production apparatus[6]), as well as of trading capital ("congested trade ") and of loan capital (except during the acute phase of the credit crisis).

(3) *Chronic mass unemployment,* which differs from the industrial reserve army of the industrial capitalism era in that it does not disappear even in the prosperity phase, growing bigger and bigger (if we disregard the cyclic movement).

These are the major aspects of the general crisis of capitalism which determine the exceptional depth, intensity and duration of the great crisis of 1929-33.

[4] The crisis of 1920-21 also occurred in the period of the general crisis of capitalism, but as already mentioned its specific nature was determined principally by the effects of the war.

[5] See *Program of the Communist International,* Stalin's Report to the Sixteenth Congress of the C.P.S.U., and the symposium, *The General Crisis of Capitalism* (in Russian).

[6] The production capacity of German industry, taking 48 hours a week as a basis, was utilized only 67.4 per cent. in 1929, and only 35.7 per cent. in 1933.

THE DEPTH OF THE CRISIS

Let us take the decline of industrial production as a measure. A comprehensive index is available for Germany only.

CHANGES IN THE INDUSTRIAL OUTLOOK OF GERMANY ACCORDING TO CYCLES [7]

Boom Year	Year of Lowest Point of Crisis	GENERAL INDEX			MEANS OF PRODUCTION			CONSUMERS' GOODS		
		Boom Year	Crisis Year	Per Cent. Change	Boom Year	Crisis Year	Per Cent. Change	Boom Year	Crisis Year	Per Cent. Change
1865	1866	15.9	16.0	+0.6	12.4	12.4	0.0	26.0	26.3	+1.2
1872	1874	22.9	21.5	−6.1	17.6	16.9	−4.0	38.0	34.3	−9.7
1885	1886	32.2	32.7	+1.6	27.7	28.3	+2.2	45.0	45.1	+0.2
1891	1892	41.4	40.0	−3.4	35.5	33.8	−4.8	58.0	57.7	−0.5
(1898)	(1900)									
1900	1901	64.7	64.9	+0.3	62.1	61.1	−1.6	75.0	72.2	−3.7[8]
1906	1908	34.3	78.8	−6.5	83.0	76.0	−8.4	89.2	87.0	−2.5
1922	1923	71.4	46.9	−34.4	70.7	43.4	−38.6	76.3	58.8	−22.9
1929	1932	103.1	61.2	−40.6	103.0	48.4	−53.0	106.2	79.4	−25.3

This table illustrates our foregoing statements most clearly:

(a) *In the era of industrial capitalism,* when German capitalism was developing rapidly, the crises in the decisive sphere of production was very mild. *During three crises there was no* decline in industrial production at all, merely a slackening in the rate of growth.

(b) In the era of industrial capitalism, when the development of productive forces was not yet limited by monopolies, the decline in the production of means of production was *not* greater than that in the production of consumers' goods, but less.

(c) *In the era of imperialism,* and particularly in the period of the general crisis, the rate of decline in industrial production during the crisis suddenly increases. At the same time the centre of gravity of the crisis shifts to Division I, as a result of the effect of monopoly and of the surplus of means of production that characterizes the general crisis.

(d) *In depth the last crisis by far surpasses all its predecessors;* the production of means of production, in particular, has dropped more than half, whereas the production of consumers' goods has declined only 25 per cent.

No general indexes calculated on this basis are available for other countries. We use as substitutes the data available for long periods of time for the *older* industries. The following table shows the *percentage decline[9] from the year of prosperity to the lowest crisis year.*

[7] Calculated by the " Institut für Konjunkturforschung " [Institute for Business Research] of Berlin.

[8] The figures refer to the years 1898 and 1900. The crisis began earlier and ended earlier in Division II, hence, the general index shows a rise whereas the two partial indexes, each separately, show a drop.

[9] The figures have been compiled by the Economic Research Section of the Institute of World Economy and World Politics, Moscow.

UNITED STATES OF AMERICA
DECLINE OF PRODUCTION IN PER CENT.

	Coal	Iron	Steel	Cotton Consumption
1857-58	1.7	20.2	—	27.4
1865	+0.5 (rise)	17.9	—	—
1874-75	9.1	27.0	+8.5 (rise)	9.6
1884-85	7.5	12.5	10.7	15.4
1893-94	6.4	27.3	18.4	19.8
1907-08	13.4	38.2	40.0	8.9
1920-21	27.5	54.8	53.0	20.0
1929-33	41.7	79.4	76.3	31.0

In essence this table reveals the same dynamics as those prevailing in Germany. The enormous decline in the output of steel and iron, the typical raw materials in the production of means of production, is particularly striking in the last crisis. The picture presented by *England* and *France* is somewhat different. In *England* the percentage decline in production was less in the present crisis than in the first post-war crisis. This is due to the fact that the general crisis is particularly acute in England; therefore, there was no real upswing there in the years 1928-29. In France, on the other hand, the crisis of 1920-21 was relatively mild (the decline in the general index of industrial output was only 11 per cent. as compared with 31 per cent. in the recent crisis), because the reconstruction of the devastated areas created a big special market for industry. But this unevenness in the case of individual countries does not alter the fact that the world crisis of 1929-33 was by far the deepest crisis in the history of capitalism!

Decisive for the exceptional depth of the last crisis was the chronic surplus of means of production, which has hit Division I particularly hard on a *world* scale, as the following table shows :

INDEX OF WORLD INDUSTRIAL PRODUCTION [10]
(1928 = 100)

	1913	1929	1930	1931	1932	1933
Means of production ...	69	110	96	82	62	75
Consumers' goods ...	81	105	98	91	89	96

In 1932, the lowest crisis year, *the output in Division I dropped some 10 per cent. below the 1913 level,* whereas the output in Division II *was still about 10 per cent. above the level of 1913.*

[10] Includes the Soviet Union. No statistics for the capitalist world, without the Soviet Union, are available for 1932-33. The figures are as follows for the previous years :—

	1913	1929	1930	1931
Means of production	69	109	94	78
Consumers' goods	81	104	93	92

As we may see by a comparison of the figures for 1931, *the inclusion of the U.S.S.R. affects the world index considerably in favour of Division I.*

Figures from the Institute für Konjunkturforschung, Special Issue No. 31, p. 67; for 1932-33, Weekly Report No. 27, July 14, 1934.

The decline in production according to divisions in the most important countries in 1932 is given in the following table.

INDEX OF INDUSTRIAL PRODUCTION IN 1932
(1928 = 100)

	U.S.A.	Germany	England	Poland	France	Japan
Division I ...	48.2	50.2	85.3	49.4	80.0	99.5
Division II ...	81.3	77.7	90.5	61.6	64.0	110.3

These figures reveal great inequalities among the different countries. The decline in the output of means of production was greatest in the *U.S.A.* and *Germany,* the two countries where the industrial production apparatus, as a result of rationalization, was the most modern and the most strongly developed prior to the crisis (in Poland the lack of capital and the complete cessation of capital imports played a great role). *France* occupies an exceptional position throughout the entire crisis : its decline in Division I was always less than in Division II. The most important reasons for this were : the late beginning and the lesser extent of rationalization before the crisis; large-scale construction of fortifications, harbours and canals during the crisis; and the importance of its luxury industries in Division II, which were particularly hit by the crisis. In *England* the decline in production was generally less because production was already at a very low level in 1928, which is taken as a basis. In *Japan* the lowest point of the crisis was reached as early as 1931.

Of the various branches of industry, the building, ship-building and machine industries suffered most under the crisis, in addition to the iron and steel industry, *i.e.,* those branches of industry chiefly producing commodities used as fixed capital. The following passage indicates the methods adopted to avoid any increase in fixed capital :

" During the last six months very few orders for machine tools were placed in Germany. They came mostly from small and medium-sized firms. The big plants and concerns have stopped all buying of production equipment. *They cover their urgent needs from the machinery inventory of the plant departments that are operating at less than capacity.*" [11]

Influenced by the chronic surplus of production capacity, *the production of means of production in some countries during the crisis has dropped to such an extent that output did not even cover current natural wear and tear.* Bourgeois authorities have already admitted that this holds true for 1931. Thus, the Institut für Konjunkturforschung writes in its weekly report of March 9, 1932, that :

" In 1931 the reduction of total existing plant in Germany's national economy due to current wear and tear and absolescence of old plants was much greater than the total replacement investments and the isolated cases of new investments. In other words, German national economy has been living on its capital in 1931."

11 H. Schoening, *" Die deutsche Werkzeugmaschinenindustrie,"* *Zeitschrift des Vereins Deutscher Ingenieure* [" The German Machine-Tool Industry," *Journal of the Association of German Engineers*], March 4, 1933.

The annual report of the American steel trust (United States Steel Corporation) for 1931 reads:

The average annual production during the ten years, 1922 to 1931, inclusive, was 43,000,000 tons, compared with a production of 26,000,000 tons in 1931.

It seems reasonable to suppose that on the basis of average demands in the United States for steel products during the past ten years the requirements of this country for maintenance and current uses alone, exclusive of development and expansion, should call for steel products in considerably greater tonnage than was consumed in 1931.—("Iron Age.")

But in 1932 steel output in the U.S.A. dropped to half that in 1931. It is therefore obvious that production was far from sufficient to cover current wear and tear.

In some cases the decline of fixed capital during the crisis may be ascertained directly. Let us cite two examples: *the American railways and the cotton industry.*

While American railways used over two million tons of new rails annually for replacement in the five years preceding the crisis, only 500,000 tons of rails were relaid in 1932.

The same holds true of U.S. railway rolling stock, as may be seen from the following table:

ROLLING STOCK ORDERS

	1929	1931	1932	(*Until Sept.*, 1933)
Locomotives ...	1,212	235	0	—
Passenger cars ...	2,303	11	0	—
Freight cars ...	111,000	11,000	2,000	—

Repairs of locomotives and cars were neglected to such an extent that the number of locomotives at present in operation is many thousands less than in the pre-crisis period. (Data obtained from various numbers of the *Railway Age*.)

NUMBER OF INSTALLED SPINDLES (IN MILLIONS) [12]

	August 1, 1929	*February* 1, 1933	*Decrease*	*Per cent.* *Decline*
Total capitalist world ...	156.7	148.4	8.3	5
England	55.9	48.0	7.9	14
U.S.A.	34.8	31.0	3.8	11
Germany	11.3	9.9	1.4	13

The textile industry declined in the leading capitalist countries, but in the colonial countries there was a certain expansion of the textile industry even during the crisis; the decline for the world as a whole therefore is less than in the three leading capitalist countries together.

Tonnage of sea-going vessels reveals a similar state of affairs:

[12] *International Cotton Statistics*, March, 1934.

WORLD SEA-GOING TONNAGE—MILLIONS OF GROSS TONS [13]

			Total	Steamships	Motorships
June, 1929	...	...	68.07	59.78	6.63
June, 1934	...	...	65.58	53.75	10.60
			−2.49	−6.03	+3.97

These figures, however, conceal the antagonistic and uneven nature of development. Almost 9,000,000 tons of *new* ships were completed from 1929-33, so that scrapped vessels represented approximately 12,000,000 tons. No less than 11,600,000 tons were laid up and withdrawn from service in the middle of 1933. But international competition and preparations for war forced the building of new and faster motorships. New ships totalling 1,200,000 tons were being built in the middle of 1934.

Taken by countries, the figures reveal the same uneven state of affairs as in the cotton industry.

LOSS OF TONNAGE BETWEEN THE MIDDLE OF 1929 AND 1934

(Millions of tons)

England	U.S.A.	Germany
2.43	1.48	0.4

Various small nations, on the other hand, increased their tonnage. The tendency to abandon world-wide division of labour is in evidence here just as in the cotton industry.

These facts and figures—which could be repeated *ad lib.*—disclose the exceptional depth of this great economic crisis surpassing all previous crises. Production would have dropped still lower *if not for the tremendous war preparations,* which provided certain sections of industry with orders. The decay of capitalism is clearly manifested by these facts.

THE ALL-EMBRACING NATURE OF THE CRISIS

The last crisis differs from all previous crises in its *all-embracing character,* as Comrade Stalin pointed out in his report at the Seventeenth Party Congress. In studying the history of previous crises, we find that there always were particular countries and certain branches of industry that were unaffected by them.[14] This crisis, through its link with the chronic agrarian crisis, has affected all countries: industrial as well as agrarian countries; imperialist nations and colonies; the means of production as well as consumers' goods; the production of food and raw materials; domestic and foreign trade; stock exchange and credit; all without exception!

Only those branches of industry *directly* involved in preparation for war: airplane construction, the artificial silk industry, etc., constitute an exception. Production rose in these branches of industry even during the crisis and their production capacity has been augmented by the construc-

---

13 *Monthly Bulletin of Statistics,* League of Nations, July, 1934, p. 292.

14 *Cf.* B. Thorp, *Business Annals,* New York.

tion of new plants, although the available plants are far from working at full capacity.

WORLD PRODUCTION OF ARTIFICIAL SILK IN THOUSANDS OF METRIC TONS [15]

1928	1929	1930	1931	1932	1933
17.4	20.8	20.0	23.4	24.0	30.2

Development was very uneven. In Japan the output of artificial silk increased from 750 tons in 1928 to 4,400 tons in 1933, according to estimates given by the League of Nations.

THE LONG DURATION OF THE CRISIS 1819658

The recent crisis is undoubtedly the longest in the history of capitalism. It is difficult to obtain exact comparative figures for the following reasons:

(a) The time of the open outbreak of the crisis can be fixed precisely (although the crisis matured for a long time in the form of an accumulation of unsold goods). On the other hand, the transition from the crisis to the depression phase is a process which is not clearly delimited and is interrupted by relapses. The time when the crisis—after reaching its lowest point—passes into the depression, can be determined only more or less arbitrarily. Only the interval of time between the *highest point of production and the lowest point of the crisis* can be stated accurately, but this low point does not signify the end of the crisis.

(b) For technical reasons: *no monthly* data of production, are available for the older cycles, only annual data. We will therefore confine ourselves to a few examples from the U.S.A.

U.S.A.—DURATION OF THE DECLINE IN PRODUCTION
(*in Months*)

Crisis				Iron	Coal	Building Contracts
1907-08	...	...	...	3	6	9
1920-21	...	...	...	16	4	9
1929-32	...	...	...	39	41	57

The long duration of the decline in production down to the lowest crisis point, which also determines the unusually long duration of the crisis as a whole, follows from the general crisis of capitalism, from the effect of monopolies, which endeavoured to prevent the drop in prices of their goods, and partly from the endeavours of the bourgeoisie to overcome the crisis rapidly by means of state measures which only resulted in a prolongation of the crisis.

THE PRICE DECLINE DURING THE CRISIS

With the exception of the post-war crisis the *price decline during the recent crisis was incomparably greater than* during any of the previous crises.[16] This tremendous price decline is the basis for a number of im-

---

[15] *Statistical Year Book* of the League of Nations, 1933-34.

[16] The fall in prices in previous crises amounted to approximately 10 per cent. *The great period of falling prices in the nineteenth century, from 1873 to 1896, was not of a cyclic character.* The price decline was the result of the great agrarian crisis and of the decrease in the value of capitalistically produced commodities due to technical progress, the rise in the productivity of labour, which was very great during this boom period of capitalism.

portant, qualitatively new factors in the crisis: depreciation of currencies, non-payment of foreign debts and cessation of capital export.[17] We must therefore deal at greater length with its causes.

During the crisis prices moved as follows in the major countries:

INDEX OF WHOLESALE PRICES [18]
(1913 = 100)

Annual Average		Germany	France (Gold Francs)	England (Economist)	U.S.A.	Japan
1929	... ...	137	127	127	137	166
1930	... ...	125	113	107	124	137
1931	... ...	111	102	89 [19]	105	116
1932	... ...	97	87	86	93	122 [20]
1933	... ...	93	81	87	94 [21]	136

These series *cannot be compared* with each other since various commodities or the same commodities weighted differently serve as a basis. But the *movement* of the price level is the same (allowing for the effect of inflation).

PRICE DECLINE IN PER CENT., FROM 1929 TO 1933

Germany	France	England	U.S.A.
	(Annual Average)		
32	36	31	31

Prices have dropped approximately by an equal percentage in all countries *where there was no great depreciation of the currency*. The causes of this big price decline are to be found not only in the acuteness of the crisis, but also in the following factors:

During the war the demand for commodities exceeded supply to such an extent that the prices of almost all commodities rose considerably above their value. This assertion seems to contradict one of the main theses of Marxism, according to which the price of commodities is determined by their value. However, this is not so. Under *extraordinary* circumstances, when demand exceeds supply for a long time, prices can and must rise above value. Only in general, only under " normal " conditions, are prices determined by their value.

" In so far as crises originate in changes in price and *revolutions in price* which *do not coincide with changes in the value of commodities*, they naturally cannot be considered in the analysis of capital in general, where prices identical with the values of commodities *are assumed*." [22]

[17] *The unevenness in the drop of prices* (the decline in monopoly prices was much slighter than the drop in prices of non-monopoly commodities; the drop in price of manufactured goods was slighter than that of agricultural commodities, etc.) is a special factor in accentuating antagonisms during the crisis. We shall discuss this later on.

[18] Monthly *Bulletin of Statistics*, League of Nations, No. 7, 1934.

[19] Inflation since September, 1931.

[20] Inflation since the end of 1931.

[21] Inflation since March, 1933.

[22] Marx, *Theorien über den Mehrwert* [*Theories of Surplus Value*], Vol. II, Part II, p. 289. My italics.—E. V.

Thus Marx considers that "price revolutions" are possible without changes in value. Moreover, in each cycle the actual market prices rise *above* value during the boom and fall *below* value during crises. The equality of total price and total value of commodities holds good only when averaged over the entire cycle. Marx says:

". . . in periods of prosperity, particularly during the period of a dizzy boom, in which the relative value of money, expressed in commodities, decreases . . . (without any other actual revolution in values), so that the price of commodities rises independent of their own value." [23]

Hence the detachment of price from value during the World War as a result of demand constantly exceeding supply in no way contradicts the theory of Marx. On the contrary, that is what had to happen. (Artificial price recovery effected by state measures—guaranteed minimum prices in the U.S.A. and in England—also played a role.) By the end of the World War, prices *in gold* had risen to more than twice the 1913 level. This excessive price rise was only half liquidated in the crisis of 1920-21; prices were then stabilized on this level, which was still much too high. The gold price index hovered around 150 in 1922-29, taking 1913 as 100. The reason why prices did not drop to about the pre-war level was *not* a decline in the value of gold compared with the pre-war period, since no technical innovations were introduced such as might have reduced considerably the labour time contained in the gold unit of weight. In our opinion, the reason for this lay in the fact that the level of very important elements in production costs; leases, rent, freight, officials' salaries, overhead expenses, taxes, etc., were fixed in long-term contracts, or by government decree. These excessively high factors in production costs kept prices high, although supply and demand tallied more or less. A second major crisis was required to destroy all these bonds and to adjust prices to the value of commodities, which had undoubtedly declined compared with the pre-war period (due to the increase in the productivity of labour). But this adjustment was a violent process which accentuated the crisis even more, and hence, overcoming the crisis was rendered more difficult. It undermined the entire international gold and credit system and it is one of the factors accounting for the exceptional character of the present depression.

REDUCTION OF PROFITS

Every crisis involves a decrease in the appropriated *surplus value,* since *the number of exploited workers drops sharply* and wage reductions cannot keep up with the fall in prices. The reduction in the total appropriated surplus value is tantamount to a reduction in total profits.

Furthermore, the heavy price decline results in *profits dropping even faster than surplus value.* The market price of commodities is not determined by the actual price of production, but by the price of reproduction! When the elements of constant capital—raw materials, auxiliary materials, etc.—drop in price during the process of production, the market price of the finished goods will not be governed by the actual expenditure, but by

[23] *Capital*, Vol. II, Chap. XX, p. 475.

the outlay necessary at the time of sale for purchasing raw and auxiliary materials, etc. Hence every turnover of capital ends in a loss when prices are falling rapidly. The workers are exploited, surplus value is appropriated, but there is no profit. The longer the production period the greater the loss.[24] Naturally idleness of production plant, which tangibly raises the cost of production, is also an important factor.

COMPANY BALANCES OF THE MOST IMPORTANT INDUSTRIAL COUNTRIES [25]

	U.S.A. Net profit of 433 industrial corporations (*Standard Statistics*) (1928 = 100)	*England* Profits (1924 = 100)	*Germany* Total profits in millions of marks
1929	113.5	120.1	315
1930	67.6	119.4	207
1931	28.0	92.5	116 (loss)
1932	7.0	75.8	73

We emphasize that these figures do not refer to profits in our sense of the term, but only to *employers' profit* (*i.e.*, after deducting interest, amortization and taxes). But this gives a roughly approximate picture none the less. It is probable that many corporations, whose credit was already jeopardized, " trimmed " their balances, *i.e.*, show a profit instead of the actual losses.

These summary figures conceal major inequalities. The deeper the crisis in particular branches of industry, the longer the process of production, the greater the loss. Let us take the U.S.A.[26] as an example. In 1932 employers' profits (profit after deducting interest on borrowed capital, taxes and amortization) were as follows in the most important branches of industry in the U.S.A. :

MONOPOLIES AS AGAINST CUSTOMERS AND PRODUCERS

	Number of enterprises	Capital (in millions of dollars)	Employers' profit	Per cent.
Food industry ...	41	785	44.1	5.6
Dairy produce ...	10	321	19.8	6.2
Bakeries ...	21	366	27.9	7.6
Tobacco ...	28	894	110.3	13.4

These two-edged monopolies, purchasing their raw materials from the unorganized farmers at very low prices and selling their commodities directly to the ultimate consumers, can therefore maintain prices at a high level. With a very short production period (in bakeries practically only

---

[24] The price decline, by cheapening the elements of constant capital, lowers the organic composition of capital, and therefore raises the rate of profit at the expense of a great loss of capital. But this effect is evident only after the drop in prices is over.

[25] *Vierteljahrsheft zur Konjunkturforschung* [*Quarterly Issue for Business Research*], Vol. VIII, No. 2, Part A, p. 98.

[26] Data taken from the *National City Bank Bulletin*, April, 1934.

one day), and with sales not declining very much, relatively speaking, they piled up respectable profits even during the crisis.

This does not hold true for all enterprises of Division II, however, as may be seen from the following figures:

	Losses in Millions of Dollars
Cotton industry	13.7
Wool industry	11.0
Other textile industries...	11.6

On the other hand, the heavy industry enterprises, with a longer production period and a greater decline in production, which produce their own raw materials or buy them at high monopoly prices from other monopolists, have sustained great losses in spite of their strong monopolist position.

	Number of enterprises	Capital (in millions of dollars)	Loss
Iron and Steel	51	4,030	160.9
Machinery plants	73	537	39.0
Automobile factories ...	20	1,382	40.5
Building materials ...	44	601	19.5
Copper production ...	14	450	10.7

We shall deal later with the effect of the decline in prices of agricultural produce.

THE CREDIT CRISIS AND ITS PECULIARITIES

Every crisis in the sphere of production is not without its effect in the sphere of credit. But the beginning of the credit crisis need not coincide with the outbreak of the crisis in the sphere of production. The distinguishing feature of the present crisis is that the open outbreak of the credit crisis occurred after a delay of two to three years. In Germany it broke out in the summer of 1931, while in the U.S.A. it assumed the dimensions of a catastrophe only in March, 1933. The far-reaching fusion of bank capital and industrial capital into finance capital *caused the big banks to mobilize all their resources to prevent the open outbreak of the credit crisis, which might have become very dangerous for them,*[27] as the bankruptcy of all the big German banks has shown. But the longer this outbreak was delayed in any one country, the more catastrophic were the forms assumed by the credit crisis. It was most acute in the U.S.A., where all the gold institutions had to close down in March 1933.

The violent outbreak of the credit crisis could not be prevented mainly because of the tremendous fall in prices which increased the real burden of indebtedness by 30 or 40 per cent. during the crisis.

The price decline meant a vast shift in the distribution of real income in favour of creditors (those living on income) at the expense of debtors (industrialists, peasants, house owners, artisans). Putting it otherwise: loan

---

[27] In the crises of the period of industrial capitalism, when the banks advanced credit chiefly on bills of exchange and their stake in a given debtor was relatively small, they drove their debtors into bankruptcy with less hesitation in order to save their claims.

capital in all its forms was to receive the same amount as before in interest and amortization out of total profits, which were greatly reduced by the crisis. This could not go on forever. There were three ways out:

(1) *Elementary cancellation of debts through bankruptcy.*

(2) *Depreciation of currency, thus adjusting the real debt burden to the lowered price level.*

(3) *Non-payment of debts,* both internal and foreign, *sanctioned by the state.*

The anarchic method of cancelling the intolerable portion of the debt burden through bankruptcy, which is the normal method under capitalism, could not be allowed to run its course during this crisis. The bankruptcies affected such commanding institutions of finance capital as the Darmstädter Bank, the Dresdner Bank, the Vienna Kreditanstalt, the Kreuger Match Trust in Sweden, the Insull Trust in the U.S.A., etc. Owing to the depth of the crisis and the tremendous price decline, the number of bankruptcies threatened to reach such enormous proportions as to involve the complete collapse of the credit system, and politically to endanger the hegemony of the bourgeoisie over the peasantry and the urban petty bourgeoisie. *The wave of bankruptcies had to be stopped.* This was done either through depreciating the currency or through governmental decrees reducing the interest rate and prohibiting sales at auction, etc., at home, and by moratoria on debts owed abroad. Thus the credit crisis grew into a bank crisis and a crisis of currencies.

THE DEPRECIATION OF CURRENCIES

Depreciation of the currencies of most countries is a *qualitatively new factor*, not found in any previous crisis.[28]

The general economic basis for the wave of inflation is the fact that the burden of domestic and foreign debts had become intolerable owing to the heavy price decline. The *immediate* cause was different in various countries. In agrarian countries with foreign indebtedness the balance of payments is negative *as a result of the heavy decline in the prices of agricultural produce, so that the net export surplus no longer meets interest and sinking funds payments on the foreign indebtedness.* In England the balance of payments was negative *for the moment* and there was a large outflow of gold owing to the sudden withdrawal of a considerable part of the foreign short-term capital invested in London. In the U.S.A., despite a favourable balance of trade, the currency was depreciated by governmental measures deliberately instituted to lighten the burden of debt,

---

[28] Previous cases of the depreciation of gold currencies, including depreciation during the post-war crisis, were almost exclusively the result of wars which had led to genuine inflation, to the issue of paper money to cover the cost of war. Present currency depreciation is *nowhere the result of " inflation " in this classical sense of the word*, which is an increase in the circulation of paper money to cover the State deficit. In some countries the banknote circulation has increased during the crisis, true enough, though it should have decreased in view of the drop in prices and reduced production. But this increase was not undertaken with the direct object of covering the budget deficit, but because cash reserves in banks and other enterprises were greatly augmented on account of the credit crisis, as is always the case in such times.

which had brought the entire credit and banking system to the verge of
destruction.

Roughly speaking, inflation proceeded in three waves. The *first wave*
caused inflation in a number of overseas agrarian countries. The *second,*
in the autumn of 1931, was marked by England's leaving the gold
standard and the adjustment of the respective currencies to the depreciated
pound sterling in all the British dominions, India and the Scandinavian
countries. The *third wave* began in the early part of 1933 with the departure of the U.S.A. from the gold standard. The process of inflation is by
no means concluded and continues in the phase of depression as well. The
situation in the middle of 1934 is as follows :

(a) *There are still four countries on a real gold standard,* that is, where
banknotes may be exchanged for gold at par whenever desired, and gold
may freely be exported : France, Switzerland, Holland and Belgium.

(b) *There is a group of countries with a formal gold standard.* In relations with other countries, the currency is exchanged on the basis of gold
parity. But this is attained not through the free movement of gold, as is
the case in countries on a real gold standard, but through the strictest
regulation of foreign trade and currency transfer, and prohibition of the
export of banknotes. In some countries, this is supplemented by the *non-
payment* of foreign debts, which we shall discuss later. This group includes Germany (after devaluation), Italy, Poland, Hungary, Rumania,
Czechoslovakia, Bulgaria, Latvia and Lithuania. In some of these countries, as in Germany, there are actually *two rates of foreign exchange* :
the official one, corresponding to the gold parity, for foreign exchange
allocated by the government; and another rate at a discount of from
twenty to fifty per cent. for marks in possession of foreigners usable only
in Germany (registered marks, etc.). Mark notes are dealt with abroad
at a discount of from twenty to fifty per cent.

(c) *All other countries have an openly depreciated currency.* These
countries comprise three groups :

(1) *The sterling bloc.* This is a group of countries closely linked economically with Great Britain, which have " tied " *their currencies* to the
pound, *i.e.,* the rate of exchange of their currencies in terms of gold is
regulated according to the quotation for the pound. To put it in other
words, in their case the British pound as it were plays the role of a world
money. This group includes all the British dominions and colonies, the
Scandinavian countries, Portugal, Argentina and Brazil.

The British bourgeoisie was doubtless forced to *abandon the gold
standard* because of the temporarily unfavourable balance of payments,
which led to a large outflow of gold. It did so very reluctantly in view of
the big profits it reaps from its position as banker to the world. This is
proved by its endeavours to procure the foreign exchange needed to maintain the gold standard by floating big loans in the U.S.A. and in France.
Conditions on the world stock exchanges did not permit the foreign secu-
rities in Britain's possession to be thrown on the market to obtain foreign
exchange, since this would have led to a catastrophic stock exchange

collapse. But when depreciation proved to be unavoidable, the British bourgeoisie derived the greatest possible benefit out of it by utilizing the depreciation of the pound in its struggle for world markets, and by re-establishing the pound's position as a world currency in spite of its depreciation (which it quickly checked by re-establishing free gold dealings). The Bank of England's gold reserves are now greater than ever.[29]

(2) *The second group constitutes the dollar bloc* : the U.S.A. and a few Central and South American states, whose currency is regulated according to the depreciation of the dollar.

Abandonment of the gold standard by the U.S.A. was not due to *monetary* compulsion, an outflow of gold which began to eat into the gold reserves, as in the case of England or Japan. (The outflow of gold at the beginning of 1933 was bound to come to a stop as soon as the relatively insignificant short-term balances of foreign banks had been withdrawn.) In general, no attempt was made to use the tremendous gold reserves—more than four billion pre-inflation dollars—to protect the currency. Departure from the gold standard was deliberately undertaken with the object of easing the untenable position of the debtors, who were collapsing under the debt burden—shifting the division of profits between industrial capital and loan capital in favour of the former.

But abandoning the gold standard alone was not sufficient to produce depreciation of the dollar. The trade balance of the U.S.A. in contrast to that of England is a very favourable one. The same is true of the balance of payments. Therefore, exceptional methods had to be applied. The U.S.A.'s favourable balance of payments was enough to maintain the new gold value of dollar notes without their being exchangeable for gold.

The issue of unbacked paper money to cover the budget deficit would have been the proper method of forcing depreciation still further. (Roosevelt had obtained the power to issue three billion dollars of additional paper money from Congress.) But Roosevelt was still afraid of this " open " inflation, and struck a path that was quite new in the history of capitalism; purchasing gold at prices higher than the current dollar rate in gold francs—artificially lowering the dollar rate of exchange. By the end of 1933 he had succeeded, through this procedure, in reducing the dollar rate of exchange by about forty per cent., at which level the dollar was actually stabilized at the insistence of dominant sections of the big bourgeoisie, without re-establishing the gold standard.

(3) The third group consists of those countries that have not " tied " their currencies either to the pound or to the dollar. Most of them are *agrarian debtor nations,* which could no longer pay interest and amortization on their foreign debts out of their export receipts in consequence of the sharp fall in prices of agrarian produce. After their gold reserves were exhausted, they were compelled to resort to inflation and to stop payments on their foreign debts. The following instance may serve as an illustration :

[29] Over £100,000,000 of gold was pumped out of India.

ARGENTINA'S BALANCE OF PAYMENT DURING THE CRISIS [30]

(Millions of dollars)

	Net favourable trade balance	Interest and Dividend payments abroad	For other[31] services	Total	Gold export	Increase in indebtedness to foreign countries
1927-28	+ 199	− 182	− 52	− 35	− 146 (import)	131
1928-29	+ 114	− 188	− 49	− 123	+ 119	38
1929-30	− 103	− 158	− 38	− 299	+ 56	167
1930-31	+ 43	− 117	− 22	− 96	+ 123	10

These figures show that net income from exports dropped from $199,000,000 to $43,000,000, whereas payments of interest and other obligations to foreign countries dropped only from $234,000,000 to $139,000,000. During the crisis Argentina paid out $218,000,000 in gold. As long as it was able to, it contracted new foreign debts to pay the interest on the old loans; but in 1930-31 it could no longer obtain any new loans. Inflation and cessation of interest payment to foreign countries became inevitable.

Thus we see that although the sharp drop in prices was the *general economic basis* for the depreciation of currencies, the concrete economic mechanism that led to inflation differed in various countries (or types of country).

A Few Words on Gold Standard Countries

It is striking that all the countries formally or in fact remaining on the gold standard *are countries that already went through the experience of very severe inflation in the post-war period* (except the typical *rentier* states, Holland and Switzerland). The tenacity with which the German, Polish, Hungarian bourgeoisie, and the like, hold on to the gold standard naturally does not imply that capitalist economy in these countries is on a sounder economic basis and less undermined by the crisis than in the U.S.A. or England. It merely means that they fear they will be unable to set any limits to currency depreciation once it sets in, because of their economic weakness. Depreciation resembling that of the post-war period would dangerously accelerate the maturing of the revolutionary crisis, since it would alienate the petty-bourgeois bank depositors and intensify the proletariat's discontent tremendously. . . .

In our publications currency depreciation is often treated much too simply as merely a means of struggle for foreign markets, as a means for supplementary exploitation of the working class, as a phenomenon which has *only* favourable aspects for the bourgeoisie. This is naturally incorrect and undialectical. *The depreciation of currency is not a remedy voluntarily employed against the crisis, but a symptom of the disease as well as an elementary factor intensifying the crisis still more.* To the first countries compelled to inflate, depreciation of the currency offers a transient advantage in the struggle for world markets, an advantage which disappears as

[30] *Statistical Yearbook* of the League of Nations, 1932-33, p. 173.

[31] Ocean freight and the like.

soon as most currencies are depreciated. The low gold prices at which inflation countries sell their goods abroad mean that they are *selling them under their value;* it signifies the impoverishment of these countries, while a few inflation profiteers grow rich. Certain sections of the bourgeoisie, principally the heavily indebted agrarians, rich peasants and industrialists, derive an advantage from inflation at the expense of loan capital; but they must run the risk of exchange fluctuations which will make all long-term calculation impossible. Inflation increases the exploitation of the workers and means expropriation of the property of the savings bank depositors (*i.e.*, chiefly the petty bourgeoisie) in favour of the big bourgeoisie. But it also involves the rapid accentuation of class antagonisms, with the threat of the petty bourgeoisie going over to the side of the revolutionary proletariat.

In contrast to the view that inflation is a remedy voluntarily employed by the bourgeoisie to overcome the crisis, we should like to emphasize the following:

The healthy, normal functioning of capitalism requires a stable gold standard currency. The fact that inflation has been introduced in an overwhelming majority of countries, that even in the phase of the present depression the process of currency depreciation has not come to a standstill, proves the far-reaching devastation of world capitalism which the crisis has entailed. Currency chaos is an element in the special character of the present depression. The almost general abandonment of the gold standard has now restricted the big shifts in the distribution of gold that took place during the crisis. The result of the struggle for gold is shown by the following table:

GOLD RESERVES OF CENTRAL BANKS AND GOVERNMENTS
IN MILLIONS OF GOLD DOLLARS [32]

July	U.S.A.	England	France	Germany	Total Europe	Asia	Latin America
1929	3,974	688	1,462	512	4,511	728	801
1933	4,009	925	3,213	58	6,922	481	367

The table reveals quite clearly the following interesting facts:

(a) During the crisis all newly-mined gold was absorbed by Europe.

(b) The debtor countries (Latin America, Asia, Germany, etc.) were obliged to part with a large proportion of their gold reserves.

(c) Within Europe, France appropriated an enormous part of the gold reserves of the world.

THE DECAY OF THE CREDIT SYSTEM AND OF CAPITAL EXPORT

Together with inflation, the debt burden, which the crisis and steep price decline had made intolerable, resulted in a disintegration of the credit system. This took on various forms:

In many countries, particularly in those which remain on the gold

[32] U.S. *Federal Reserve Bulletin.*

standard either formally or in fact—the debt burden was reduced by state intervention: prohibition of sales by court order (sheriff sales) and reduction of the interest rate. Moreover, government credit has taken the place of private capitalist credit to an ever greater extent—guarantee of savings bank deposits and reorganization of bankrupt banks, which are transformed into semi-governmental institutions. The net result is a tremendous shrinkage in the total volume of credit. Short-term indebtedness throughout the capitalist world shrank from 57 billion marks in 1931 to 25 billion marks at the end of 1933. (Reichskreditgesellschaft estimate.)

Payment of *international* debts became impossible owing to lack of gold or of an adequate export surplus, and to a large extent had to be abandoned. Reparations and inter-allied debts are no longer being paid. A large number of nations have declared a complete or partial moratorium on government loans.[33] Several nations have declared a moratorium even on private debts, *e.g.,* Germany (standstill agreement in regard to short-term debts and loans), Austria, Hungary and a number of South American countries.

The natural consequence of this general non-payment of foreign debts is an almost complete *cessation of capital export,* even after the acute credit crisis had been passed and capital became available in the imperialist countries for export purposes.

NEW ISSUES OF CAPITAL FOR FOREIGN COUNTRIES [34]

	1928	1929	1930	1931	1932	1933
U.S.A. (millions of dollars) ...	1,325	763	1,020	255	27.0	1.6
Great Britain (millions of pounds):						
Colonies	219	159	127	37	29.0	30.0
Foreign countries ...	86	54	70	9	0.3	8.0

Capital is now exported abroad only when foreign policy and preparations for war demand it. (England's loans to the dominions and to Argentina, the French loans to Rumania for equipping the latter's army, and the loans of the U.S.A. to the government of Chiang Kai-shek). The cessation of the " normal " export of capital, which is one of the cornerstones of imperialism, shows how deeply capitalism has been shaken by the crisis. *The cessation of capital export is an important factor in the exceptional nature of the present depression.* This does not imply the cessation of the struggle for capital investment, however, the best proof of which was Japan's protest in April 1934 against the investment of capital in China by other nations.

The collapse of the credit system also manifests itself in the peculiar fact that a tremendous abundance of *short-term funds* is paralleled by a

---

[33] Almost all the countries of Central and South America, the Balkan States and the countries of Central Europe (Germany, Austria and Hungary).

[34] *Statistical Yearbook* of the League of Nations for 1932-33 and 1933-34.

lack of *long-term credit,* with the issue of stock and bonds at an extremely low level.[35]

The decline is general, continuing in 1933, except in Great Britain. The trend is highly uneven : the U.S.A. declined over 90 per cent., while France and England lost only one-half. In Japan the issue of capital increased threefold in consequence of the war boom. (Data from *Statistical Year-book* of the League of Nations for 1933-34, p. 226.)

The Bank of France has 25 billion francs of *non-interest bearing deposits.* The American government was able to dispose of short-term treasury notes at an interest rate of 0.12 per cent. per annum. Worry over the *safety* of capital and fear of tying up capital in long-term investments under the generally prevailing conditions of political and economic insecurity outweigh the desire to invest at greater advantage. The property of money to become potential capital, the characteristic feature of capitalism, asserts itself with ever greater difficulty.

THE SHRINKAGE OF FOREIGN TRADE

Every cyclic crisis entails a drop in foreign trade. In this crisis, however, the shrinkage is extraordinarily great. The reasons for this are as follows :

(a) *The fight for markets* has brought about a situation in which every commodity that can be produced at home at all is produced within the country under tariff protection, or with imports prohibited. This holds true both in industry and in agriculture.[36]

(b) Preparations for war have the same effect.

(c) In many countries *the lack of foreign exchange* necessitates the reduction of imports.

(d) *The almost complete cessation of capital export.*

WORLD FOREIGN TRADE IN BILLIONS OF PRE-INFLATION GOLD DOLLARS [37]

			1928	1929	1930	1931	1932	1933
Imports	...	...	34.7	35.6	29.8	20.8	14.0	12.5
Exports	...	...	32.8	33.0	26.5	18.9	12.9	11.7

World foreign trade has shrunk to about one-third, approximately half of the loss being due to the drop in prices, and the other half to the reduced volume of trade. The drop in total value continued in the years 1933-34 as well.

[35] ISSUE OF CAPITAL—EXCEPT FOR REFUNDING

				U.S.A. Dollars	Gt. Britain Pounds	France Francs	Germany Marks	Italy Lire	Japan Yen
				(In millions)					
1929	...	...	...	10,183	254	19,245	2,664	7,280	2,662
1932	...	...	...	1,862	113	14,432	972	3,647	3,818
1933	...	...	...	936	133	10,429	—	3,344	6,617

[36] This led to the most insane state of affairs : England subsidizes sugar-beet cultivation, although enormous quantities of sugar are stored all over the world; Germany subsidizes the cultivation of vegetable oil plants, and so forth.

[37] The difference between import and export consists of freight charges, interest losses and differences in price between exporting and importing countries. The figures are taken from the statistics of the League of Nations.

The shrinkage of foreign trade proceeded unevenly, of course. Some countries, such as Japan, were able to increase their share of world trade during the crisis, while the shares of Germany and the U.S.A. diminished.

In many cases the shrinkage of foreign trade was the cause of inflation, as we have shown above. Conversely, protection of the currency in countries on an actual or nominal gold standard led to further shrinkage of foreign trade. The whole mechanism of international trade is out of gear. Commodities are no longer exported from countries where they can be produced most cheaply to countries where their production is most costly. Foreign trade is more and more regulated on the principle of a " net balance " between any two countries, i.e., every country buys from every other only as much as the other takes in exchange, so that no net balance need be paid in gold or foreign exchange. A kind of international " barter in kind " develops: the U.S.A. exchanges wheat for coffee with Brazil; Hungary exchanges wheat for timber with Austria; Japan exchanges cotton goods for raw cotton with India, etc. Not a trace is left of the free trade that was typical of the period of rising industrial capitalism.

This gives rise to the *ideology of " autarky."* The shrinkage of foreign trade, the tendency to abandon the world-wide economic division of labour, involves reduced productivity of labour and is a sign of the progressing decay of capitalism.

CHAPTER III
THE WORLD AGRARIAN CRISIS

T H E industrial crisis ran its course interwoven with the chronic agrarian crisis persisting since the end of the War. This deepened and prolonged the industrial crisis, and accentuated the agrarian crisis, making it more general. All the countries of the world and all branches of agriculture : cereals, stock-raising, dairy farming, industrial crops, were affected most acutely by the agrarian crisis. Its social and political consequences are stupendous; the peasantry of the entire bourgeois world is in motion. The tradition, formerly so natural, hegemony of the bourgeoisie over the masses of the peasantry—with whose help it was usually able to crush the revolutionary movement of the proletariat—is endangered. The bourgeoisie is compelled to resort to complicated and perilous manœuvres to divert the peasant masses temporarily from the revolutionary road. For the Communist Parties the agrarian crisis has opened the road to the exploited rural masses.

In this chapter we shall analyse the agrarian crisis principally from the economic standpoint. Its social and political effects will be dealt with later.

The basic cause of the agrarian crisis is the same as that of cyclic industrial crises : the contradiction between social production and private appropriation, with its contingent poverty and restricted consumption for the masses. In this sense, agrarian crises are " capitalist crises," as Lenin said. The outward form is also the same : *both are overproduction crises,* which involve a drop in prices and the wholesale bankruptcy of producers.[1]

There are, however, very important differences. Whereas industrial crises under capitalism recur periodically at intervals of eight or twelve years, *there is no such periodicity in agrarian crises.* The history of capitalism records only two general agrarian crises of long duration : the European agrarian crisis of 1873-95 and the present *world agrarian crisis.* (Former agrarian crises, such as the English crisis after the Napoleonic wars, were of a local character. Before railways were built there was no *world market* for agrarian produce, merely isolated markets limited by the undeveloped state of transportation.) The following problems must therefore be cleared up :

(a) Why are there no periodically recurring crises in agriculture as in industry?

[1] AGRICULTURAL SALES INCOME

				U.S.A. (Millions of dollars)	Germany (Billions of Marks)
1929	...	...	...	...	11,918	10.2
1933	...	...	...	...	5.143	6.5 (1932-33)

Number of Sheriff Sales of Peasant Farms in Germany

1930	1931	1932
4,318	5,798	6,961

Yearbook of Agriculture, 1933, Quarterly Vol. 9, No.1, p. 25.

(b) Why do agrarian crises outlast several industrial cycles?

(c) What connection is there between agrarian crises and industrial crises?

(d) What is the difference between the present agrarian crisis and that of the nineteenth century?

We shall endeavour to answer these questions as briefly as possible:

(a) There are no periodically recurring agrarian crises because *the simple production of goods and production for the producer's own use predominates in agriculture.* Although the capitalist mode of production has been predominant for over a hundred years, although the peasant producers were subjugated by capital and exploited by it in a thousand different ways, and although agriculture has been long carried on largely by capitalist lease-holders in the advanced capitalist countries (England), nevertheless even to-day the bulk of the agricultural produce on the market is not produced by capitalists, but by peasants. Peasant agriculture to-day still outweighs capitalist agriculture.

Another factor is the backwardness of agriculture in general: its low organic composition of capital and the relatively minor role played by fixed capital (the " material basis " of crises, as Marx says) even in capitalist agriculture. If the organisation of agriculture were as capitalist as industry, with the role of fixed capital just as large, and if the retarding effect of ground rent did not operate, agricultural production would exhibit the same cyclic movement as industry.

(b) The duration of the agrarian crisis, persisting through several industrial cycles, is also due mainly to the slight development of capitalism in agriculture. The specific conditions of agricultural production account for the fact that production is not reduced at the outbreak of the crisis as it is in industry. The crisis does not take on the form of a sudden decline in production, but of the accumulation of large, unsold stocks, with production unrestricted.[2]

The reasons for this are as follows: Since the production costs in large-scale capitalist agriculture are much lower than on peasant farms operating under the same natural conditions, the former can continue production at a profit for a long time, even during the crisis. The peasants, however, are *compelled* to continue production on the old scale until production involuntarily declines owing to the degradation of agriculture. The peculiarities of agricultural production lie in the circumstance that the percentage of the fixed costs that do not vary with the scale of production

---

[2] The League of Nations index of world foodstuffs production (cereals, meat, wine, coffee, tea, cocoa, etc.) reveals the following picture (1925-29, taken as 100):—

1925	1926	1927	1928	1929	1930	1931	1932	1933
98	97	99	103	103	104	102	104	103

We see that the tremendous drop in prices during the last four years has not brought about a reduction in output. Nor was there a reduction in the output of textile fibres or rubber. Some countries (mainly the European importing countries) have increased their agricultural output, while the exporting countries (U.S.A. and Canada) have reduced their output considerably. The size of the annual crop is another important factor, of course.

is much higher than in industry.[3] Ground rent in the form of leasehold payment and mortgage interest, amortization interest on buildings and machinery, fodder and replacement of draft animals, taxes and finally wages of the full-time labourers, which total at least seventy per cent. of the individual costs of production, remain almost unchanged when the area under cultivation is reduced. Therefore, restriction or total cessation of operations in agriculture involves far greater losses than in industry. In addition, it is very difficult for the peasant to find employment for his own labour power and that of his family off his farm, without abandoning it altogether. The peasant, therefore, continues production even when he can make only a minimum living wage. All endeavours made hitherto to induce agricultural producers to restrict their production voluntarily have failed because of this circumstance. Moreover, the prices of agricultural produce fluctuate according to the results of the harvest, temporary price rises awakening hopes for improvement and inducing the producers to stay on their farms. These are the most important causes accounting for the long duration of agrarian crises.

(c) Although the dynamics of agrarian and industrial crises differ, industry and agriculture constantly react on each other. *Every industrial crisis makes the situation in agriculture worse,* since the demand for industrial raw materials declines, while the demand for foodstuffs, particularly those of better quality (meat, milk, butter, eggs) drops as a result of the declining income of the working class. Prices, therefore, sink. But this does not yet mean an agrarian crisis. Conversely, the course of industrial cycles changes under the influence of the agrarian crisis, which greatly restricts the capacity of the agricultural population to purchase manufactured goods. The agrarian crisis tends to accentuate and prolong industrial crises, while the boom phases grow shorter and less pronounced.[4]

(d) The most important economic and political question is the difference in character between the present agrarian crisis and the great agrarian crisis of the nineteenth century. Before we answer this question, however, we must dwell in brief on the important *role that ground rent plays in agrarian crises.* We presume that the reader is acquainted with the Marxian theory of ground rent and we shall therefore deal only with the role of ground rent in the agrarian crisis.

Ground rent is that portion of the surplus value appropriated in agriculture which does not enter into the establishment of the average rate of profit, owing to private ownership of land, but is taken by the landowner as rent. This is made possible by the fact that the organic composition of capital in agriculture is lower than the average of the total capital

---

[3] How the proportion of these fixed charges increases with decreasing income is shown by the following official data for the U.S.A. (in millions of dollars):—

		Gross Income	Interest	Per Cent.	Taxes	Per. Cent.
1929	...	11,913	554	4.7	777	6.5
1932	...	5,143	510	10.0	620	12.0

[4] Kondratiev's wrong theory of " long cycles," which was largely accepted also by Trotsky, is based on the effect of the great nineteenth century agrarian crisis upon industry.

of society. If not for this there would be no absolute rent, merely differential rent. Theoretically, it is assumed that the capital invested in agriculture (the capital of the capitalist lessee) yields the average rate of profit, and that the landowner takes only that part of the surplus value gained by the lessee which represents the latter's profit over and above the average rate of profit on his invested capital.

But the landowner does not get the economic rent, which varies according to the yield of the harvest, and the course of prices. *The amount of rent is not fixed annually after accounts are settled, but is fixed in the lease or in the purchase price,*[5] *on the basis of the results of previous years.* As soon as the lease is signed, or the land bought on credit, subject to a corresponding mortgage, the rent signifies a definite fixed charge for the future, as far as the lessee or landowner is concerned, representing an element in his individual production outlay but not of the social cost of production. If the price of agricultural produce falls while the cost of production remains unchanged, the lessee or the indebted landowner is unable to pay the excessive lease rent or mortgage interest. He is ruined, although his own costs of production would allow him to make an average profit if he had no rent or not a too high rent to pay (in the form of lease rent or mortgage interest).

This is the special role that rent plays in an agrarian crisis. *Not the existence of rent in general* (which is a *constant* burden on agriculture), *but the fact that it is fixed at too high a level,* hits agricultural producers most severely during crises.

This accounts for the long duration of the agrarian crisis, since reducing *ground rent, fixed* on the basis of former high prices, to a level that corresponds to the fallen prices is a long drawn-out process, involving the wholesale ruin of the agricultural producers. (We will deal with the usury rent that poor farmers have to pay in the chapter devoted to the social effects of the crisis.)

We return once more to the difference between the two great agrarian crises.

Engels characterizes the agrarian crisis of the nineteenth century as follows:

"But everything is transitory. The trans-oceanic steamboats and the railroads of North and South America and India enabled very peculiar stretches of land to enter into competition upon the European grain markets. There were on the one hand the North American prairies, the Argentine pampas, steppes, made fertile for the plough by nature itself, virgin soil, which yielded rich harvests for years to come even with primitive cultivation and without any fertilization. Then there were the lands of the Russian and Indian Communist communities, that had to sell a portion of their product, and an increasing one at that, to obtain money for the taxes wrung from them by the pitiless despotism of the state, very often by means of torture. These products were sold without regard to their cost of production, sold at

[5] The *price of land* (apart from the sum expended on clearing and improving the soil) *is nothing but ground rent capitalized at the current rate of interest.*

the price offered by the dealer, because the peasant absolutely had to have money when tax day came around. And against this competition—of the virgin prairie soils and of the Russian and Indian peasants ground down by taxation—the European tenant farmer and peasant could not maintain themselves at the old rents. Part of the soil of Europe fell definitely out of competition for grain growing, the rents fell everywhere. . . . Hence the woes of the agrarians from Scotland to Italy, and from Southern France to East Prussia. Fortunately, far from all prairie land has been placed under cultivation. There is enough left to ruin all the great landed estates of Europe and the small ones into the bargain." [6]

We see that the agrarian crisis of the nineteenth century was *not a world crisis* like the present one, but a *European* crisis. There was no agrarian crisis in North and South America nor in Australia. It was not an *all-embracing crisis* like the present one, but a crisis of grain production.[7] Stock-raising and industrial crops were not affected by the crisis. *It was a crisis within the capitalist system, whereas the present crisis is part of the general crisis of capitalism itself.*

Engels' hope that there was enough prairie to " ruin all of European landed property, including the small proprietors," did not materialize. The agrarian crisis was surmounted within the framework of capitalism. But what is of decisive importance is that the manner in which the agrarian crisis was overcome in Europe in the nineteenth century does not apply to the present agrarian crisis.

How was the previous agrarian crisis in Europe overcome?

We can distinguish the following ways :

(a) The agricultural centre of gravity was shifted from cereals to stock-raising, together with the importation of cheap fodder (Scandinavia, Holland, Belgium, Western Germany), while ploughed land was turned into pasture and meadow (England).

(b) Considerable reduction in the cost of production was effected by rationalization. The substitution of green fallow land for bare fallow land, the introduction of better crop rotation, deeper ploughing (the iron plough), improved machinery, artificial fertilizers and seed improvement were the chief means employed. While large sections of the middle

---

[6] Footnote to page 842, Vol. III, Chap. XLIII of *Capital,* evidently written at the beginning of the nineties. The preface to Vol. III is dated October, 1894.

[7] This is best shown by the price movements in the *British* markets, which at that time could rightly be considered as the world market, during the agrarian crisis of the nineteenth century.

WHOLESALE PRICES IN LONDON

Annual Average	Cereals			Livestock Products	
	Wheat (112 lbs.)	Oats (112 lbs.)	American Corn (480 lbs.)	Prime Beef (8 lbs.)	Pork (av. 8 lbs.)
	s. d.	s. d.	s.	s. d.	s. d.
1851-75 ...	12 5	8 8	33	4 3	4 2
1876-82 ...	10 1	8 5	26	4 11	4 5
1883-1900 ...	7 1	6 6	23	4 8	3 6

Data taken from Sering: *Internationale Preisbewegung und die Lage der Landwirtschaft in den aussertropischen Ländern* [*International Movement of Prices and the Condition of Agriculture in Non-Tropical Countries*], Berlin, 1929.

peasantry, who lacked the necessary funds for such rationalization, were ruined, the big capitalist agricultural enterprises and the rich peasants succeeded in *reducing the cost of production through higher yields per acre,* in this way managing to get through the period of low grain prices.

(c) Production costs were reduced through reductions in the cost of the means of production supplied by industry. This was still in the epoch of free competition, when advances in labour productivity benefited the consumers.[8]

(d) Grain prices were raised artificially through the introduction of protective tariffs, in grain importing countries of Continental Europe, such as France, Italy and Germany.

(e) Finally, in the course of a long drawn-out process—against the bitter resistance of the landowners—the level of ground rent adapted itself to the new price level, and the agrarian crisis was overcome.

The ways and means of overcoming the agrarian crisis of the nineteenth century (with the exception of the last method) *are not applicable in the present agrarian crisis since they can be effective only under the conditions of advancing capitalism.* This necessary prerequisite was a great increase in the consumption of animal husbandry products due to the rapid increase in the industrial (urban) population of Europe and to the swift expansion of colonial exploitation, which gave rise to a broad stratum *of people living* on unearned income and which enabled the European bourgeoisie to maintain a numerically growing labour aristocracy. Therefore the crisis in European grain production could be overcome on an *ascending curve*: through a rise in commodity production and through specialization in agricultural crops; through expanding reproduction; technological progress (improved means of production), agricultural advances (better utilization of the soil), etc. The level of European agriculture at the end of the great nineteenth century agrarian crisis was undoubtedly higher than at the beginning of the crisis. Under capitalism this progress was achieved, of course, at the cost of proletarianizing millions of formerly independent peasants. But these proletarianized peasants were able to earn a living partly in the rapidly developing industries of Europe which at that time gave employment to millions of new workers, and partly in the overseas immigration areas. . . .

At the present time it is impossible to overcome the agrarian crisis on an ascending curve.

(a) There are no opportunities for extending the consumption of animal husbandry products in the period of the general crisis of capitalism. Chronic mass unemployment, the decline of the labour aristocracy in number and position, the tendency to reduce the number of workers employed by industrial capital in the advanced capitalist countries, the rapid impoverishment

---

[8] The English Sauerbeck Index moved as follows during the agrarian crisis:—

	1871-75	1891-95
Mineral raw materials	115	68
Textiles	100	56

The price " scissors " operated only in the case of agricultural products, but not for animal husbandry products.

of the urban petty bourgeoisie under monopoly capitalism, the expropriation of pensioners and savings bank depositors through inflation—in
short, the tendency to reduce the consuming power of the urban masses
makes this impossible.

The rapid expansion of industry in the nineteenth century gave rise to
a greatly increased demand for raw materials, and to wider cultivation of
industrial crops. At present, we see a reverse process : the catastrophically
low prices[9] of raw materials have led to a rapid restriction of the area
under cultivation.

AREA UNDER INDUSTRIAL CROPS IN THE CAPITALIST WORLD [10]
(in millions of acres)

	1929-30	1930-31	1932-33
Sugar beet	5.48	4.84	4.37
Tobacco	5.98	5.98	5.12
Cotton	83.10	76.35	72.00
Jute	3.44	1.86	2.15
Hemp	1.16	0.86	0.67

(b) Technically, the lowering of production cost through *rationalization,* through the employment of improved means of production, etc., is
possible now as well. But the unbelievably low wages paid agricultural
labourers render such rationalization unprofitable from the standpoint of
private business. The overwhelming majority of agricultural producers
lack the necessary capital. The collapse of the credit system makes the
partial acquisition of the necessary working capital impossible, at least for
the present. The capital that does enter agriculture expands the area
under cultivation in the overseas countries through improved technique
(tractors, combines), thus accentuating the crisis for the peasantry, since
it leads to an increase in production and makes liquidation of the enormous stocks in hand,[11] which keep prices down, still more difficult.

[9] PRICES OF IMPORTANT INDUSTRIAL RAW MATERIALS IN GOLD FRANCS
(per hundred pounds)

July	Cotton New Orleans	Jute London	Rubber New York	Raw Silk Yokohama	Hemp London	Copra London	Soya London
1929 ...	97	36	110	23	82	27	13
1932 ...	30	12	15	6	34	12	5
1933 ...	39	13	29	7	41	10	5

Coffee, tea and cocoa suffered a similar price decline.

[10] Yearbook of the Agrarian Institute in Rome, 1932-33.

[11] Up to 1933 stocks of agricultural produce increased, or remained almost undiminished in
magnitude. Only the catastrophic crop failure in the northern hemisphere in 1934 will lead to
a reduction in carry-over, but if the bad harvest does not recur, this will exert only a passing
effect.

WORLD STOCKS OF AGRICULTURAL PRODUCE
(In April of Each Year)

	1929	1930	1931	1932	1933	1934
American cotton (thousands of bales) ...	2,879	3,870	7,000	9,930	11,174	9,236
Wheat (millions of bushels)	497	518	600	584	526	483
Sugar (thousands of tons) ...	6,190	6,125	8,453	9,091	8,903	8,046
Tea (millions of pounds)	260	210	242	213	276	251
Coffee (millions of bags)	15.4	37.5	31.1	36.9	26.9	—
Rubber (thousands of tons) ...	245	426	547	646	646	673

(Data from the *London and Cambridge Economic Service*, Quarterly Supplements.)

(c) Reductions in the price of the means of production used in agriculture are impeded by production and distribution monopolies which maintain high prices. The " scissors " between the prices received by the agriculturists for their commodities and the prices they have to pay for their means of production is wide open.[12]

(d) The maintenance of high agricultural prices in the importing countries by means of tariffs, etc., meets with the obstacle of the limited consuming power of the urban population. Under the influence of higher prices, production expands so rapidly (as is clearly proved by the example of Germany and France in 1933) that domestic production meets domestic requirements, so that tariffs and quota measures become ineffective.

(e) The adjustment of rent to the changed price situation also proceeds in an anarchic fashion in this crisis, involving the ruin of millions of agricultural producers and a *degradation of agriculture,* which was not a general phenomenon in the previous agrarian crisis.

The degradation process in agriculture is manifested in various forms in the several countries: reduced use of artificial fertilizers, inadequate replacement of agricultural machinery and implements, reduction in livestock inventory and deterioration in its quality, poorer land cultivation and smaller crop yields, the decay and neglect of the peasant farm in general.

The process of degradation in agriculture comprises two phenomena differing economically and socially.

A more or less voluntary extensive *development of capitalist agriculture* —adjusting methods of production to the changed price situation, such as the substitution of horse-drawn ploughs for tractors, since gasoline is expensive while oats are cheaper and unsaleable; reduced use of artificial fertilizers, since it does not pay to use them at prevailing low crop prices;

[12] DATA ON PRICES OF AGRARIAN AND INDUSTRIAL PRODUCTS

| | U.S.A. (1909-14=100)a | | | Germany (1913=100)b | | |
	Prices of farm produce	Prices of goods bought by farmers	Ratio	Agricultural produce	Manufactured goods	Ratio
1929 ...	138	152	91	—	—	—
1930 ...	117	144	81	—	—	—
1931 ...	80	124	65	111	136	82
1932 ...	57	107	53	97	118	82
1933 ...	63	109	58	93	113	82

A few European countries (France, Switzerland, Sweden) were able to prevent the growth of a " price scissors " by means of high tariffs, import prohibitions and the establishment of governmental minimum prices. This holds true on paper at least, since the poor peasants receive much lower prices in the countryside than those quoted on the commodity exchanges.

(a) *Monthly Summary,* U.S. Dept. of Agriculture, April, 1934.

(b) *Vierteljahrshefte,* Vol. 9, No. 2, B.

the return to manual labour in place of complicated machinery,[13] since wages have dropped very steeply.

Furthermore, forced general deterioration of the peasant farm, since the peasant's net income is not enough to maintain simple reproduction in spite of the greatest personal privations suffered by his family; the dying cattle cannot be replaced, worn-out implements cannot be renewed, etc. Decrease in labour output in agriculture, limitation of production for the market and the trend to confine production to the needs of the peasant household proper.

We see that the methods successfully adopted in the nineteenth century to overcome the agrarian crisis cannot be applied to-day. *The present agrarian crisis is part of the general crisis of capitalism and cannot be solved within the framework of the capitalist system of society.* (Naturally enough, temporary improvement, as in 1924-28, is possible and even probable.) The agrarian crisis has led to an unprecedented wholesale ruin of the toiling peasantry, to the pauperization of the poor peasants and agricultural labourers, and to a revolutionary mass movement of the toiling agricultural population.[14]

That is why the only solution (temporary though it may be) of the agrarian crisis at all conceivable within the framework of capitalism— ruining all the *"inefficient"* (*i.e.,* the poor and middle) peasants, and driving them off the land; transferring their land to the elements possess-

13 DECLINE IN USE OF AGRICULTURAL MACHINERY

	1928	1929	1930	1931	1932	1933
U.S.A. Domestic sales of agricultural machinery (millions of dollars) ...	—	458	381	192	65	—
Germany. Domestic sales of agricultural machinery (millions of marks) ...	245	215	155	100	25	— (first six months)
Poland. Domestic orders for agricultural machinery (1928=100)	100	77	25	10	2.2	2.9
Imports of agricultural machinery (1928=100)	100	70	36	17	4.9	5.2

The major portion of the decline is, of course, accounted for by the fall in prices. The decline in actual sales, however, is also tremendous.

SALES OF AGRICULTURAL MACHINERY IN THE U.S.A. (UNITS)*

	Tractors	Combines	Harvesters	Threshers
Highest annual figure in the period				
1921-29	160,637	19,666	53,219	14,662
1931	93,632	8,172	22,675	5,280

No later figures are available, but the decline in the operations index number of the agricultural machinery industry from 93 in 1931 to 37 in 1932 and 42 in 1933, shows that sales declined still further.

The drop in sales of machinery in the western agricultural districts of Canada is still more acute. Sales of units were as follows† :—

	Tractors	Threshers	Combines
1928	17,143	6,247	3,657
1933	777	182	77

* *Farm Implement News,* June 22, 1933.

† *Canadian Farm Implements,* December, 1933.

14 In subsequent chapters we shall deal with endeavours to overcome the agrarian crisis artificially, as well as with its social and political consequences.

ing more capital; letting the " superfluous " land lie fallow and restricting production to fit the restricted, " able to pay " demand, on the pattern of the industrial trusts—is impracticable for the bourgeoisie.[15]

In the epoch of the maturing revolutionary crisis, the bourgeoisie, confronted by a proletariat which is rising to storm the ramparts of capitalism, cannot force the solution of the agrarian crisis by deliberately hastening the wholesale ruin of the toiling peasantry. Hence the search (vain though it be) for another solution of the agrarian crisis; hence the experiments and manœuvres of the bourgeoisie!

---

[15] Such a solution was proposed by some of the ideologists of the American bourgeoisie. See, for instance, *Harvey Baum*, by E. Shullead and B. Ostrolenk, Philadelphia, 1928; or *The Surplus Farmer*, by B. Ostrolenk, New York, 1932. Roosevelt, afraid of the farmers' revolts, struck out along the opposite road.

CHAPTER IV
THE CRISIS IN THE COLONIES

T H E colonies are most acutely affected by the crisis. This follows from their *position* as colonies, as subjugated areas. The Theses of the Second Congress of the Communist International " On the Colonial Question " state that " in the main, European capitalism draws its power not so much from the European industrial countries, as from its colonial dominions." Capital in the imperialist countries shifts a considerable part of the crisis burdens to the colonies and hence the crisis is especially deep and devastating there. The most important factors in this situation are the following:

(a) The overwhelming majority of the colonies and semi-colonies are *agrarian countries*. They therefore suffer the full force of the chronic agrarian crisis and its accentuation as a result of the industrial crisis.

(b) Imperialism has largely turned the colonies into raw material appendages of the home countries. A number of colonies and semi-colonies are *one-crop countries,* whose economic life depends on the sale of one (or a few) commodities in the capitalist world. Egypt, for instance, produces cotton, Australia—wool and wheat, India—rubber, Cuba—sugar, Brazil —coffee, etc. These countries are extraordinarily limited in their opportunities for economic manœuvring. Overproduction has led to an enormous drop in prices,[1] which is ruining them. They now have to sell two to six times the quantity of their major export commodity to industrial countries for the same amount of money they received before the crisis. In consequence their export surplus no longer sufficed to meet the interest on their foreign debts; their balance of payments became unfavourable, and they were therefore compelled to turn over their gold reserves, small as they were to the imperialist usurers.[2] In this way they fall into still

---

[1] Some examples of the drop in prices of typical colonial commodities:—

(In gold francs per 100 lbs.)

	Rice (Saigon 1st) London	Cane Sugar (Cuba) New York	Tea (Ceylon) London (per lb.)	Coffee New York	Copra London	Soya London
Dec. 1928 ...	14.8	11.1	1.45	93.5	29.7	14.1
Dec. 1932 ...	5.6	4.3	.45	43.0	12.5	5.6

	Cotton (bales) Alexandria	Rubber New York	Jute 1 London	Raw Silk New York (per lb.)
December, 1928	196	93.5	40.8	26.7
December, 1932	45	16.8	11.5	7.5

[2] *Gold reserves of some of the colonial and semi-colonial countries (in millions of their respective currency units)*:—

	Brazil (Milreis)	Argentine (Pesos)	Mexico (Pesos)	Dutch East Indies (Gulden)
End of 1928	1,242	641	39	170
End of 1932	129 (1930)	215	10	104

greater dependence on the latter, succumbing to inflation,[3] which makes
the burden of their debts (contracted in foreign currency) even heavier.
Let us take India as an example.[4]

FOREIGN TRADE OF INDIA, YEAR ENDING MARCH 31
(Millions of rupees)

		1929	1930	1931	1932	1933
Net export surplus	...	860	790	620	348	34
Net gold imports	...	212	143	125	—	—
Net gold exports	...	—	—	—	580	683

(c) The price " scissors," which accentuates the crisis in agrarian countries, in general, strikes the colonies with particular force:

PRICE INDICES (1913 = 100)

	U.S.A.	Germany	England		Colonial Commodities			
	Manu-factures		Pig-iron	Coal	Indian Cotton (London)	Jute	Tea	Cane Sugar (New York)
						(London)		
1929	136	157	132	122	114	102	138	71
1930	127	150	126	120	74	69	112	53
1931	111	186	110	114	59	54	74	48
1932	101	119	109	113	65	52	65	33

These figures, however, are far from giving a correct picture of the
increase of non-equivalent exchange between the colonies and the imperialist countries during the crisis, since they give the prices received
by the European dealers in colonial products, *i.e.,* the prices ruling on the
exchanges. The prices the peasants receive in the colonies dropped even
lower. With the prevailing oversupply the big international monopolies,
such as Unilever, themselves fix the prices that their buyers are to pay for
the commodities in the colonies.

" Capitalism has succeeded in somewhat easing the position of industry . . .
*at the expense of the peasants in the colonies and in the economically weak
countries* by still further forcing down the prices of the product of their
labour, principally of raw materials, and also of foodstuffs." [5]

(d) Most of the colonial and semi-colonial countries either have a silver
currency, or silver (sometimes, as in China, copper as well) forms the
legal circulating and paying medium at home, while a formal gold
standard exists in commerce with foreign countries. The tremendous fall
in the price of silver during the crisis enabled the imperialist countries
to obtain raw materials from these countries at exceptionally low prices.

These factors resulted in the rapid impoverishment of the colonial

[3] The colonial and semi-colonial countries occupy first place in regard to the extent of
currency depreciation. By the middle of 1934 currency depreciation (per cent. of gold) was as
follows: Mexico, 67; Argentine, 66; Columbia, 65; Uraguay, 54; Brazil, 58; Bolivia, 58;
China, 52 (per cent. of 1929 rate of exchange), etc.

[4] Official figures: *Statist,* November 11, 1933, page 670.

[5] Stalin, *Report at the Seventeenth Congress of the Communist Party of the Soviet Union,
Socialism Victorious,* p. 8.

peasantry : accelerated transfer of the land to the hands of the landlords;[6] a growing hunger for land; growing " over-population " in the country-side, which is enhanced by the accelerated return to the land of urban artisans ruined by the development of domestic capitalist industry and by foreign competition, as well as of workers thrown out of employment by the industrial crisis.[7]

Impoverishment is further intensified by the manifold exploitation of the peasantry. The feudal landowners, village usurers, the native and the imperialist bourgeoisie exploit the colonial peasantry in various ways :

> " The disadvantages of the capitalist mode of production, with its de-pendence of the producer upon the money price of his product, thus coincide here with the disadvantages arising from the imperfect development of the capitalist mode of production." [8]

This general characterization of colonial economy by Marx is even more true of the era of crisis. Chronic starvation and periodically recurring famine are now the lot of hundreds of millions of colonial peasants. Slavery is on the increase; it is an every-day occurrence for parents to sell their daughters into slavery.[9]

The degradation of agriculture is especially pronounced in the colonies. The manifold exploitation of the peasants deprives them of so much of their hard-earned income that they are not even able to continue the process of simple reproduction. The peasants are unable to buy the neces-sary quantities of urban fertilizers needed for the intensive cultivation so indispensable in the thickly populated areas of China. Livestock is diminishing, while its quality grows worse. In many regions of China the irrigation system, the basis of Chinese agriculture, is falling into decay. Imports of rice and wheat are increasing, while the area under poppy cultivation for opium production is expanding in Kuomintang China. In the one-crop countries specialization is being reduced and production for one's own needs is returning.

This general impoverishment of the population in the colonies during the crisis in many ways modifies the process of the development of the consumers' goods industries in the colonies and semi-colonies. The pro-cess of expansion of light industry undoubtedly continues during the crisis. The shrinkage in the capacity of the market to absorb local manu-factures is compensated for by the fact that the impoverishment of the

---

[6] Korea may be taken as an example: The proportion of the area cultivated by landlords rose from 54.1 per cent. to 56.4 per cent. between 1928 and 1932. The number of landless tenant farmers rose from 1,191,000 in 1926 to 1,393,424 in 1931. (Figures are taken from Mif, *Hegemony of the Proletariat in the Colonial Struggle for Emancipation* [in Russian].)

[7] In India, where periodic censuses have been taken for decades, the proportion of the agricultural population—in contrast to imperialist countries—is constantly higher. The same is obviously true of China, where no census is taken.

[8] " *Capital*," Vol. III, Chap. XLVII, p. 944.

[9] " In the suburbs of Kiangfu and on the shores of the Sienyang Ho (Shensi Province) a ' human market ' has been established, where girls under ten are sold for two to three dollars per head. The price for girls above ten years is five dollars." (*South China Morning Post*, November 22, 1932.)

population increases the demand for the *cheapest kinds of commodities* of inferior quality, which are produced by the colonial (and Japanese) industries.

Moreover, the great currency depreciation in colonial and semi-colonial countries, particularly the drop in the price of silver, served as protection against the competition of foreign goods. As early as 1931, the yearly report of the Bank of China stated:

"In the last three years Chinese industry has manifested signs of improvement, owing to the cheaper price of the goods of domestic industries as compared with that of imported goods, which is a result of the fall in the price of silver." [10]

These factors operated to produce an increase in domestic production and a sharp decline in the import of manufactures in many of the colonies and semi-colonies (the rise in tariffs also plays a certain role). The following figures[11] show this is true in the case of China:

	Textiles			Cigarettes		Matches	
	No. of cloth looms	Output (1,000 pieces)	Import of cotton goods (million yds.)	Output (1,000 packages)	Imports (millions)	Output (1,000 cases)	Imports (1,000 cases)
1929 ...	25,818	14,658	868	750	9,547 (including Manchuria)	600	8,424 (including Manchuria)
1933 ...	39,564	20,122	372	1,123	250 (excluding Manchuria)	800	73 (excluding Manchuria)

Numerous new plants for knitted goods, rubber goods, soap, caps, enamelware, paper, ink, pencils, as well as electric bulbs, radio sets, cement, bricks, and the simplest kinds of machinery, etc., have been established during the crisis especially in the Shanghai and Hongkong areas. (On the other hand, the depreciation of silver reduced the imports of foreign machinery, hampering the development of industry, particularly those industries owned by Chinese.)

Similar phenomena are observed in the other colonial and semi-colonial countries. (Many new textile factories erected in the interior of India; the growth of the textile, boot and shoe, and other industries in Brazil and Chile during the crisis.) But the following factors must be emphasized in our estimate of this course of development:

(1) The crisis is extremely severe in the branches of industry that produce semi-finished goods for export: raw silk, tea, oil-seed mills, etc.

(2) The erection of factories by *foreign* capital is the principal factor in increased production in light industry and the growth in the number of enterprises, thus increasing dependence upon imperialism.

(3) The growth of light industry (though limited in extent) is attained

[10] Index of imported manufactured goods in Shanghai, in silver (1926 = 100):—

1929	1931	1933
110	160	153

[11] Figures taken from an article by Gamberg, *The Position of Chinese Industry During the Crisis*. (In Russian.)

through a big rise in the rate of exploitation of the colonial proletariat—wage reductions, lengthening of hours of work, increased labour intensity —which capital was able to force through despite the workers' resistance. The ruin of the artisan trades and the uninterrupted impoverishment of the toiling peasants under the hammer-blows of the crisis and of manifold exploitation by the landowners, imperialists, domestic bourgeoisie and usurers, continued to throw new hands into the industrial labour market, making more difficult the often heroic struggle against capital of the colonial proletariat—largely consisting of women and children, and drawn directly from the village.

CHAPTER V

UNSUCCESSFUL ENDEAVOURS TO OVERCOME THE CRISIS ARTIFICIALLY

D u r i n g the last five years the bourgeoisie has made innumerable efforts to overcome the crisis artificially. They all proved to be failures, as was to be expected. Both the general crisis of capitalism and the cyclic overproduction crises are consequences of the " natural laws " of capitalism, as Marx often puts it. The *general crisis* of capitalism only expresses the fact that the capitalist system of society, as a historically transient form of society, is now passing through the period of its unevenly proceeding revolutionary collapse. No artificial measures can alter this.

The cyclic overproduction crises represent the violent outbreak of capitalism's contradictions but at the same time they also involve their temporary solution. The endeavours to mitigate the crisis, or to hasten its end, lead in the final analysis to a prolongation of the crisis.

How is a cyclic overproduction crisis overcome? The most important factors are the following :

Production is so greatly restricted that consumption exceeds production.[1]
Part of the surplus products is physically destroyed.

The drop in prices reduces the price total of commodities to the social requirements. Surplus stocks of commodities are absorbed. Prices do not decline further. Cheapening of the elements of constant capital increases the utilization of total capital.

During the crisis wages are cut, the intensity of labour increased, labour conditions grow worse, causing a temporary decrease in consuming power. At the same time, however, better utilization of capital (as the prerequisite condition for the resumption of investment) and an expansion of the market for Division I are made possible.

The credit crisis reduces social capital through bankruptcies and company reorganizations, thus increasing the profit rate on the capital remaining. The prerequisites are present for new capital investments in the sphere of production. At the same time the credit crisis eliminates the insolvent debtors; the credit chain, broken during the crisis, and mutual " confidence " are re-established. Large amounts of loan capital are once more available for the resumption of real accumulation. Crisis passes into depression.

The bourgeoisie is just as unable to comprehend the overproduction crisis as it was a hundred years ago. Hundreds of books, hundreds of thousands of articles on the crisis have been published by bourgeois

[1] The question might arise as to where this consuming power comes from if production is so restricted. This question is not hard to answer. The bourgeoisie and those living on unearned income, government officials and a large part of the salaried employees continue consumption during the crisis on almost the same level as before. The unemployed live on their savings plus unemployment insurance.

writers within the last five years, without having advanced the understanding of the latter in the slightest degree. Sometimes this is acknowledged by the ideologists of the bourgeoisie themselves.

Wagemann, director of the German Institute of Business Research,
wrote as follows in the *Wochenbericht* [*Weekly Report*] of December
26, 1932 :

> "In many places the outbreak of the acute credit crisis has affected the
> foundations of economic development and thus interrupted the organic
> course of the depression. Such events affecting national economy from the
> outside cannot be foreseen by research methods any more than earthquakes,
> fires, etc. Nor are their consequences . . . subject to any quantitative predic-
> tions."

Under the heading "*Bankruptcy of National Economy, the Manchester Guardian* of September 1, 1931, wrote :

> "We know more of the velocity of an electron than we do about the
> velocity of money. We know far more about the cycle of the earth about
> the sun and the sun about the universe than we do about the cycle of trade.
> We can predict the movements of unseen and inconceivably remote heavenly
> bodies with vastly greater accuracy, than we can predict the end of the
> trade slump."—("Manchester Guardian," January 9, 1931.)

In contrast to this total confusion in the heads of economists, each section of the ruling class deliberately pursued the aim of making economic
policy serve its own interests. Victory in the struggle among these conflicting interests was finally gained by the financial oligarchy, monopoly
capital, concealed though it was behind all sorts of manœuvres.

The bourgeoisie sees in the crisis *chiefly the unsaleability of its commodities at profitable prices.* All the measures suggested for overcoming the
crisis moved within this circle.

"*Our goods do not sell because of overwhelming foreign competition,*"
declares the capital producing for the home market. Hence, tariff rises,
quotas and import prohibitions to surmount the crisis.

"*We cannot sell our goods abroad,*" the exporters cry. Hence, government subsidies, freight rebates and state-organized dumping.

"*The value of our currency is too high,*" shout the exporters of all
countries, demanding inflation (or more inflation wherever it exists
already).

"*The value of our currency is too low,*" cry the importers of foreign
raw materials, the creditors and the coupon-clippers. "Only maintenance of the gold standard ensures economic stability, credit and a way
out of the crisis."

"*Our production costs are too high,*" industrial capital cries. Hence,
wage cuts, a longer working day, labour speed-up—the effort to overcome the crisis at the expense of the workers, which restricts the capacity
of the domestic market to absorb manufactures still further.

"*Our selling prices are too low because of unrestricted competition,*"
the monopolists say. Hence, government aid in the formation of mono-

polies (England), compulsory cartels, prohibiting the establishment of new enterprises (Germany), government sanction of cartel prices, minimum prices fixed by the government. This artificial maintenance of high monopoly prices,[2] increases the profit of monopoly capital, but it slows up the liquidation of surplus stocks, and prolongs the crisis.

" Consuming power must be increased," demand the leaders of the trade unions and Social-Democratic economists. " The crisis is a result of under-consumption." The capitalists should increase wages, the state should put more money in circulation, and should put through public works. Then the capacity of the domestic market will increase and the crisis will be over.

This agitation foundered on the resistance of capital, which is not disposed to accept the nonsensical plan of paying higher wages out of its own pocket to be able to sell more goods. (Roosevelt manœuvres with this catch phrase for demagogic reasoning.)

" This crisis is due to insufficient credit." The state should provide for credit expansion. Efforts in this direction have failed. (Hoover's Reconstruction Finance Corporation.) The " credit-worthy " capitalists do not require any additional loan capital in view of the diminished business during the crisis. Those who do require money to pay old debts are not " credit-worthy."

" The burden of debts is ruining us," cry the debtors. Hence, reorganization (of course only of the biggest enterprises) through state subsidies, governmental purchase of shares, reduction in the interest rate and relief of the debt burden through inflation.

" The crisis can be overcome only by re-establishing free circulation of commodities in the world market." Tariffs should be reduced, quotas, import and export prohibitions should be abolished and international credit and capital export should be restored.[3] This policy was advocated by the British bourgeoisie at the beginning of the crisis. It failed because the bourgeoisie of every country (and the British bourgeoisie with increas-

---

[2] In some countries the " free " prices and those that are fixed, i.e., the cartel prices, are combined in the indices of the government institutes of business research. The maintenance of high monopoly prices is clearly shown in the following table :—

	Germany (1928 = 100)		Austria (1923-31 = 100)		Poland (1928 = 100)	
	Cartel prices	Free prices	Cartel prices	Free prices	Cartel prices	Free prices
1928	102	107	—	—	—	—
1929	105	97	99	100	108	94
1932	84	48	93	73	105	53
1933(a)	84	48	94	73	93	49

The difference in prices is tremendous. In reality, the difference is probably less, since the official cartel prices are secretly evaded and underbid by the individual cartel members in various ways.

(a)Ten months.

[3] The re-establishment of " free trade " as it existed before the crisis would benefit the strongest imperialist industrial countries, but would place the weaker countries at a disadvantage. It would not solve the crisis, since the purchasing power of the capitalist world as a whole would not be raised in the least.

ing determination) endeavoured to monopolize its domestic market. They succeeded in destroying the world market in the old sense. There are no longer world market prices in the old sense, the international division of labour is being more and more restricted and foreign trade is shrinking. The ideological expression for all this is the senseless catchword " autarky."

We do not wish to tire the reader by prolonging this list. The conflicting interests of the various strata of the ruling classes led to a constant struggle around the state's economic policy, to uninterrupted parliamentary " log-rolling," to increasingly frequent cabinet crises, and to an uncharted zig-zag policy, which is one of the bases for the fascization of the state.

Roosevelt's " New Deal " represents the most grandiose effort to overcome the crisis by governmental measures. The essence of this policy is:

(a) Saving the credit system from utter collapse by a government guarantee of deposits;

(b) Reducing the burden of debts by 40 per cent. through the depreciation of the dollar;

(c) Artificially raising the prices of agricultural produce through a reduction of output prescribed and subsidized by the government;

(d) Furthering the organization of monopolies by means of the Codes, which in many cases amount to compulsory cartels;

(e) Combating unemployment by undertaking big public works and by reducing the working hours per week;

(f) Regulation of wages: fixing minimum wages in the Codes, which in practice became maximum wages.

As we know, the effort led to a very sharp rise in industrial output in the summer of 1933 (accumulation of stocks and increased purchases by the rich in anticipation of the inflationist rise in prices), and to a sharp relapse in the autumn of 1933. This was followed by a gradual renewed improvement in the first half of 1934 and by a new decline beginning with July. Since housing construction as well as the renewal and increase of fixed capital are very slight up to the present and the purchasing power of the working class has not increased, the artificial increase of production clashed with the limited capacity of the market and collapsed after a few months had elapsed. In the final analysis the increase of production remains within the bounds that the inner forces of capitalism would have reached; its progress, however, was no longer more or less even, but followed an unsteady zig-zag.

All the efforts to overcome the crisis artificially failed in the long run. The fact that the acute phase of the crisis came to an end and passed into the depression of a special kind, is not due to the manœuvres of the bourgeoisie. It was effected by the inner forces of capitalism tending to overcome the cyclic crisis, which were reinforced by the increased preparations for war and (in some countries) temporarily by inflation.

A few words on the efforts to overcome the agrarian crisis artificially. Their main object was *a rise in prices*. The methods attempted in the importing countries differed from those in the exporting countries.

In the *importing countries* an effort was made to make domestic prices independent of the movement of world market prices, through quotas, increased tariffs, import prohibitions, and so forth. This policy was pursued chiefly by the West European countries: Germany, France, Italy, etc. By 1933 this policy had succeeded in making domestic prices two to three times higher than world market prices.[4]

This development of prices led to an expansion of the farmed area; the increased harvest, however, soon covered the domestic demand[5] (reduced by the crisis), and protectionism became ineffective. The new drop in prices could be halted only by the introduction of government-fixed prices (France, Germany. Czechoslovakia) and the organization of state control of the grain trade.

In the exporting countries, the endeavour was made to raise the world market price through purchasing the surplus quantity and keeping it off the world market: Canadian Wheat Pool, Federal Farm Board in the U.S.A., coffee valorization in Brazil, etc. All these efforts ended in failure, since production continued to increase, stocks accumulated still further, and the organizations could not stand the burden. Either they went bankrupt (Canadian Wheat Pool), or the bourgeoisie no longer desired to bear the losses (Farm Board in the U.S.A.); prices again fell steeply.

This experience shows that *prices cannot be maintained at a high level unless production is restricted*. A campaign was begun for voluntary restriction of the area under cultivation (particularly in the U.S.A.); bonuses were paid for reduction in cultivated area and efforts were made to conclude international agreements for restricting the production or export of various agricultural commodities. These efforts also failed by and large, although the prices of certain commodities produced chiefly on capitalist plantations (rubber, sugar, tea) rose considerably in consequence of restricted production. The enormous weight of fixed costs (Chapter III) renders restriction of production difficult in agriculture. Effective control is scarcely possible in view of subdivision into millions of small farms. It proved impossible to restrict production according to plan as was indicated in the chapter on the agrarian crisis.

[4] Prices in Gold Francs, July, 1932

	Berlin	Paris	London	Chicago	Buenos Aires
Wheat per 100 lbs.	13.4	14.8	5.4	4.7	4.0
Pork per 100 lbs. (on the hoof) ...	47.7	66.2	—	23.6	—

(Yearbook of the Agrarian Institute in Rome, 1932-33.)

[5] Germany may serve as an example. The area under wheat cultivation increased from 4,000,000 acres in 1929 to 5,700,000 acres in 1933.

Domestic Production Met the Country's Needs As Follows (in per cent.):

	1926	1929	1932
Wheat	48	72	97
Meat	91	94	99
Butter	70	72	85

Hence, as early as two years ago, a bad harvest was awaited as a blessing. The *Minneapolis Tribune* (U.S.A.) wrote :

"We, who learned to pray for our daily bread, are now praying that it be taken away from us; a heresy as peculiar in the field of theology as in the field of economics."

A similar contradiction exists between the entire ideology of agricultural education, whose aim is to teach how to get the biggest crops, between the traditional system of state awards to farmers with the biggest crops, and the agitation and legislation for reducing the cultivated area and the crops by prohibiting the use of larger quantities of fertilizer (American cotton regions), and the like.

Finally, the only recourse left was the systematic, wholesale *destruction of agricultural produce of every kind*. In 1933, 24,700,000 acres of ripe cotton (approximately one-quarter of the total area) was ploughed under in the U.S.A. In Brazil ten million bags of coffee (almost the total annual world requirements), are burned, dumped into the sea or used as road construction material every year.

Tea is not gathered; rubber trees are not tapped. Whole shiploads of oranges were dumped into the sea in London. Five million hogs were bought by the U.S. government and destroyed in the autumn of 1933. In Denmark, 1,500 cows were slaughtered weekly and converted into fertilizers. In Argentine, hundreds of thousands of older sheep were killed and abandoned to make room for the young; the cost of transportation to the slaughter houses would have exceeded the money received for them. And so forth and so on! All this is happening at a time when millions upon millions of unemployed and their families are starving and are clad in rags. *Never before in the history of mankind has anything like this ever occurred*. The decay of capitalism—the contradiction between the productive forces and the production relationships is tangibly obvious to every peasant and worker!

The long and tedious process of the degradation of agriculture and the crop failure of 1934 will finally bring about the reduction of stocks so ardently desired and will raise prices somewhat.[6] This will only be a short interlude, however. In a year or two overproduction stimulated by the higher prices, will be still greater than at present. A solution of the agrarian crisis within the framework of the capitalist system of society is nowhere in sight; at most, only a temporary mitigation of the crisis may occur.

*   *   *   *   *

The principal results of the efforts to overcome the crisis artificially (and of all capitalist economic policy during the crisis) is the intervention of the state in every detail of economic life in favour of the ruling classes in general, and of monopoly capital and the big agrarians in particular. Monopoly capital makes use of its control of the state machinery to effect a systematic shift of national income in its favour and to rob the state

[6] The effects of the crop failure upon the condition of the toiling peasants will be dealt with later.

treasury in various ways and under all sorts of pretexts. " State capitalism " tendencies have grown considerably. A transition from monopoly capitalism to a " state war-monopoly capitalism," as Lenin called capitalism in the period of the World War, is taking place to a certain extent.

In fact the present situation of capitalism very much resembles that during the World War. First, *because the preparations for the next world war dominate the economic policy of all nations more and more.* The economy of most capitalist countries, especially of Japan and Germany, already manifests pronounced features of war economy, which inevitably involves increasing the role of the state in economy.

Second, *the rapid maturing of the revolutionary crisis,* the threat to the bourgeoisie's domination, compels the latter to consolidate its state power for the purpose of better defence. The resulting fascization of the state apparatus is connected with the strengthening of state-capitalism tendencies.

We shall endeavour to indicate the chief outlines of the strengthening of state-capitalism tendencies.

(a) *The suddenly increased role played by the government budget.* While the value of the products of society (according to bourgeois terminology : the national income) has dropped very heavily as a result of production restrictions and the fall in prices, a large part of it, unchanging in magnitude, was appropriated by the state and redistributed.[7] This means that the proportion of the national income taken by the state has increased.

(b) *Foreign trade has in essence become a concern of the state.* The innumerable restrictions of foreign trade (tariffs, quotas, prohibitions, allocations of foreign currency, barter between nations, etc.) have created a situation in many countries (Germany, the Baltic states, and Japan) which very much resembles a state trade monopoly.

(c) *Credit has actually become state credit;* in most nations (chiefly Germany and the U.S.A.) the banks are governmental or semi-governmental banks and in every respect depend on the state.

(d) *The state has acquired increasing control over the distribution of labour power* (" voluntary " labour service in the U.S.A., Germany, etc.; state measures for creating work).

[7] Budgets of the Most Important Countries During the Crisis
(in millions of the respective currency units)

	U.S.A.		Japan		England		Germany		France	
	1929	1934	1929	1934	1929	1934	1929	1934	1929	1934
Expenditures	3,848	7,105	1,815	2,309	818	830	8,002	6,647	455,000	505,000
National Income(a) ...	80,500	39,800	—	—	3,849	3,381	75,400	46,500	245,000	206,000
Governmental expenditures in per cent. of national income ...	4.8	17.8	—	—	21.3	24.6	10.5	14.3	18.4	24.5

(a) In every case the figures for the national income of the previous year are taken for comparison.

(e) *The prices of many commodities are determined by the state* : directly through price fixing by the state (all the prices of agricultural commodities in Germany); indirectly through the organization of obligatory cartels and through foreign trade and currency policy.

The effect of this and other kinds of state interference is that the profits of each enterprise (and even of some commercial transactions) depend on the rapidly growing number of governmental measures. *In general,* all government measures tend to benefit monopoly capital, but in individual cases, very much depends on the bureaucrats, rapidly growing in number, who " interpret " and enforce the laws and the decrees. The importance of these bureaucrats (and their corruption) has grown immensely. Although this basis is general, the differences between the various countries are often far-reaching. We shall return to the same question in later chapters.

CHAPTER VI
THE SPECIAL NATURE OF THE PRESENT DEPRESSION

IN his report to the Seventeenth Party Congress, Comrade Stalin stated that "industry in the principal capitalist countries had already passed the lowest point of decline and did not return to it in the course of 1933."

The following table shows this in figures:

INDEX OF INDUSTRIAL OUTPUT (1928 = 100) [1]

	Capitalist world (June)	U.S.A.	England	Germany	France	Japan	Poland
Month of highest output in 1929	109.8	114.4	107.9	107.2	113.4	—	105.8
1929 (average)	106.0	107.2	106.0	100.4	109.4	111.4	99.7
1930 ,,	90.5	86.5	97.9	90.1	110.2	105.6	81.8
1931 ,,	77.9	73.0	88.8	73.6	97.6	100.7	69.3
1932 1st quarter	69.5	62.5	80.1	62.0	79.5	101.0	52.2
2nd ,,	64.2	54.7	89.4	61.3	74.0	104.8	54.5
3rd ,,	63.3	55.3	82.7	59.6	73.2	107.2	54.0
4th ,,	67.4	59.5	90.0	61.8	76.1	118.7	54.0
1933 1st ,,	66.6	56.5	89.9	64.1	80.8	120.9	48.2
2nd ,,	75.7	70.9	91.7	67.6	85.8	125.7	55.2
3rd ,,	82.6	82.6	91.8	70.8	87.4	129.0	58.0
4th ,,	75.3	67.3	99.5	73.4	84.3	138.1	60.1
1934 1st ,,	80.5	73.0	103.3	81.8	82.7	132.6	60.2
2nd ,,	—	76.5	104.1	87.7	79.5	—	63.8
Lowest point in 1932	61.5 (July)	52.3 (July)	82.7 (2nd quarter)	58.5 (August)	72.4 (July)	91.4 (May, 1931)	46.5 (March, 1933)

Industrial output in most countries reached its lowest point in the middle of 1932. Some countries, such as Japan (war and inflation boom), reached it as early as 1931, while others, like Poland, passed it only at the beginning of 1933.

The lowest point in the price decline was reached somewhat later, in 1933; the fall in prices is still continuing in some countries possessing a stable currency.

Price formation is greatly distorted owing to currency depreciation. Recalculation on a gold basis at the rate of exchange is impracticable since the rise in prices during inflation always lags considerably behind the depreciation of the currency.

The accumulation of stocks of agricultural products (see table in Chapter III) came to a standstill at the same time. The stocks of *industrial*

---

[1] The figures are taken from League of Nations statistics. Figures of world output have been taken from the data of the Berlin Institute of Business Research.

raw materials began to diminish. *The stocks of industrial finished products diminished considerably,* falling below the normal level by the end of 1932.[2]

WORLD STOCKS OF INDUSTRIAL RAW MATERIALS

	April	1929	1930	1931	1932	1933	1934
Tin (1,000 tons)		27	41	60	62	52	22
Lead „ „ U.S.A. ...		—	41	116	151	173	198
Zinc „ „ „ ...		35	90	140	138	137	105
Petroleum (millions of barrels)		599	639	591	560	504	502
Copper (1,000 tons)		324	—	586	701	647	506

The figures are taken from the *London and Cambridge Economic Service;* figures for copper from the *Berliner Börsenzeitung* of August 2, 1934. (1929-30 —annual average.)

No statistics are available for the stocks of manufactures in other countries; the trend, however, is undoubtedly similar. The continuing drop in prices prompted all enterprises, particularly the wholesale and retail trade, to reduce inventory to a minimum. During 1933, the world economic crisis had thus reached a stage which is ordinarily described as a transition to the depression.

MARX ON DEPRESSION

In Marx's analysis of cycles, the focus of interest is always the crisis, as that phase of the cycle in which all the contradictions of capitalism break out openly and violently, the capitalist system of society is shaken to its very foundations, the proletariat is freed of the illusions arising during the prosperity phases, and the historically transient nature of capitalism is strikingly demonstrated. The other phases of the cycle interested Marx principally as phases preliminary to the next crisis. That is why only scattered remarks on the depression are found in Marx's works. Parenthetically the *term* "depression," characterizing a certain phase of the cycle, is not found in Marx's works at all. (When the term is used it is used in the *English* sense of "crisis.") Marx uses the expression "stagnation," "state of rest," "the phase of the industrial cycle that follows a crash,"[3] and "the melancholic period." However, Marx's meaning is clear, and it is useless to quibble about words.

Marx characterizes the phase of depression in greatest detail in the following passage:

"... in the phase of the industrial cycle following immediately after a crisis, when masses of loan capital lie fallow. At such moments, when the process of production is restricted (production in the English industrial districts was reduced by one-third after the crisis of 1847), when prices of commodities are at their lowest level, and when the spirit of enterprise is paralysed, the rate of interest is low, indicating nothing but an increase of loanable capital precisely as a result of the shrinkage and paralysis of industrial

---

[2] INDEX OF STOCKS OF MANUFACTURES IN THE U.S.A. (1923-25 = 100)

	1929	1930	1931	1932
December	119	120	108	96

[3] *Capital*, Vol. III, Chap. XXX, p. 567.

capital. That less currency is required when the prices of commodities have fallen, the number of transactions decreased, and the capital put into wages contracted; that, on the other hand, no additional money is required for the function of world money after the debts to foreign countries have been liquidated, partly by the export of gold and partly by bankruptcies; and that, finally, the volume of discount business diminishes with the number and amounts of the bills of exchange themselves—all this is quite obvious. Hence the demand for loanable money capital, either for means of circulation or payment (the investment of new capital is still out of the question) decreases and it becomes relatively abundant. But the supply of loanable money capital also increases positively under such circumstances, as we shall see later." [4]

Let us enumerate the most important features of this quotation :

Production is restricted.
The spirit of enterprise is crippled.
Prices of commodities are at their lowest level.
Loan capital lies idle in vast amounts.
The rate of interest is extremely low.

All these features were undoubtedly present in 1933. The crisis passed into depression, not an ordinary depression, but one of a " *special kind.*"

Stalin on the Present Depression

" Does this mean that we are witnessing a transition from a crisis to an ordinary depression which brings in its train a new boom and flourishing industry? No, it does not mean that. At all events at the present time there are no data, direct or indirect, that indicate the approach of an industrial boom in capitalist countries. More than that, judging by all things, there cannot be such data, at least in the near future. There cannot be, because all the unfavourable conditions which prevent industry in the capitalist countries from rising to any serious extent still continue to operate. I have in mind the continuing *general* crisis of capitalism in the midst of which the *economic* crisis is proceeding, the chronic working of the enterprises under capacity, the chronic mass unemployment, the interweaving of the industrial crisis with the agricultural crisis, the absence of tendencies towards any serious renewal of fixed capital which usually heralds the approach of a boom, etc., etc.

" Apparently, what we are witnessing is the transition from the lowest point of decline of industry, from the lowest depth of the industrial crisis to a depression, not an ordinary depression, but to a depression of a special kind which does not lead to a new boom and flourishing industry, but which, on the other hand, does not force it back to the lowest point of decline." [5]

What is of decisive importance is the following : *Considered mechanically, the present depression is hardly to be distinguished from all preceding phases of depression, as characterized by Marx;* [6] considered dynamically, there is a fundamental difference : *the present depression* (in contrast to " normal " depressions) *does not furnish a sufficient basis for a*

[4] *Capital*, Vol. III, Chap. XXX, pp. 569-70.

[5] Stalin, Report at the Seventeenth Congress of the C.P.S.U., *Socialism Victorious*, pp. 8-9.

[6] The principal difference is the completely disrupted state of the monetary and credit system at the present time.

boom in capitalist economy. The special nature of the depression consists in the deformation of the industrial cycle under the influence of the general crisis of capitalism.[7]

This deformation is clearly evident in the entire development of capitalist economy since the lowest point of the crisis, in the middle of 1932. In the cycles of rising capitalism a few months sufficed to raise production and business from the bottom of the crisis to the peak of the preceding boom phase. In some cases (see Chapter III) there was no drop in production at all during the crisis, but merely a retardation of the rate of growth. Up to now in the period of imperialism it usually took one or two years for the previous peak to be reached again after the bottom point of the crisis.

What do we see to-day?

More than two years have elapsed since the crisis touched bottom, but the volume of the capitalist world's industrial output is still twenty per cent below what it was in 1928; after two years of recovery, production is still much more below the preceding peak than at the lowest point of the crisis in former cycles.

It is also obvious that *the ascending line of economy again snapped in the summer of 1934.* There is a pronounced relapse in the U.S.A., as in 1933; German economy is heading for a catastrophe; in France the slow decline continues; in England improvement has come to a standstill, etc. There is no doubt that in the third quarter of 1934 the volume of industrial production is lower, and the condition of capitalist world economy as a whole is worse, than a year ago.[8]

It is obvious that *the contradiction between the productive forces and the production relationships is so acute in the present period of the end of capitalist stabilization that increased production prematurely hits a snag in the market's limited absorption capacity before the boom phase is reached.*

The inner mechanism of capitalism was effective enough to overcome the lowest point of the crisis, to bring about the transition to a depression, and in some countries to create a limited revival; but it does not prove to be effective enough to produce a real boom, a prosperity phase.

---

[7] This deformation was manifested as early as the cycle of 1921-29; the boom was *not general.* Some countries (England, for instance) and whole industries (coal, shipbuilding, cotton) participated in the boom only to a very slight extent. The boom would have been even slighter if not for the necessity to make good the devastations of the war.

[8] It should be emphasized that the transition from the crisis phase to the depression phase of the industrial cycle does not mean an improvement in the economic position of the agricultural countries in general. In countries (such as the Balkans, South America and China) where industry represents no more than 10-20 per cent. economically, an increase of even 25 per cent. in industrial output involves an improvement of no more than 2.5—5 per cent. in the total economy of the country. *Should the condition of agriculture grow worse at the same time* (crop failure), then in spite of the transition to the depression in the field of industry *the whole economic condition of the country will grow still worse.* The depression involves an improvement in every case only for the industrial countries. For the agrarian countries it may be accompanied by further deterioration depending upon the actual conditions.

We must now determine why the rise in production once begun is now prematurely blocked by the market's absorption capacity at the present time. The decisive factors are as follows:

(a) The " material basis " of the boom is the expansion of the market for goods of Division I, especially the expansion and renewal of fixed capital in the process of real accumulation. (See Chapter I.) The chronic failure to utilise in full the available production apparatus and the chronic surplus of industrial capital characterize the period of the general crisis of capitalism. Germany serves as an example:

UTILIZATION OF CAPACITY OF GERMAN INDUSTRY

(in per cent.) [9]

1929	1930	1931	1932
67.4	52.2	44.5	35.7

Thus, even in the year of maximum production, 1929, the production apparatus of German industry worked at only two-thirds of capacity. The other capitalist countries present a similar picture. Needless to say, the bourgeoisie is reluctant under such circumstances to renew or increase fixed capital except in the armament industries, because the existence of unutilized plants reduces the rate of profit, the surplus value being divided among an unnecessarily large capital. But without it a boom is impossible.

(b) The great crisis led to a tremendous process of centralization. The establishment of monopolies,[10] the monopolist nature of capitalism, has developed enormously. In some countries (Germany, England, U.S.A.) the formation of monopolies was aided by governmental measures. But the stronger the monopolies, the stronger also the brakes on technical progress and the slighter the incentive to renew fixed capital.

Naturally, this does not mean that technical progress has come to a stop altogether; under capitalism this is impossible. (Even the feverish improvement in *armament technique* would be impossible without certain technical progress in other spheres of industry.) The following seems to us to be the qualitatively new element: owing to low wages and the great surplus of fixed capital *only such technical improvements are introduced as secure a very great reduction in production costs, i.e.,* a particularly great reduction in the labour power required. A slight reduction in the cost of production is not enough to induce new investments of capital.

(c) The increased formation of monopolies lessened the fall in prices of monopoly goods (see above). Trade monopolies and the rise in turnover and consumption taxes resulted in *retail prices dropping much less than*

[9] *Vierteljahreshefte,* Vol. 7, No. 2, p. 119. As a rule forty-eight working hours a week are taken as complete utilization of capacity.

[10] Some of the international cartels and trusts collapsed during the crisis; in the period of depression a revival of the tendency to establish (or re-establish) international monopolies may be noticed. During the crisis, the organization of monopolies within individual countries proceeded at an accelerated rate with the aid of State measures.

wholesale prices.[11]   This restricted sales to the ultimate consumer, which *in the final analysis* also determine the level of production in Division I.

(d) In previous cycles, the capitalist market expanded through drawing the independent peasant producers, working largely for their own needs, into the capitalist exchange of commodities.   In this connection Lenin says :

> " The fundamental process of the formation of a home market (*i.e.,* the development of commodity production and capitalism) is social division of labour.   This means that, one after another, various forms of working up raw materials (and various operations in this process) become separated from agriculture and become independent branches of industry which exchange their products (now become *commodities*) for the products of agriculture. Thus, agriculture itself becomes an industry (*i.e.,* production of commodities) and the same process of specialization takes place in it." [12]

The differentiation and disintegration of the peasantry proceeds along with the spread of commodity production; an agricultural bourgeoisie is formed on the one hand, and an agricultural proletariat on the other, whereby the capitalist market continues to expand notwithstanding the impoverishment of wide sections of the peasant population.

> " The transformation of the peasantry into an agricultural proletariat thus creates a market chiefly for consumers' goods, while its transformation into a rural burgeoisie creates a market principally for means of production. In other words, labour power becomes a commodity in the lower groups of the ' peasantry,' while the means of production become capital in the upper groups." [13]

In the present depression the following change has taken place : the process of " depeasantizing," as Lenin calls it, *i.e.,* drawing the agricultural producers into the capitalist market is essentially completed in the most highly developed capitalist countries : the U.S.A., England and Germany.   In the present agrarian crisis the process of differentiation develops into the wholesale ruin of the small and middle peasants.   At the present time, however, this process is interlinked with the degradation of agriculture as already indicated in Chapter III—and hence there is *no* expansion but a decrease of the capitalist market.   Sales of the means of production are reduced because horses and human labour replace machinery, the use of artificial fertilizers is declining, and so forth.   The transformation of the peasantry into an agricultural proletariat does not create a market for consumers' goods since the proletarianized peasant chiefly increases the army of the unemployed!   The chronic agrarian

11 Comparative wholesale and retail prices, annual average (1913 = 100) : —

	U.S.A.		Germany		Poland	
	Wholesale	Retail	Wholesale	Retail	Wholesale	Retail
1929	137	171	137	154	127	113
1933	95	132	93	119	81	87
Reduction in per cent. ...	31	23	30	23	37	23

(*League of Nations Statistics*)

12 Lenin, *Selected Works*, Vol. I, " The Development of Capitalism in Russia," p. 223.

13 Lenin, *Collected Works*, Russian edition, Vol. III, " The Development of Capitalism in Russia," p. 120.

crisis is one of the main obstacles in the path of a boom! (The crop failure of 1934 will increase the misery of the toiling people in the countryside enormously; the rise in prices—relatively insignificant due to the pressure of large stocks—will not compensate for the loss in the size of the harvest even for most of the landowners and rich peasants.)

(e) In former cycles the capitalist market was enlarged extensively by drawing new regions into the capitalist mode of production: by the conquest and opening up of colonies. To-day the world is already partitioned; there are no more rulerless regions to conquer. Intensive exploitation of the colonies as markets is hampered by the development of consumers' goods industries in the colonial and semi-colonial countries themselves, a process which has not stopped even during the crisis.

(f) During the period of imperialism the export of capital was one of the most powerful levers for expanding the boundaries of the capitalist market. All export of capital means supplementary *sales of goods*,[14] which would be impossible if the respective countries had to pay the equivalent of the delivered goods at once. *At present the export of capital has almost completely ceased.*[15]

The main reasons for this are as follows:

1 *Economically*: the crisis has shown that with the present tendency to abandon the world economic division of labour, with the chronic agrarian crisis and with tariff walls, it is very difficult for the capital-importing debtor countries to transfer the interest or the profit on the foreign capital invested there, since the creditor countries do not want to buy the debtor countries' goods.

2. *Politically*: the world is close to the second round of wars, but the coalitions of countries for the next world war are not yet definite. Each country faces the menace of *strengthening its future enemy* through the export of capital, and losing its capital in the war.

The prospect of an impending war hampers replacement of the " morally obsolete " fixed capital; the capitalists expect that war with its enormous demand and high prices will render even obsolete plants, now fit to be scrapped, profitable.

But the world is also close to the second round of revolutions. The menace of the proletarian revolution impedes capital investments in general, and capital export in particular. The bourgeoisie tries to keep its capital in liquid form; it sacrifices higher profits for greater security.

(g) *The huge decline in the income of the working class* as a result of mass unemployment, reduced earnings, increased taxes, and so on, is one of the most important factors limiting the market for consumers' goods. The transition to depression has done very little to change this. *Production has increased, the number of exploited workers has increased, but the total purchasing power of wages has scarcely risen.*[16]

[14] Only in very rare cases is capital exported in the form of gold; as a rule it assumes the form of commodity export.

[15] See Chapter II for data.

[16] For details see next chapter.

The *changed character of rationalization* during the crisis plays a great role in this regard.

Before the crisis the task that capital set its scientists, technicians, organizers and speed-up men, was approximately as follows :

"Reduce my production cost per unit. If that can't be done without increasing the quantity of goods produced, don't worry about it. Sales are my affair. There is always a market for a good commodity at a low price."

The crisis has taught capital that in the period of the general crisis of capitalism there are very narrow limits to the expansion of the capitalist market. The crisis has taught capital that in many cases the cost of production in the "thoroughly rationalized" plants equipped for mass production, where the entire process is mechanized and runs on the conveyor system, has risen to a far greater extent owing to the reduced output, than in the less modern plants.

In the crisis, capital therefore set its scientists, technicians, organizers and speed-up men the following task :

"*Reduce the cost of production per unit provided that this does not lead to an increase in the quantity of commodities produced,* since there is no prospect of increased sales." Or still more concretely : "Attain lower production costs with the plant running at far below capacity, as at present."

Scientists, technicians, engineers and speed-up men have carried out capital's orders. Although plants were running at far below production capacity the cost of production has dropped considerably.

Of the methods employed for this purpose, the following seem to us to be most important :

(1) Concentrating production in the best plants of the monopolist organizations and closing down the inferior plants. *Within the plant* only the latest machinery is used, while the others are shut down, or vice versa, the conveyor is abandoned for more primitive methods of production better suited to the limited sales.

(2) Choosing the workers who are "best" : from the standpoint of capital, workers who accept speed-up and increased intensity of labour with as little resistance as possible.

(3) *Increased intensity of labour accompanied by severe reductions in wages.* Part-time work[17] in various forms enables capital to increase the intensity of labour to the maximum during the actual working day. And if the workers are rapidly and prematurely worn-out by this murderous speed-up, capital need not worry; the millions of unemployed always provide plenty of fresh material for exploitation.

(4) The division of the labour process into separate, absolutely simple movements and the extensive mechanization of the labour process reduces

---

[17] In America, the workers work only two or three days a week in the coal, iron and steel, automobile and other industries, although the factory runs full-time. The factory's labour time does not coincide with the labour time of the employed workers. The factory "employs" double the number of workers it can accommodate, but most of them work only every other day. This was the case in many branches of industry in the U.S.A., even during the boom period.

the number of skilled workers who are more difficult to replace, and converts the great mass of workers into easily replaceable unskilled and semi-skilled workers.

Thus, new forms of rationalization enabled monopoly capital to increase the workers' output during the crisis considerably and to make the proletariat bear the burden of the crisis to a large degree.

This peculiarity of crisis rationalization is an important element in the special nature of the present depression. The reduction of production costs at the expense of the workers lessens the incentive to renew fixed capital, thus limiting the expansion of the market for the means of production, while lowering wages narrows the market for consumers' goods.

*   *   *   *   *

To sum up, the transition to the stage of depression has increased the return on capital. Capital succeeded, as Stalin says, in improving its position somewhat at the expense of the workers, at the expense of the peasantry, and at the expense of the colonies. This was also the case in previous depressions. But formerly the better return on capital led to large new investments, to the expansion of the market for Division I, and hence for Division II as well, and thus to a new boom. This is not the case now. New investments of capital are reduced to a minimum; the " material basis " for a boom is lacking. That is why increased production strikes the snag of the limited market after a few months, commodities do not find an adequate sale, the stocks of manufactured goods again pile up[18] and a new setback occurs. These setbacks would have been still greater and industrial production still lower if the rapidly growing preparations for war did not provide a supplementary market even though it be of an unproductive character.[19]

THE OUTLOOK

In recent years the economic prerequisites for the revolutionary collapse of capitalism have developed by leaps and bounds. The contradiction between productive forces and production relationships has become palpable. The bourgeoisie is incapable of utilizing the productive forces created by it; there is a chronic surplus of capital together with a surplus of population, closed down plants and starving armies of unemployed. The large-scale " methodical " destruction of capital and of every kind of commodities shows how far the decay of capitalism has proceeded. The finance oligarchy, in trying to improve its position at the cost of all the remaining sections of the population is expropriating the weaker capitalists and the petty bourgeoisie through concentration of capital and, in using the state apparatus dominated by it to plunder the entire population, accentuates

[18] This is most clearly shown in the U.S.A. The index of stocks of finished goods, which had dropped to 96 by December, 1932, rose to 110 in December, 1933 (192 for textiles).

[19] The quantitative extent of the increased preparations for war may be determined approximately, but only through very complicated calculations. We estimate that from 10 to 40 per cent. (depending on the individual countries) of the increase in industrial production of 1933 was due to war preparations.

the contradictions between productive forces and the production relationships still further. It restricts ever more the consuming power of society and intensifies the general crisis of capitalism.

The same causes that entail the particular nature of the present depression also determine the further course of capitalist economy. The general crisis of capitalism, the end of temporary stabilization and the ensuing aggravation of imperialist and class contradictions, as well as the general instability of all relations, will produce another and still greater deformation of the industrial cycle. Except for a few countries, perhaps, the present depression will drag on for many years, with brief booms and sharp relapses, without passing into a period of prosperity, *and finally, it will be succeeded by a new, deeper and more devastating economic crisis.* . . .

Such would be the outlook if the outbreak of world war and *the outbreak of a proletarian revolution were delayed for many years to come.* This, however, is highly improbable. Dissatisfied with the slight improvement in the return on capital in the present depression of a special kind, the bourgeoisie will look to war as a way out. The proletariat, whose situation in the depression is hardly any better than it was in the crisis, will—with the help of the toiling peasantry and the oppressed colonial peoples—seek its way out in the offensive against the rule of the bourgeoisie.

CHAPTER VII

THE SOCIAL CONSEQUENCES OF THE ECONOMIC CRISIS

ACCENTUATED STRUGGLES WITHIN THE RULING CLASSES

C R I S I S and depression have seriously deranged the capitalist system of society. The inner conflicts among all the sections of capitalist society have become very acute.

The economic basis for this is the decrease in total profits during the crisis. As outlined above, the total appropriated *surplus value* has diminished during the crisis because the increased rate of exploitation did not compensate for the reduction in the number of workers exploited. The effect of the prolonged and heavy drop in prices during the crisis was that goods were very often sold at a loss. The workers were exploited, but capital realised no profit. Under these circumstances the struggle for the division of the profits (or losses) necessarily became extremely sharp. This struggle is proceeding along various contradictory lines. All sections of the bourgeoisie in countries of agricultural imports combat the artificial maintenance of high ground rents, which raise the price of foodstuffs, make wage-cutting difficult, and hamper the reduction of production costs, thus hampering their ability to compete in the world market.

Agrarians and peasants, the industrial bourgeoisie and the petty bourgeoisie fight jointly for the reduction of interest charges against loan capital, against the coupon-clipping class. The finished goods industries combat the raw material monopolies, the peasants fight against the big trading monopolies, and so on.

The struggle revolves around tariff policies, price policies, the incidence or shifting of taxes, government orders, subsidies, credits, etc.—*in short, control of the state*. In some countries, such as Germany, Japan and Austria, this struggle is already taking the form of political murders and armed struggles. The " crisis in the ruling class " is unmistakable.

IMPAIRMENT OF THE CONDITION OF THE URBAN PETTY BOURGEOISIE

The situation of all sections of the urban petty bourgeoisie has grown considerably worse. The *" independent" strata* : artisans, café owners, small shopkeepers, doctors, and the like, have suffered a catastrophic diminution of income, largely because of the impoverishment of the proletariat, which furnishes most of their clientèle. The growing competition of the co-operative societies, of department and chain stores, direct sales to consumers by capitalist bakeries, milk companies, canning plants, and so on, account for an ever-increasing share of the shrunken market. Most of the independent petty bourgeoisie fall more and more into debt to capital; they grow poorer and go bankrupt. Hence, the popularity of the fascist demagogy : " Break the chains of interest slavery," " Abolish department stores," among these groups.[1]

THE SOCIAL EFFECTS OF THE CRISIS UPON THE NON-INDEPENDENT PETTY-BOURGEOIS STRATA

The condition of the non-independent petty-bourgeois sections, the so-called " new middle classes," is still more disastrous. The crisis threw engineers, chemists and technicians out of industry *en masse*. The rationalization of office work threw millions of clerical employees out of work. Armament expenditures increase rapidly, but the bourgeoisie can find no money for cultural purposes. Wholesale unemployment exists among teachers and scientific workers. Those who still hold positions have had to accept salary reductions. Since there is a shortage of funds, teachers receive no salaries, sometimes for years on end; this occurs not only in such countries as China and Rumania, but in Chicago and other big cities of rich America as well. Tens of thousands of college graduates are glad to earn some sort of living as street sweepers, waiters or odd-job workers.

THE SOCIAL EFFECTS OF THE CRISIS UPON THE VARIOUS SECTIONS OF THE PEASANTRY

In Chapter III we dealt with the agrarian crisis as a whole. Now let us examine its effects upon the toiling peasantry.

Although all agricultural producers are affected by the fall in prices, by the growing burden of too high rents, intolerable debts and high taxes, it is a matter of course that (except for the agricultural labourers) the crisis hits the middle and small peasants worst of all. The reasons for this are as follows :

(a) The production costs of the small farm are higher than those of the capitalist large-scale farm. With the present state of prices the peasant produces at a loss, at a price level of agricultural commodities, allowing big farms to yield a profit.

(b) The rent paid by the peasant as tenant of a landlord's acreage is always " usury rent " in the sense that it not only swallows the excess of appropriated surplus value over and above the average profit, but the entire profit and even part of the wages as well.

(c) The rate of interest that the toiling peasants must pay the small provincial savings bank and village money-lenders is usurer's interest; it is considerably higher than the interest the big landowner pays on his mortgage, obtained at the original source.

(d) The *" price scissors "* hits the middle or small peasant much harder than it does the big producer, since the former is obliged to sell his commodities to the provincial trader (whose debtor he very often is) below the prevailing market price, or else his selling price is dictated by the big

---

[1] The number of artisans has diminished during the crisis, as far as one can judge, but the number of " independent " small shopkeepers *has not* decreased, since more and more of the unemployed are resorting to street hawking to eke out a miserable existence.

monopolies (dairy companies, flour mills and slaughter houses). At the same time he buys his manufactured articles from middlemen at higher prices. For the toiling peasants, therefore, the gap in the "price scissors" is much wider than that in the official indices based on wholesale prices. When minimum prices for agricultural produce are fixed by the state, they are gotten only by the big landowners and the rich peasants, whereas the middle and the small peasants have to sell their produce cheaper.[2]

(e) The taxes the toiling peasants have to pay are considerably higher per acre or in proportion to their income than those paid by the landowners and rich peasants, who are able, through their dominating position in the governmental and communal machinery, and through their "connections," to shift the tax burden largely to the shoulders of the toiling peasantry.

(f) Ninety-nine per cent. of the *aid* which the capitalist state offers "argiculture" in the form of cheap credit, remission of debts, subsidies, and so on, is obtained by the big landlords and rich peasants; the toiling peasants are left empty-handed.

Thus the agrarian crisis hits the middle and poor peasants most heavily all along the line.

The effects of the agricultural crisis can therefore be formulated from the class point of view as follows:

The process of continued differentiation characteristic of all capitalism —the sinking of part of the middle and poor peasants into the ranks of the village poor and the proletariat, and the rise of a very tiny section into the ranks of the rich peasantry—is intensified in the agrarian crisis to the point of *mass ruin of the poor and middle peasants.* The toiling peasants are expropriated at a rapid rate. More and more of the land passes into the hands of the banks, usurers and speculators; the former owner becomes an exploited tenant on what was formerly his own land.[3]

The degradation of agriculture, which is discussed in Chapter III, strikes the middle and small peasants most of all. Their income—after deducting taxes, rent and interest—is not enough to maintain simple reproduction even in spite of the greatest personal privations and the strenuous labour of the entire family. Worn-out machinery cannot be renewed, livestock that dies cannot be replaced. The peasants incessantly sink lower and lower into hopeless misery.

This holds true for the "independent" middle and small peasants. The situation of the village poor, who cannot live without extra earnings

---

[2] A minimum price of 127 francs per quintal of wheat was established in France in 1933; but the peasants received only 80 to 90 francs. (See *Statist,* April 21, 1934.)

[3] The percentage of farmers in the U.S.A. working leased land exclusively was as follows, according to census data:—

1900	1920	1925	1930
35.3	38.1	38.9	42.4

In 1930-34, this process of dispossessing the farmers from their land continued at an even faster pace. At the present time probably as many as 50 per cent. of the farmers in the U.S.A. are working leased land. (The farmers who lease other land in addition to their own are not included in these figures.)

from wage labour, is desperate. The almost complete standstill of build-ing construction, mass unemployment in industry, and the compulsory enrolment of the unemployed as " auxiliary labour " on the farms of well-to-do peasants (Germany), all make it impossible for the village poor to find the extra employment as wage labourers that is absolutely neces-sary for them to make a living. Their position is hopeless and starvation is daily at their door.

Marx already pointed out that in agriculture the replacement of workers by the machine is irrevocable. Before the general crisis of capitalism, the labour power released in agriculture could find employment in industry. To-day this is no longer the case. During the industrial crisis, the tide of unemployed workers, of industrial workers deprived of unemployment insurance, began to flow back from the cities to the countryside, to their relatives, in order to escape death from starvation. Opportunities for the village poor to get employment become still rarer. *The more difficult it is to find employment, the stronger the drive of the poor rural population to cultivate land themselves, so as to utilize their idle labour power* and keep from starving. While millions of former peasant proprietors were deprived of their land during the crisis, other millions strove to lease small plots of land at usurer's rentals, thus retarding the adjustment of land rent to the changed price level still further.

A few concrete examples suffice to show the impoverishment of the toiling peasantry in various countries. We cite bourgeois sources exclu-sively :

U.S.A. (Arkansas) :
    The last remnants of their meagre harvests are now used up. The live-stock is taken off to the woods—to end there. The children cannot go to school, for they have no clothes. The Red Cross is the last hope.[4]

U.S.A. (Oklahoma) :
    Debts which they will never be able to pay and the mortgage foreclosures are rapidly reducing the number of independent farmers. They have become tenants. Large areas of Oklahoma are now in the hands of the insurance societies, whose wage-workers the farmers now are.[5]

Canada (Saskatchewan) :
    In South Saskatchewan the farmer received in the middle of January 35 cents for a bushel of wheat No. 1, the best quality, and 15 cents for poor quality. Few of them have much to sell. There are some who do not receive sufficient from the sale of their wheat to pay the threshing costs. In those parts in which such conditions exist, the poorer classes of farmers are reduced to a ration of rough house-baked bread with syrup, alternated by a few potatoes, for their sustenance. Cases have been cited in which fried field-mice and other earth-inhabiting creatures and soup of Russian thistles have been the only means of preventing death by starvation.[6]

Italy
    " *Polenta* must take the place of honour as of old, and there must be little

---

[4] *Chicago Tribune*, quoted in *Literary Digest*, February 28, 1931.

[5] London *Times*, November 17, 1930.

[6] *Ibid*, February 19, 1930.

bread and hardly any meat in the peasant diet. I see no other way out of our present troubles." [7]

"Fortunately, the Italian people is not used to several meals a day, and since its standard of living is modest, it feels shortage and privation much less." [8]

Hungary

Two years ago a Hungarian illustrated paper printed a picture of a horse found on a country road with a rag tied to it; wrapped in the rag there was a horse's passport together with a letter which read:

"I have completed my autumn work with this horse. I have no fodder to keep it through the winter. I cannot sell it because there are no buyers. I haven't the heart to kill it. I'm letting it go free; perhaps somebody will take it in and feed it."

Conditions in a large German village in Hungary, with 2,000 inhabitants, are described as follows in an article by L. Leopold in the *Pester Lloyd,* November 19, 1933:

"Only one paper is received in the whole village. The total annual consumption of pencils is ten dozen, including the school. The barber relates: 'There isn't any money at all left in the village. The peasants haven't a red cent and get a shave only for big holidays. . . . The people here have no money. Hardly a few pengo in the whole village. They gradually stopped counting in money terms. Since the village shopkeeper himself has no cash and cannot buy either wheat or rye, nobody even talks of money prices.'"

Japan

"The agrarian crisis, which has ensued since the end of the war, has never been paid so little attention as now. Its results have been a decisive reduction of the number of peasant landlords, the growth of conflicts between tenants and landlords, the desertion of the farmers by the progressive youths and girls, the continued deficit in the peasants' budget and the continuous accumulation of unpayable debts. . . . The farmer is disillusioned by the repeated relief campaigns, which in the long run are undertaken at his expense, and had no other effect but to perpetuate the conditions of his suffering." [9]

These quotations could be continued indefinitely. Everywhere we have the same picture—the consistent impoverishment of the exploited rural population under the blows of the crisis. Discontent is widespread and finds expression in numerous peasant revolts, to which we shall return later.

It is self-evident that the 1934 crop failure—hailed with delight by some of the landowners—has turned the miserable condition of the village poor and of the small peasants, who always must buy additional foodstuffs, into a disaster. The situation of the middle peasants, whose harvest *this* year was not enough to meet their own requirements, has grown still worse. The rise in prices that followed the crop failure benefits only a

[7] The fascist professor, Bizorrero, in *Corriere Paduano* of June 11, 1931, quoted in the *Economist,* August 29, 1931.

[8] Mussolini, speech in the Senate, December 18, 1930.

[9] S. Washio in the *Trans-Pacific,* December 7, 1933.

small upper crust of landowners and rich peasants, but entails still greater misery for the exploited sections of the rural population.

THE IMPOVERISHMENT OF THE PROLETARIAT

The absolute and relative impoverishment of the proletariat proceeded at an accelerated rate during the interval between the Sixth Congress and the Seventh. In spite of the growing resistance of the proletariat, in spite of great, stubborn, often bloody strikes (particularly in 1933 and 1934), the capitalist offensive *proved successful on the whole.* Capital has largely succeeded—to an uneven degree in different countries, and by varying methods—in making the proletariat bear the burden of the crisis.

The impairment of the workers' conditions proceeded along the following main lines in all countries :

(a) Increase in the number of unemployed (and part-time workers).

(b) Reduction in the *real wage* of the employed workers.

(c) Increased intensity of labour.

(d) Curtailment of social insurance.

We must definitely emphasize the fact that the official figures used by us below, as the only ones available for investigating the condition of the working class, *have been falsified in many cases.* The bourgeoisie endeavours to have the conditions of the working class appear in a better light. In many cases this falsification can be proved from the official figures themselves. In most cases, however, exposure of the frauds requires more space than we have at our disposal. But the impairment of the conditions of the working class is clearly evident even from bourgeois statistics.

(a) MASS UNEMPLOYMENT AND INCREASED LABOUR OUTPUT DURING THE CRISIS

There are no reliable statistics of unemployment throughout the world. Unemployment among agricultural labourers and semi-proletarians is nowhere recorded. We can only reproduce the official statistics and prove by a few examples how they are falsified.

PERCENTAGE OF UNEMPLOYED INDUSTRIAL WORKERS

	1929	1930	1931	1932	1933	1934 (first six months)
Germany (trade unions)...	13.2	22.2	34.3	43.8	44.7 [10]	17.5 [11]
Austria (receiving dole)	12.8	16.2	20.2	27.2	31.1	29.4
Belgium („ „)	1.3	3.6	10.9	19.0	17.0	19.0
Canada („ „)	5.7	11.1	16.8	22.0	22.3	19.4
Denmark	15.5	13.7	17.9	31.7	28.8	24.7
U.S.A. (trade unions) ...	12.0	21.0	26.0	32.0	31.0	23.0
Norway („ „) ...	15.4	16.6	22.3	30.8	33.4	37.3
Holland (insured) ...	7.5	9.7	18.7	29.9	31.4	30.7
England (prolonged unemployment)	8.2	11.8	16.7	17.6	16.4	14.8
England (together with the " temporarily stopped ")	11.8	16.8	23.1	25.5	23.2	17.4

[10] Last figures of the General Federation of Trade Unions in Germany, May.
[11] Statistics of the German Labour Front.

These figures do not give a complete picture of the prevalence of unemployment. Unemployment among agricultural labourers and poor peasants, and part-time *work* (although the latter is very widespread) are not listed. None the less they show that the officially listed percentage of unemployed rose everywhere up to and including 1932 and that the percentage of unemployed is much higher than in any of the preceding crises.

Of particular importance, however, is the fact that *the transition to the period of depression and the increase of industrial production in 1933 was accompanied by a disproportionately slight reduction in the percentage of unemployed.*

The explanation for this peculiar fact is that the *trend towards the reduction of the number of workers employed by industrial capital,* as Marx uses the term—agriculture, industry, building, transport—a tendency pointed out by us before the crisis, at the Sixth Congress of the Comintern,[12] *has been increased considerably by crisis rationalization in the highly developed capitalist countries.*[13] In other words, in the period of the general crisis of capitalism, the process of displacing workers as a result of increased productivity and intensity of labour (a process which is inherent in capitalism) can no longer be compensated by an increase of production. At increasingly short intervals the expansion of production clashes, as we have pointed out above, more and more sharply with the limits of the capitalist market which grows increasingly narrow with the continued development of the general crisis of capitalism and with the chronic aggravation of the contradiction between the production and sales possi-

---

12 E. Varga, *Die Wirtschaft des Niedergangsperiode des Kapitalismus nach der Stabilisierung* [*Economy in the Period of the Decline of Capitalism After Stabilization*]. Chapter III, 1928.

13 *The trend of the number of workers* employed in industry to diminish, *even before the crisis,* is evidenced by the following figures:—

NUMBER OF WORKERS EMPLOYED IN INDUSTRY AND IN CRAFT TRADES IN GERMANY

(in millions)

(In enterprises employing more than five workers)

1925	1926	1927	1928	1929	1930
9.5	7.6	8.9	9.1	8.3	7.5

We see that the number of workers employed was far behind that of 1925. (All the figures are *official.*)

The tendency towards reduction of the number of productive workers, producing value and surplus value, is most clearly shown in the United States. The following official census figures illustrate this particularly well:—

Workers (in thousands)

	1919	1925	1929	1931
Agricultural workers(a)	2,336	—	2,733	—
Railwaymen	1,960	1,786	1,694	1,283
Miners	888	—	788	—
Industrial workers	9,041	8,384	8,839	6,523
	14,225		14,054	

Even during the peak of the boom in 1929 the number of workers exploited by industrial capital did not equal the total for 1919, although the index of industrial production (mining + industry) was 83 in 1919 and 119 in 1929 (1923-25=100). An increase of more than 40 per cent. in the volume of industrial production was achieved with a reduction in the absolute number of workers employed.

(a) Figures for 1920 and 1930.

bilities. To-day the correctness of Engels' thesis, written forty years ago, is proved with special clearness :

" The daily increasing speed with which production can to-day be increased in all fields of large-scale industry is offset by the continually increasing slowness with which the markets for these increased products expand. What the former turns out in months, the latter can scarcely absorb in years." [14]

Hence, because of lack of a market, it is impossible to have such an expansion of production as could—except for cyclic fluctuations—prevent a reduction in the number of employed workers in the most advanced capitalist countries.

The following table compiled by the National Industrial Conference Board, a bourgeois institution, may serve as an illustration of this development in the U.S.A.:[15]

(1923-25 = 100)

	Production	Employment	Labour hours	Wages paid	Output per worker	Output per working hour	Labour cost per unit of output
1923	101	104.2	106.5	103.4	97.3	95.0	102.3
1924	94	96.2	93.9	95.7	97.7	100.1	102.1
1925	105	99.6	99.9	100.9	105.1	104.8	96.5
1926	108	101.4	101.6	104.3	106.5	106.3	96.6
1927	106	98.8	98.0	102.0	107.1	107.9	96.6
1928	112	97.2	97.0	101.8	114.8	115.0	91.3
1929	119	101.1	101.8	107.7	117.8	117.0	90.7
1930	95	87.8	80.7	87.4	108.4	117.9	91.9
1931	80	74.4	64.4	66.0	107.7	124.4	82.2
1932	63	62.0	48.3	45.3	101.2	130.3	72.1
1933	76	66.2	52.0	47.5	114.8	145.0	63.4

This table indicates quite clearly the roots of the growing chronic mass unemployment and the economic basis for the declining trend in the number of workers employed in the industries of highly developed capitalist countries (and in production as a whole).

In the course of ten years the output per worker has increased by 17.5 per cent. and the output per worker-hour by 50 per cent. (The smaller increase in the output per worker is due to the *shorter working day* during the crisis; *up to 1929 the rise in the output per worker and per hour run parallel.*) The increase in output was particularly steep during the crisis owing to crisis rationalization. The output per hour increased from 118 to 145 during the interval 1931-33. As a result, an increase in the production index from 63 in 1932 to 76 in 1933 (*i.e.*, by 20 per cent.) was accompanied by a rise in the index of employment by 4.2 or only six per cent. If as many workers had full-time employment as in 1923, with the present output per worker in American industry, production would be fully 50 per cent. greater. And *if as many workers were now employed as in the*

[14] *Capital*, Vol. III, Chapter XXVII, p. 518.

[15] *National Industrial Conference Board Bulletin*, Feb. 20, 1934, p. 10.

*last prosperity year, 1929, the volume of production would exceed that of
1929 by 25 per cent.* and be almost double that of 1933. In fact, *it would
be much more than double,* since the increase in the output per worker
would undoubtedly continue still further. But even the most optimistic
ideologists of American capitalism would not have the courage to prophesy
such an increase in production. This means that American industry will
never again employ as many workers as it did in 1919 or even in 1929.
This means that the process of discharging workers from American industry, as well as from agriculture and mining, which began in 1919, will
continue. This means that chronic mass unemployment will tend to increase, aside from cyclic fluctuations.

The increase in output per worker in the U.S.A. as a result of crisis
rationalization was most strikingly shown in the period preceding the
general introduction of part-time work through the N.I.R.A.[16]

OFFICIAL STATISTICS OF AMERICAN INDUSTRY

(1923-25 = 100)

	Volume of Industrial Production	Employment	Wages
May 1932	61	61	46
May 1933	80	60	42

In the course of one year production was increased 31 per cent., while
the number of workers employed dropped, and wages fell by ten per cent.

This great increase in output per worker during the crisis is not peculiar
to American industry alone.

The German Institute of Business Research gives the following figures
for the increase in output per worker per hour for the whole of German
industry.[17]

1925	1928	1929	1930	1931	1932
87.3	100	106.6	115.6	121	124.4

OUTPUT PER PIT-WORKER IN GERMAN COAL MINES [18]

(1913 = 100)

1925	1928	1929	1930	1931	1932	1933
103.6	126	134	144	163	180	187

It is clear that such an increase in output must eventually lead to a
further reduction in the number of employed workers in Germany as
well.

A similar trend is seen in England. Industrial production in 1933 was

[16] N.I.R.A.—the National Industrial Recovery Act; the law empowering the President of
the United States to regulate industry by means of decrees. (" Codes.")

[17] *Wochenbericht,* July 5, 1933. *Deutschlands wirtschaftliche Lage an der Jahreswende,*
1933-34.

[18] Reichskreditgesellschaft [*The Economic Position of Germany at the Close of* 1933].
Glückauf, June 3, 1934.

98.5 (1924 = 100) according to the official Board of Trade Index, whereas the index of employment was only 86.3.

A rapid increase in the output per worker also took place in the coal-mining industry in France.[19]

AVERAGE OUTPUT PER SHIFT IN POUNDS

1930	1931	1932	1933
1,350	1,588	1,725	1,875

Finally, let us take the increase in output per worker during the crisis in the Japanese textile industry, which is the country's major industry.[20]

	Cotton Yarn Output Bales per worker per month	Number of employed workers per 1,000 spindles
1927	1.23	35.3
1929	1.46	27.5
1930	1.51	23.5
1931	1.75	20.6
1932	1.85	20.1

NUMBER OF WORKERS PER 100 LOOMS

	Men	Women	Total
1927	132	660	792
1929	122	494	616
1930	113	430	543
1931	90	357	447
1932	79	368	447

Parallel with the trend towards reduction in the number of workers employed by industrial capital, who directly create value and surplus value, the number of workers employed in trade, banking, etc., who do not create value, tends to increase. This is best seen in Great Britain:

SHIFT IN NUMBER OF PRODUCTIVE AND NON-PRODUCTIVE WORKERS EMPLOYED IN GREAT BRITAIN [21] (IN THOUSANDS)

	Industry, Mining, Building and Transport	Per Cent.	Trade, Banking, etc.	Per cent.
1928	7,940	77.2	2,344	22.8
1929	7,926	73.4	2,875	26.6
1930	7,507	71.9	2,933	28.1
1931	7,024	69.9	3,021	30.1
1932	6,890	69.1	3,077	30.9
1933	7,111	69.2	3,165	30.8

As we see, the number of non-productive workers *increased* by 300,000,

[19] Data of the Coal Committee.

[20] Data of the Japanese textile cartel, *Japan Advertiser*, Special Supplement, January, 1933.

[21] Taken from the *Labour Gazette*. From the total number of workers listed as employed on a certain day in the various branches of industry the average number of unemployed are deducted.

during the crisis, whereas the number of productive workers creating value and surplus value diminished by 800,000. The decay of capitalism is manifested here most strikingly.

*   *   *   *   *

Owing to the lack of reliable data it is impossible to ascertain definitely the absolute number of unemployed. The official figures record only the number of " registered " unemployed. Since the cuts in unemployment insurance have eliminated the incentive for the workers to register, statistics give a completely false (or deliberately falsified) picture of unemployment. The following figures are interesting (but not reliable), therefore, as showing *the trend of world employment but they must not be taken as absolute figures.*

WORLD UNEMPLOYMENT
Index [22]

					Number in millions [23]	
1929	...	...	...	100	March 1931 ...	21
1930	...	...	...	168	December 1932	28
1931	...	...	...	241	March 1933 ...	30
1932	...	...	...	297	March 1934 ...	32.5
1933	...	...	...	279		

That the number of unemployed is falsified, as in Germany for example, is proved by comparing the following figures (all of them official).

	August 1929	August 1933 [24]
	(in millions)	
Number of employed according to sickness insurance fund statistics	18.77	12.72
Unemployed	1.27	4.12
Total	20.04	17.84

Two million two hundred thousand workers have simply disappeared from German statistics in the course of four years; they are neither employed nor officially unemployed. To this there must be added some hundred thousands representing the difference between the number of workers who have reached the working age and the old workers, who have dropped out of the labour market either through death or disability.[25] Finally, there are the hundreds of thousands of small peasants,

[22] *International Labour Review*, April, 1934.

[23] *Wirtschaft und Statistik* [*Economy and Statistics*], May, 1934.

[24] In order to " trim " the statistics, the fascist government included various categories of forced labourers (who receive no wages) in the sickness insurance statistics, so that the " corrected " number of employed was announced as 13,725,000 in August, 1933.

[25] According to German official estimates, the number of persons reaching the working age was (in thousands):

1930	1931	1932	1933	Total
664	575	594	745	2,538

To offset this, the number of deaths between the ages of fifteen and fifty-five are less than 200,000 per annum.

artisans, petty shopkeepers, who were robbed of their "independent" existence in the crisis and thrown into the ranks of the unemployed.

To sum up: chronic mass unemployment, this terrible scourge of the proletariat in the capitalist countries of to-day, is not a transient cyclic phenomenon. The transition to depression has mitigated it to only a small extent. *It is impossible to place the army of unemployed in production again,* as was the case with the industrial reserve armies in boom periods before the crisis of capitalism. This would require a production level far exceeding that of 1929, of which, however, there is no likelihood.

Thus the situation has arisen which Marx foresaw as a hypothesis:

" *A development of the productive forces which would diminish the absolute number of labourers.* [The number of workers employed is under discussion.—E. V.], that is, which would enable the entire nation to accomplish its total production in a shorter time, *would cause a revolution,* because it would put the majority of the population upon the shelf." [26]

The development of productive forces has reached this stage; the period of the general crisis of capitalism is the period of the social revolution.

(b) THE REDUCTION OF REAL WAGES

Bourgeois wage statistics are so falsified and so unreliable that they give no picture of the lowering of real earnings even of workers who are fully employed. All the calculations given below must therefore be used with the greatest reserve. In order to avoid any charge of exaggeration, we have taken, in all doubtful cases, the figures that are more favourable to the workers.

The wages of the full-time workers were reduced in three different ways:

(1) Elimination of " wages above agreement schedules." [27]

(2) Lowering of *collective agreement wages.*

(3) Increase in *taxes and wage deductions.*

Germany:
DECLINE OF AVERAGE EARNINGS IN THE BUILDING TRADES FROM AUGUST 1929 TO AUGUST 1932 (in per cent.) [28]
(For all cities with more than 100,000 inhabitants)

	Bricklayers	Carpenters	Semi-skilled building workers	Excavation workers
Reduction in per cent. of gross earnings ...	41.8	34.9	33.5	33.9

Between August 1932 and August 1933 (*i.e.,* already under the fascist regime) the collective agreement wages in the building trades were further reduced some 5 per cent.

---

26 *Capital*, Vol. III, Chap. XV, p. 309.

27 " Wages above agreement rates " are used in these statistics to mean additional wages which piece-workers receive over and above the hourly wage fixed by the collective agreement.

28 *Wirtschaft und Statistik*, No. 17, 1933, p. 544.

Reductions in the collective agreement wages of other trades were somewhat smaller. Between October 1929 and February 1933 typical wage cuts were as follows: skilled workers in the metal industry 18.1 per cent.; chemical industry 18.7-18.9 per cent.; textile workers 13.9-15.5 per cent. In addition, earnings above the collective agreement rates were cut 5-8 per cent.

The wages paid the workers are further reduced, moreover, during the crisis by numerous new taxes and imposts,[29] which together comprise about five per cent. of wages.

The reduction in money wages of the fully employed worker totals from 25 to 52 per cent., depending on the branches of industry. Wage cuts for the higher-paid trades were greater than for the lower-paid ones.

Compared with this the official cost of living index (1913-14 = 100):

	1921	August 1934	Rate of fall
Total	158.8	123.3	22
Rent	126.2	121.3	4.5
Food	154.5	118.5	23

The official figures *doubtless* list the drop in the cost of living too high rather than too low.[30] But even if we accept the official figures, we get a drop in real wages of from 5 to 32 per cent. in the case of the full-time workers.

The full-time workers represent a minority of the German working class, however. According to trade union statistics, average employment was as follows in 1932 (in per cent.):

Full-time workers	Part-time workers	Totally unemployed
33.6	22.6	43.8

The total income of the German working class as a whole, including the unemployed, has diminished enormously during the crisis, especially since unemployed insurance benefits have been cut at a rapid rate and the burden of maintaining the unemployed has been shifted to an increasing extent to the shoulders of the employed workers.

The total income of workers, office employees and civil servants was as

---

[29] (a) Increase in social insurance deductions: rise of 1.5 per cent. of wages in unemployment insurance contribution;

   (b) " Crisis tax " (newly introduced): one per cent. on wages exceeding 100 marks per month;

   (c) " Aid to married people ": all unmarried workers have to pay 2 per cent. on monthly earnings of from 75 to 150 marks, and 3 per cent. on monthly earnings of from 150 to 300 (more than half the industrial workers are unmarried);

   (d) " Donations to work creation ": " voluntary " (!) contribution of 1 to 2 per cent. of wages (now abolished);

   (e) Winter aid donation: approximately one hour's wages per month;

   (f) Numerous " collections," compulsory subscriptions to the fascist press, etc.;

   (g) Citizen tax: six marks per annum.

[30] Particularly rent, which remained relatively stable, has been inadequately weighted. Moreover, the prices of those foods that the worker now buys, because of his diminished money income, sank less than the average while some, such as margarine, have risen sharply.

follows, according to the estimate of the Institute for Business Research (billions of marks) : [31]

1929	1930	1931	1932	1933
44.5	41.0	32.5	25.7	26.1

The decline from 1929 to 1933 is 41 per cent. To this we must add an increase of at least 5 per cent. in taxes and deductions, hence a total *decline in money income of 46.6 per cent.*

The decline would be still greater for the *workers alone* since there is less unemployment among the higher employees and civil servants, and the latter's wages are cut much less. Even assuming that all the official figures and the official calculations of a drop of 21 per cent. in the cost of living are correct, we find a *net reduction of 26 per cent in real wages for all workers, office employees and civil servants.* The actual reduction in the real wages of workers alone is undoubtedly a few per cent. higher. According to our estimate, the real income of the German working class has declined about one-third during the crisis.

United States

Real wages of the full-time workers as well as the income of the working class as a whole declined considerably in the United States during the crisis

AVERAGE WEEKLY EARNINGS OF ALL INDUSTRIAL WORKERS [32]

	1928	1929	March 1933 (Minimum)	March 1934	Decline in Per Cent. since 1929
	27.88	29.17	14.56	20.49	29.8
Cost of living [33] (1923 = 100) ...	100.8	100	71.8	78.5	21.5

It must be emphasized that this cost of living index, like the German one, is based on a standard of living that is much too high, and inapplicable to the period of crisis. For instance, only 33 per cent. of total expenditure is allocated for food. Hence the rise of 20 per cent. in the food index between March 1933 and March 1934 is quite independently reflected in the total index.

The American census of manufactures enables one to calculate the *rate of surplus value* in industry with some degree of accuracy on the basis of wages paid and the increase in value due to production. The result is as follows :

TREND OF THE RATE OF SURPLUS VALUE IN U.S. INDUSTRY [34]

1899	1909	1919	1921	1923	1925	1927	1929	1931
128	130	122	106	118	128	133	152	147

Konjunkturstatistisches Handbuch [*Handbook of Business Statistics*] 1933, p. 80, for 1933, cf. *Wochenbericht* [*Weekly Report*], No. 23, September 3, 1933.

[32] Data from the *National Industrial Conference Board Bulletin.*

[33] Index of the *National Industrial Conference Board Bulletin.*

[34] *Cf.* Appendix for the method of calculation.

We can see that the rate of exploitation shows a decidedly rising trend. The drop in the crisis year 1921—and to a slighter extent in the present crisis—*does not denote a diminution in the exploitation* of the *productive* workers, who create surplus value, but indicates a relatively higher proportion of wages paid to the unproductive, supervising, guard and office personnel, due to plants being operated at far below capacity during the crisis.

The impairment of the condition of the working class in the U.S.A. was largely due, however, to the *tremendous unemployment*. According to various estimates (there are no official statistics) the number of totally unemployed has exceeded ten million for many years. Part-time work is likewise widespread. This enormous unemployment is manifested in the huge decline of wages paid.

INDEX OF WAGES PAID IN BIG AMERICAN INDUSTRIES [35]
(Federal Reserve Board, 1923-25 = 100)

1929	1930	1931	1932	1933	1934 (first 4 months)
109	89	68	46	49	61

Thus, the total wages paid in 1933 was only 45 per cent. of the 1929 level. This enormous drop is not mitigated by any sort of unemployment insurance. The workers ate up their savings[36] they sold their automobiles, furniture, houses and fell into the hands of their creditors. In "rich" America, millions are homeless and starving; they become tramps and sink to the level of the *lumpen*-proletariat.

In conclusion some data on the impairment of the condition of the workers in Japan :

TREND OF REAL WAGES IN JAPAN [37]
(1926 = 100)

	1929	1930	1931	1932	1933	March 1934
Hourly wages ...	98.6	96.2	91.3	88.1	85.1	83.5
Actual earnings ...	103.9	98.7	90.7	88.1	89.2	91.6
Cost of living (1914 = 100)	—	—	135.5	136.8	145.6.	149.0 (May)

The increase in the actual amount of earnings while wages per hour

[35] These figures are based on data supplied monthly by the big plants which together employ approximately three million workers. We have reason to believe that wages in small enterprises, in agriculture and trade, have dropped at least as much.

[36] SAVINGS BANK DEPOSITS AND DEPOSITORS IN THE U.S.A.

	Deposits (millions of dollars)	Number of depositors (thousands)
June, 1929	62,764	28,218
,, 1933	39,268	21,421

Thus, almost seven million depositors consumed all their savings between 1929 and 1933. The total sum of the deposits dropped 23,500,000,000 dollars in four years. There is no doubt that it is largely the workers who ate up their savings. Inflation further reduced what remained by 40 per cent.!

[37] Data from the Economic Bureau of the Mitsubishi concern.

decline is due to the overtime and night work prevalent in the armament industries. In recent years *real wages* fell by 20-25 per cent. even according to these figures taken from capitalist sources.

We can dispense with figures for other countries, as they present the same picture.[38]

The wages of agricultural labourers have declined to an even greater extent than those of industrial workers. Here are a few instances.[39]

	Canada	U.S.A.	New Zealand
		(Wage per day)	(weekly wage)
	(1914 = 100)	(1927 = 100)	(1914 = 100)
1929	194	99	179
1932	106	49	125
1933	100	48	115

We can easily form an idea of the frightful poverty of the agricultural labourers in the capitalist world when we take into consideration the enormous unemployment in agriculture, the absence of any sickness, accident or unemployment insurance in most countries and the reports on the conditions of the peasantry quoted above.

(c) CUTTING DOWN SOCIAL INSURANCE

In the last four years social insurance has been cut all along the line in every country. Unemployment insurance exists only in England, practically speaking (and there it is reduced by the Means Test). In all other countries where unemployment insurance existed, nothing but miserable shreds of it are left.

Germany may serve as an example. By forced labour, by discharging workers in whose families there is a wage earner, by hiring workers who draw an unemployment dole, by stopping unemployment relief to Communists and Social-Democrats, and by imprisoning the unemployed in concentration camps, unemployment insurance has been practically abolished by the fascists.

REGISTERED UNEMPLOYED IN VARIOUS CATEGORIES (IN PER CENT.)

	Receiving unemployment insurance	Receiving crisis relief	Public welfare relief	Receiving no relief
January, 1929 ...	78.8	5.1		
June 1934	10.5	33.0	32.0	24.5

But the number of those receiving no relief in fact exceeds 50 per cent. since, as we have shown above, at least 2,200,000 and probably 3,000,000 unemployed do not register at all, having given up all hope of ever getting work or unemployment relief.

Paralleling the withdrawal of relief, the amount of relief itself was cut

---

[38] According to official data the real wages of full-time workers have declined least of all in England and Sweden.

[39] Data from the *Statistical Yearbook* of the League of Nations, 1933-34.

for all categories. As the cities have no funds, public welfare relief has been reduced to the most pitiful alms. Similar cuts have been made in all other forms of social insurance.

(d) Working Hours

A few words about working hours. Motivated by fear of the millions of unemployed, the bourgeois governments and the reformist trade unions in many countries have advocated a compulsory reduction of working hours, the " planned distribution of work " (naturally with a corresponding reduction in earnings). This was carried out on a large scale only in Roosevelt's " Codes," which *on the whole,* however, only sanctioned the existing state of affairs. In 1932, the working hours per week in the factories of the U.S.A. averaged 34.8.[40] But this average covered the most glaring disproportions. In 1932, nine factories in the woollen industry worked 60 hours a week in the night shift, two factories 65 hours, and one 67.5 hours (likewise in the night shift). In the cotton industry, 39 factories worked 11 hours daily in the night shift and ten factories 12 hours.[41]

Capital's complete indifference to the fate of the workers (and the uneven employment index in different factories) is shown by the fact that *in Britain, with hundreds of thousands unemployed in the very same branch of industry,* not only part-time but also overtime is worked. The following table gives British data for September 1933.[42]

	OVERTIME		PART-TIME	
	Per cent. of workers	Overtime hours per week	Per cent. of workers	Number of hours less per week
Worsted industry	26.5	6	12	11
Woollen industry	23.0	7	16	10
Shoe industry ...	16.0	7.25	37	9.5

There are similar phenomena in France. Although part-time work is quite general, there are plants where the hours of work are inhumanly long. The laundries and millineries of Paris work up to 18 hours a day, confectioneries 12 hours, and so on. Overtime is worked regularly in the armament plants. No doubt this is also the case in other countries that do not publish such detailed statistics.

(e) Increasing the Intensity of Labour

We have furnished exhaustive data above on the increased labour output during the crisis. This increase was due almost exclusively to the increased *intensity* of labour. Productivity of labour probably increased only in exceptional cases, since on the whole no improved machinery was introduced during the crisis. The most important methods employed to increase the intensity of labour were as follows : speeding up machinery;

[40] *Survey of Current Business,* January, 1933, p. 28.

[41] According to the official figures of the U.S. Labour Department, cited in the *American Federationist,* organ of the A.F. of L., February, 1933, p. 184.

[42] *Labour Gazette,* October, 1933.

increasing the number of looms operated by one worker in the textile industry; introducing the conveyor and running it at a faster rate; " scientific " management (Bedaux): increasing the supervising staff, introducing the espionage system, fines, etc.

(f) FORCED LABOUR

Finally, we should like to point out a *new* phenomenon: the ever-wider growth of various forms of " voluntary " forced labour, to which youth is subjected in an increasing number of countries. It is furthest developed in Germany and in the U.S.A. The youths are quartered in camps and employed as unskilled labourers (road building, drainage, canals, military fortifications, and so on), at the same time undergoing military training. Another form of forced labour is the allocation of un-employed workers to rich peasants on whose farms they have to work through the summer for food, lodging and a little pocket money. In case they refuse to undertake this work, they are deprived of unemployment or welfare relief. The forced labour system which has existed in the colonies for a long time, is now being more and more extended in various forms to the most advanced capitalist countries.

(g) THE FRIGHTFUL CONDITIONS OF THE WORKERS IN THE COLONIES

The conditions of the colonial workers have doubtless grown worse more rapidly than those of the workers in the imperialist countries. Colonial capital has cut wages and impaired labour conditions by using the most brutal force. There is no statistical data that is at all usable. We must confine ourselves to a few concrete instances taken at random from bour-geois sources.

Cuba :

" Labourers are working for 10 cents a day throughout Cuba, and large numbers are unable to get jobs even at that wage. . . . Families carrying children in their arms are seen asleep in vacant doorways others prowl about garbage pails for something to eat." [43]

Porto Rico :

" It is estimated that there were about 200,000 unemployed family heads on the island; since the average family has 5.6 persons, about 1,120,000 persons are affected, two-thirds of the total population of 1,600,000. " [44]

India :

" Taking the City and Island of Bombay, it is seen that 5 out of 84 mills have been scrapped. . . . Twenty-nine mills have been closed down. . . . The total number of unemployed workers is thus easily more than 61,000. . . .

" In other words, for every 100 persons employed, there are 70 workers who are thrown out of employment. . . . In the midst of the closure of 29 mills no less than 14 mills are working night shift. . . .

[43] *Herald Tribune*, January 25, 1934.
[44] *The New York Times*, April 8, 1934.

" Forty-eight out of the remaining 50 mills which are working have made cuts varying from 7 per cent., to 44.5 per cent. . . .

" There are only two mills in Bombay which have so far made no direct cut in wages. But these have been put on the rationalization basis by giving more looms and spindles to the workers. . . ." [45]

" Unemployed coolies from the tin mines and the rubber estates drift through the streets like ghosts. . . . Thousands of Chinese and Indian labourers are being repatriated every month. . . . Every Mohammedan store has its crowd of beggars. . . . Chinese women hide behind the pillars of the shops watching their children invade the parked cars with their hands to their mouths as a sign of hunger, mumbling broken petitions between their spread fingers. . . ." [46]

The quotations could be continued endlessly.

[45] *Bombay Chronicle*, February 8, 1934.
[46] *Manchester Guardian*, February 17, 1933.

CHAPTER VIII
THE RISE OF THE SOVIET UNION

T H E six years since the Sixth Congress have shown the workers of the whole world, through the example of the Soviet Union, what it really means to have the productive forces freed from the shackles of the capitalist mode of production. For in these six years the Dictatorship of the Proletariat—which Kautsky and Co., the lackeys of the bourgeoisie, claimed had " stabilized hunger and suffering "—has rendered possible rapid progress in the technical, economic, social and cultural fields such as the world has never known. The gigantic First Five-Year Plan, which the bourgeoisie and the Social-Democrats called a fraud or at best a utopia, was completed in four and a quarter years. In order to measure the tremendous extent of the progress which has been made in these six years, let us sketch the principal features of the Soviet Union's situation in the fiscal year 1927-28.

Compared with the leading capitalist countries, the Soviet Union was a decidedly *backward country in the field of technology.* Only the simplest machines could be made within the country itself. The decisively important means of production : lathes, tractors, combines, automobiles, airplanes, chemicals, etc., were not made in the country. Agricultural technique was completely backward, very little different from that of the pre-war period; even the wooden plough was still widely used.

In the economic field the Soviet Union was still an *agrarian country* in 1927-28. Agriculture accounted for 51.3 per cent. of the gross value of production, industry for only 48.7 per cent. (The situation had scarcely changed compared to the pre-war period; at that time agriculture accounted for 57.9 per cent. and industry for 42.1 per cent.[1])

At that time the Soviet Union was largely dependent on the capitalist countries economically, because it had to import the principal means of production. Industry still produced articles of consumption primarily; *only 27.2 per cent. of the gross value of industrial production represented means of production, while 72.8 per cent. were articles of consumption.*[2]

A boycott by the capitalist countries could therefore have cut off technico-economic progress. Development of the country's defences was also dependent on the outside capitalist world. Equipping agriculture with modern instruments of production, without which the transition to socialist agriculture is impossible, was out of the question.

The problem that Lenin had posed still faced the Bolsheviks in all its magnitude : *Either catch up with the capitalist countries economically and surpass them, or perish.*

At that time capitalism still possessed strong roots in the Soviet Union.

[1] Stalin, *Report to the Sixteenth Congress of the C.P.S.U.*
[2] *Ibid.*

Some 12 per cent. of industrial production was still in private hands, while some 17 per cent. of the industrial workers were employed by exploiters.[3] Still more important: private ownership dominated agriculture. There were about 24,000,000 peasant farms, with a tendency to further division. They comprised roughly:

7,000,000 poor peasants,
16,000,000 middle peasants,
1,000,000 kulaks.

The kulaks owned about 10 per cent. of the land, and they exploited at least one-quarter of the agricultural population, either directly as workers, or indirectly through renting out draught animals and machines, through usurious loans, etc. In the middle of 1928, Stalin said:

" . . . raising the level of individual small and middle peasant production . . . is still the chief aim of our work in the sphere of agriculture." [4]

The transition from this policy of improving the small and middle *individual* peasant farms, of combating and limiting the capitalist elements,[5] to the policy of liquidating the kulaks as a class, on the basis of thorough collectivization, was only contemplated as yet.

This means that the great question which had been posed by Lenin— " Who will defeat whom "—had not yet been finally settled in the Soviet Union, *that possibilities still existed for the restoration of capitalism!* Even after the Sixth Congress of the Comintern, Stalin said in this connection:

" Do the conditions exist in our Soviet country that make the restoration of capitalism *possible?* Yes, they do exist. That, comrades, may appear strange, but is a fact. We have overthrown capitalism, we have established the dictatorship of the proletariat, we are intensely developing our socialist industry and are closely linking it up with peasant economy; but we have not yet torn out the roots of capitalism. Where are these roots implanted? They are implanted in the system of commodity production, in small production in the towns, and particularly in the villages. As Lenin said, the strength of capitalism lies ' in the strength of *small production,* for unfortunately, small production still survives in a very, very large degree, and small production *gives birth* to capitalism and to bourgeoisie, constantly, daily, hourly, spontaneously and on a mass scale.' [*Collected Works,* Russian edition, Vol. XXV, p. 173.] Hence, since small production is a mass phenomenon, and even a predominant feature of our country, and since it gives birth to capitalism and to a bourgeoisie constantly and on a mass scale, particularly under the conditions of N.E.P., it is obvious that the conditions do exist which make the restoration of capitalism possible." [6]

[3] Larin, *Private Capital in the Soviet Union,* Moscow, 1927. (In Russian.)

[4] Stalin, *Leninism,* Vol. II, " The Results of the July Plenum of the Central Committee of the C.P.S.U.," p. 48.

[5] " The proletarian state power has succeeded in keeping within narrow limits the young capitalist shoots unavoidably sprouting in town and country on the New Economic Policy foundation." (Resolution of the Sixth Congress on " The Situation in the Soviet Union and the C.P.S.U.")

[6] Stalin, *Leninism,* Vol. II, " The Right Danger in the C.P.S.U.", p. 60.

In this regard Lenin said:

" As long as we live in a small-peasant country there will be a firmer economic basis for capitalism in Russia than for communism. That must always be kept in mind. Everyone who has carefully observed village life as compared with the life in the city, knows that we have not eradicated the roots of capitalism and that we have not undermined the basis, the foundation of our internal enemy. . . . Only when the country is electrified, only when industry, agriculture and transport are placed on the technical basis of modern, large-scale industry—only then will our victory be complete." [7]

Viewed dynamically, the Soviet power still rested essentially on two contradictory foundations at that time:

" on the basis of large-scale socialist industry which *destroys* the capitalist elements, and on small, individual peasant farming, which generates capitalist elements." [8]

In the social sphere: the condition of the industrial working class had already improved considerably, but average yearly earnings were still only 843 roubles; there still was considerable unemployment, housing conditions were still very bad, and the large-scale construction of workers' dwellings had only begun. *The condition of the agricultural workers and of the village poor* was far from uniform; their dependence on the kulaks and their exploitation were very great in many districts, where the local Soviet machinery was under the latter's influence. The kulaks conducted an active struggle against the Soviet Union by refusing to deliver grain, and there were moments in 1928 when the alliance of the working class and the middle peasantry was imperilled.

The technical specialist personnel of all kinds, with the exception of the army, still consisted predominantly of old, bourgeois elements, very many of whom were hostile to the Soviet Union. In many cases, as the Shakhty trial proved, this went as far as active counter-revolutionary sabotage, under instructions from *emigré* whiteguards or the general staffs of foreign countries.

Progress in the cultural field was already very great; yet only 58 per cent. of the population could read and write. The workers and sons of workers studying at the universities were still very slight in number; the bourgeoisie's monopoly of education was still unbroken. Development of the various national cultures had only begun.

This, in the roughest outlines, is the picture of the Soviet Union at the time of the Sixth Congress. *The six years that have elapsed since then have involved an unprecedented change, giant progress, in all fields,* the results of which were summarized as follows by Comrade Stalin at the Seventeenth Congress of the C.P.S.U.:

" During this period, the U.S.S.R. has become radically transformed; it has discarded the features of backwardness and mediævalism. From an agrarian country it has become transformed into an industrial country. From

[7] Lenin, *Collected Works*, Russian edition, Vol. XXVI, pp. 46-47.

[8] Symposium, *From the First to the Second Five-Year Plan*, Stalin, " The Results of the First Five-Year Plan," p. 115.

a land of small individual agriculture it has become a land of collective, large-scale, mechanized agriculture. From an ignorant, illiterate and uncultured country it has become—or rather it is becoming—a literate and cultured country, covered with a network of higher, middle and elementary schools operating in the languages of the nationalities of the U.S.S.R." [9]

Let us illustrate this for the entire period from 1928 to 1934.

In the field of technology: construction of the most complicated machines and tractors has been commenced (motors, tractors, combines, giant turbines, blooming mills, rotary printing presses, airplanes, etc., etc.). The chemical industry has been newly created; this is the only country in the world where synthetic rubber is produced on a factory basis. Production of the most complex metal alloys has been undertaken, etc.

In the field of economics: *industrial production has increased by leaps and bounds,* and thousands of new industrial plants have been established, which in size and modernity exceed those in European countries, and are equalled only in the U.S.A.

GROWTH OF INDUSTRIAL PRODUCTION [10]

(1929 = 100)

	1928	1929	1930	1931	1932	1933	1934 (Plan)
Soviet Union	79.4	100	129.7	161.9	184.7	201.6	243.9
Capitalist world [11] ...	93.7	100	87.1	73.1	62.6	71.1	70.0

The volume of industrial production has tripled during six years. During the same period, production in the capitalist world has decreased 30 per cent. It is now approximately on the 1913 level, whereas production in the Soviet Union has more than quadrupled since then. This one contrast is enough to demonstrate the absolute superiority of the Soviet system over the capitalist system! Trotsky's counter-revolutionary chatter to the effect that the economy of the Soviet Union is " regulated " by the economy of the capitalist world has been proved completely false. The rise of industrial production in the Soviet Union has proceeded untouched by the severest industrial crisis in the capitalst world.[12]

The reason why there is no over-production crisis in the Soviet Union, and why there cannot be any, is as follows:

Under capitalism, the extent of production is determined in the long run by the consuming power of society, " by the poverty and restriction

9 Stalin, Report at the Seventeenth Congress of the C.P.S.U., Socialism Victorious, p. 24.

10 We supplement the figures given by Stalin, with data for the year 1928, and for the 1934 plan, according to the State Planning Commission data.

11 From the figures of the German Institute for Business Research (*Special Bulletin*, No. 31, and *Vierteljahrshefte*, 1934, II, B), recalculated from a 1928 to a 1929 basis. For 1934, *my estimate is used.*

12 The agrarian crisis made it more difficult to export agricultural products; the industrial crisis hampered the export of raw materials, but likewise reduced the purchase price of industrial goods. On the whole the influence of the crisis in the capitalist countries on the economy of the Soviet Union was very slight.

of consumption of the masses." In the Soviet Union the reverse is true : *the expansion of consumption is governed by the extent of production* (and by the requirements of socialist accumulation). There is no *social* obstacle to limitless increase in the consumption of the working population of the Soviet Union, until the latter is many times greater than at present. The sole limitation is the magnitude of production itself. In other words, there is *no market problem in the Soviet Union* in the capitalist sense of the term; when production increases, the consuming power of the population increases parallel with it.[13]

The following figures show *the conversion of the Soviet Union from an agrarian country into an industrial country.*

RATIO OF INDUSTRY AND AGRICULTURE IN THE TOTAL PRODUCTION OF THE SOVIET UNION (AT 1926-27 PRICE LEVEL).

	1928	1929	1930	1931	1932	1933	1934 (Plan)
Industry	53.1	54.5	61.6	66.7	70.7	70.4	79.2
Agriculture ...	46.9	45.5	38.4	33.3	29.3	29.6	20.8

The transformation of the Soviet Union from an agrarian country to an industrial country is shown not only in this rapid increase in the proportion of industrial production, but in *the changed relationship between Divisions I and II as well*. There is a very rapid proportional increase in the production of the means of production. Although, as we have shown above, the exceptional severity of the crisis in capitalist countries is determined precisely by the extremely large decline in the production of the means of production, although the bourgeoisie issues the slogan of stopping the expansion of production capacity and, finally, although it is precisely in the leading capitalist countries that an anarchic (and in many cases organized) destruction of the means of production has taken place during the crisis, in the Soviet Union every effort is exerted to develop the production of the means of production. These efforts are meeting with complete success, as the following figures show :

RATIO OF DIVISIONS I AND II IN LARGE-SCALE INDUSTRIAL PRODUCTION OF THE SOVIET UNION (AT 1926-27 PRICE LEVEL)

	1928	1929	1930	1931	1932	1933
Division I	46.7	48.5	52.6	55.4	57.0	58.0
Division II	53.3	51.5	47.4	44.6	43.0	42.0

Between 1928 and 1933 the proportion of *machinery* production in the total value of industrial production has risen from 13.3 per cent. to 26.1 per cent. *More than one-quarter of total industrial production is the production of machinery,* something which has probably never been the case in any capitalist country.

And this fundamental reconstruction of Soviet industry, the new con-

---

[13] Because of the necessity for rapid expansion of the productive apparatus, *i.e.*, for using a very large part of the value produced for socialist accumulation, consuming power, that is, the demand for consumers' goods, actually exceeds the supply. Hence the temporary " goods famine " at times.

struction of thousands of factories, of powerful central power stations, canals, railroads, and great new crities in former waste areas, *has all been created by the workers of the Soviet Union themselves.* In the years 1929-33 alone, sixty billion roubles were invested in industry in the Soviet Union, at a time when new capital investments in the capitalist world had fallen almost to zero. The means for industrializing the country were obtained not with the help of foreign loans,[14] not by plundering colonies, as in most capitalist countries, but through the enthusiastic work of the toilers of the Soviet Union.

What made it possible for the Soviet Union to carry through this tremendous task with its own forces? It is the *dictatorship of the proletariat,* the superiority of the Soviet system to capitalism, that performed this miracle. The most important factors in this respect are the following:

(a) *There are no parasites in the Soviet Union.* The wide class of landowners, bourgeoisie, coupon-clippers, priests, etc., and the enormous train of servants and hangers-on they maintain, does not exist. There are no English lords with their town palaces and country manors, with their hundreds of stewards and servants, cooks, chamber-maids, stable-boys, masters of the hounds, hunters, governesses, chauffeurs, pilots, etc. The whole insane, stupid luxury—the ruling classes, the daily new costumes of the bourgeois ladies, the display of wealth in jewelry and the like— the dictatorship of the proletariat has swept all these idle trappings of bourgeois society beyond the borders of the Soviet Union. There is no equality of income, indeed; high output gets higher pay. The stage of communism, when everyone will consume according to his needs, and work according to his abilities, has not yet been reached. A few outstanding writers, architects, physicians, have relatively high incomes. These are exceptional cases; in general the standard of living of a factory director, who has millions of rubles at his disposal, or that of a People's Commissar, is no higher than that of an intermediate official under capitalism. This is not asceticism, but the *conscious temporary limitation of the entire population's needs,* to make possible a speedier tempo of socialist construction!

(b) *In the Soviet Union there are no unemployed.* While half of those seeking employment in capitalist countries are unable to find work because the rotting system of capitalism, undermined by the fever of the crisis, is unable to give the workers jobs, every healthy person in the Soviet Union, without exception, is at work. Although in capitalist countries it is considered distinguished to lead an idle life, in the Soviet Union it is considered a disgrace not to work if one is able to.[15]

(c) *In the Soviet Union every worker feels responsible for production.* The mechanical class discipline of capitalism, the speed-up system, is

[14] The slight commodity credit that the Soviet Union gets abroad is quite insignificant compared to the investments made.

[15] According to the laws of the Soviet Union social pensioners (invalids, the aged, etc.) may work as workers or employees without any reduction in their pensions, and without receiving a lower wage or salary for the same work than that paid to " ordinary " workers.

replaced by a voluntary socialist discipline of work, which the workers impose upon themselves, as the ruling class. Socialist competition, the system of shock brigades, and the moral pressure of the majority of workers, who are consciously striving to make their factory progress, sweep along with them the minority of workers, only recently recruited from the villages, who are still less advanced. The workers, especially the Party members, feel that they share responsibility for the factory's success; in many meetings the collective experience of the workers is gathered and used for the benefit of the factory. The relationship between the workers and the factory is totally different from that under capitalism.

(d) *The economy of the Soviet Union is directed methodically.* The "overhead waste" of the capitalist mode of production : the cost of competition, of advertising, of bad investments, the periodically recurring destruction of values in crises, etc., do not exist in the U.S.S.R. The entire output of the population is usefully employed.

(e) *To these must be added the intensive utilization of the already available means of production.* The superiority of Soviet economy to capitalist economy is demonstrated particularly clearly in the *degree of utilization* of the means of production. Under capitalism, in general, the utilization of production equipment 48 hours a week is regarded as full employment; but in the Soviet Union, where work is done in three shifts of seven hours each, 147 hours a week is so regarded. We can illustrate the significance of this by taking the British cotton industry as an example. The British cotton industry has 52,000,000 spindles, of which only 39,900,000 were in use in 1932, for 35 hours a week, *i.e.,* 1,400,000,000 hours a week. In the Soviet Union, with the customary full utilization of all spindles 147 hours a week, they would work 7,620,000,000 hours a week, or more than five times as much! *With the full utilization customary in the Soviet Union, the English textile industry could produce one and a half times the total world demand for cotton goods.*

The methodical complete utilization of all productive forces by the proletariat as the ruling class made it possible to *double the national income in five years.* The latter rose from 25,000,000,000 rubles in 1928 to 50,000,000,000 in 1933. And since there are no parasite classes in the Soviet Union to squander a large part of the national income on meaningless luxury, since there is no wholesale destruction of values such as takes place under capitalism, a very large part of the national income can be used for socialist accumulation while raising the living standards of the entire population. In this way the Soviet Union was able, with its own forces, to convert the country from a backward agrarian land into a leading industrial country. *Only the dictatorship of the proletariat could accomplish this!*

New industrial construction covers *all parts of the territory of the Soviet Union,* from the polar regions to the deserts of Central Asia. Industrial centres have risen everywhere in the midst of the peasant population, which is of great importance in solving the problem of agriculture.

During these years a real revolution has taken place in agriculture!
The voluntary union of the toiling peasants into collective farms has
turned a country of backward peasant agriculture into a country of the
most modern large-scale farms.

DEVELOPMENT OF COLLECTIVIZATION

	1928	1929	1930	1931	1932	1933	1934 (June 1)
Number of collective farms (in thousands)	33.3	57.0	85.9	211.1	211.05	224.5	233.5
Number of collectivized farmsteads (in millions)	0.4	1.0	6.0	13.0	14.9	15.2	15.7
Collectivization of peasant farms in per cent. ...	1.7	3.9	23.6	52.7	61.5	65.0	70.8

Some 230,000 *large-scale collectivized enterprises have taken the place
of* 16,000,000 *peasant farms.* This was paralleled by the establishment of
big Soviet farms on hitherto uncultivated land. This transformation
would have been impossible without the tremendous progress in the
production of the most modern agricultural machinery.[16] Only because
the advantages of machine farming could be demonstrated to them in
practice through experience, did the poor and middle peasants voluntarily
decide to give up their private farms and to unite in collectives.

As a result of these changes the *" private sector "* is rapidly disappear-
ing from Soviet economy. In industry the proportion of the private sector
is now no more than one per cent. (The concessions of foreign capitalists
have outplayed their part and almost all of them have been taken over
by Soviet industry.) In agriculture the proportion of individual peasant
farms is about 15 per cent., and is constantly decreasing.[17]

*The collectivization of agriculture signifies a fundamental turn of the
village towards socialism.* Before collectivization there were approximately
1,000,000 kulaks in the agricultural population, exploiting 7,000,000 poor
peasants. (Large differences in income also existed among the middle
peasantry, depending upon the possessions of the individual peasants.)
*The basis for exploitation disappeared with the pooling of the land and
means of production*[18] *in collective farms,* and the acceptance of poor

[16] In 1933 the Soviet farms and collective farms had the following mechanical equipment:

Tractors	Combines	Motor trucks
204,100	25,000	24,400

In 1928 there was scarcely any such machinery employed in agriculture!

[17] Collectivization has progressed furthest in regions where grain cultivation predominates,
because there the advantages of collective farming are greatest. At the opposite pole are the
nomad peoples, still numerous in the territory of the Soviet Union, where one cannot even
speak of collectivization as yet.

[18] Collectivization, as is generally known, was temporarily overdone, in that the milch-
cows and smaller livestock serving the needs of the family itself were collectivized together
with the means of production and the draught animals. In many cases communes were
formed with complete community of property, income and consumption, instead of working
associations (" artels "). The Party opposed these excesses, which were historically premature.
(Cf. Stalin's famous article, *Dizzy with Success,* March, 1930.) Instead it issued, and is also
putting into practice, the slogan that every collective farmer should have at least one cow of
his own.

peasants as members enjoying full rights. There is no longer any necessity for the poor peasant to let himself be misused by private exploiters; the kulaks, whose land and means of production have been pooled in the collective farms, are no longer able to exploit the labour of others. *The kulaks are thus liquidated as a class.* The size of the agricultural population's income now depends primarily on the *number of days of work done on the collective farm* and on the quality of work of the whole collective!

As a result, at the present time, *the middle peasant* who, as Lenin said, felt attracted as a *working* man toward socialism, but as a *small producer* felt attracted to the old, familiar capitalism—is no longer the *central figure in the Soviet village. Now, the central figure is the collective farmer,* whose working conditions approach those of the industrial worker more and more closely (work in large enterprises, in brigades, in socialist competition, and with modern machinery), and whose whole attitude toward life is undergoing a corresponding change.   Lenin said the following in this regard :

" The middle peasant in a communist society will come over to our side only when we improve his standard of living. If to-morrow we could procure 100,000 first-class tractors, supply them with gasoline and mechanics (and, as you all know, that at present is a sheer fantasy), the middle peasant would cry, ' I am for the *communia! ' * [19] (*i.e.,* for communism)." [20]

With the change of the basic masses of peasants from small commodity producers to collective farmers, and the step-by-step transformation in their psychology, there also disappears the former intellectual influence of the petty bourgeoisie on the industrial working class, which Lenin considered so important a factor.

It is obvious that this tremendous change in class relationships could not be brought about without the bitterest resistance by the kulaks, without " revolutionary overhead costs."[21] The establishment of political sections in the tractor stations, to which tens of thousands of the best Party members were sent for day-by-day contact with the collective farmers, serves to facilitate the transition from individual to collective economy, as well as to liquidate the remainders of the kulak's ideological influence upon the collective farmers.

The present situation of the Soviet Union is summarized as follows in the Theses and Resolutions of the Seventeenth Party Congress :

" Already during the first Five-Year Plan period, thanks to the heroic struggle of the working class, the foundation of socialist economy was laid, the last capitalist class—the kulaks—was defeated and the basic masses of

[19] " *Communia* " is the term used by the peasants and repeated by Lenin.—*Ed.*
[20] Stalin, *Leninism,* Vol. II, " A Year of Great Change," p. 177.

[21] The major overhead cost was the great decline in the number of cattle, partly because the kulaks and the elements influenced by them slaughtered *very much* cattle during the collectivization campaigns, and in part because the transition from the individual keeping of livestock to big collective livestock ranches required a change in working methods which could not take place without some friction. At the present time the number of cattle is again increasing rapidly.

the peasantry—the collective farmers—became a firm support of the Soviet government in the countryside. The U.S.S.R. finally established itself on the socialist road." [22]

The position of the working class in the Soviet Union has improved very much in every respect during the years since the Sixth Congress. While chronic mass unemployment is constantly on the increase in the capitalist countries (aside from cyclic fluctuations), unemployment has been completely liquidated in the Soviet Union, and there is a permanent shortage of workers, although the number of workers and employees increased from 11,600,000 in 1928 to 23,400,000 in 1934, or more than 100 per cent. While wages were cut in the capitalist world, *the average earnings of an industrial worker in the U.S.S.R. have risen from 843 rubles in 1928 to 1,610 rubles in 1934*, although the working day has been reduced to seven hours (six hours for workers underground and in occupations injurious to health). Social expenditures are being reduced everywhere else, but in the Soviet Union they rose from 1,063,000,000 rubles in 1928 to 5,871,000,000 in 1934.[23]

However, it is not at all necessary to cite figures to demonstrate the tremendous improvement of the position of the working class during these years. One can see it with one's own eyes. *Torn shoes and patched clothes no longer prevail in the streets of the cities.* Hundreds of thousands of new dwellings and large, wholly new cities shelter the workers. Millions of workers engage in sports or occupy themselves with music. Hundreds of thousands who used to be manual workers have become technicians, factory directors and inventors.

The enormous achievements in the cultural sphere are known to our readers, and are acknowledged even by the bourgeoisie of the whole world. Illiteracy has been almost completely liquidated in the Soviet Union; seven years of compulsory school attendance now prevails.

NUMBER OF STUDENTS

	Elementary schools (Millions)	Intermediate schools (Thousands)	Universities, etc. (Thousands)
1928	11.9	2,415	180
1934	19.7	6,991	471

The number of pupils attending intermediate schools has increased tenfold in six years, and of those in the schools of higher learning has almost tripled!

Although under capitalism a worker who got as far as university study was looked upon as a rarity, 51.4 per cent. of the university students in the Soviet Union in 1933 were workers.

The result of this gigantic cultural progress is the *final abolition of the*

[22] Resolution on "The Second Five-Year Plan of Development of the National Economy of the U.S.S.R.," *Socialism Victorious*, p. 639.

[23] In 1934 approximately every fifth worker spent his vacation in a sanatorium or rest-home.

education monopoly of the specialists of bourgeois origin. The Soviet Union already has its new intelligentsia, stemming from the working class and working for socialist construction with all its might.

Under capitalism the selection of those capable of the highest mental achievements is made only from the narrow circle of the ruling classes. The son of a poor peasant or of an ordinary worker—although he may possess the genius of a Newton, a Hegel, or a Marx—finds the road to the development of his talent closed by the bourgeoisie's monopoly of the means of education. The sons of the ruling classes, on the other hand, no matter how unfit they may be for mental work, are helped by private tutors, by bribes, and by connections, in getting their university degrees. *In the Soviet Union, the selection of those fitted for the highest mental achievements takes place from among the entire people.* Every worker and every peasant is offered the opportunity of developing his abilities and, what is more, each is assisted in his efforts to educate himself. Every talent is discovered, whether in man or woman, young or old, a Russian or a member of any other nationality in the Soviet Union. *This systematic selection of all the talented from the entire population* (not merely from the narrow circle of the ruling classes) *ensures the future mental superiority of the Soviet Union to the capitalist world in all fields: technique, science and art.*

The cultural advance embraces *all the nationalities in the Soviet Union.* The uncultured state forced upon the peoples of Russia by the Great Russian chauvinism of the tsarist era making it impossible for them to develop a national culture, has been done away with. Dozens of nations have been awakened to a new cultural life. Newspapers, magazines and books are being printed in the languages of the formerly oppressed nations, and schools of all grades are established in these languages. An entirely new cultural world is being created.[24]

The gigantic advances of the Soviet Union in all fields—the undeniable fact of the superiority of the country of the dictatorship of the proletariat to the capitalist world—has enormously increased the Soviet Union's revolutionary influence upon the proletariat and the exploited strata of the agricultural population in the capitalist countries, as well as the oppressed colonial peoples. The apologists of capitalism have the greatest difficulty in discovering any arguments to counteract the growing drive of the proletariat to follow the Russian example. Even the mere recording of all the slanders, lies and distortions that the bourgeoisie uses to combat the revolutionary influence of the Soviet Union would lead us too far afield. We propose only to characterize the methods briefly.

1. *The method of gross lies and slander* (Kautsky, the Archbishop of Canterbury, etc.): There is no material or cultural progress in the Soviet

---

[24] The sale of books is fantastically high, compared with that in capitalist countries. Nineteen million copies of Gorky's books were sold during the past few years. Single novels by other writers attain editions of over one million copies. Scientific works appear in editions of as high as 50,000 copies. Total daily newspaper circulation has risen from 8,800,000 in 1928 to 38,500,000 in 1934.

Union. The Five-Year Plan is a swindle; the statistics of the Soviet Union are forged. Suffering is widespread, and millions are dying of hunger.

2. *Denial of the socialist character of the Soviet Union* : The material advances are recognized as a fact, but the social are not. Kautsky says : Not the dictatorship *of* the proletariat, but *" dictatorship of a minority over the proletariat."* Trotsky's characterization : " Degeneration and Thermidorianism." The following line of argument, by Dan, is characteristic of this " finer " falsification, intended to mislead the workers of the capitalist world.

" The elimination of the private economic sector by no means signifies that the capitalist trends in Soviet economy have been successfully destroyed. Capitalism, as a system of social relations in the productive process, is characterized by certain very definite traits. The immediate producers are no longer owners of the means of production, which, on the contrary, as ' capital ' stand in opposition to them and rule them. It is not the immediate producers who determine the tasks and conditions of their own work, but the owners of ' capital,' who appropriate a part of their work as surplus value and who occupy the position of a ' ruling class ' with respect to them. However much the cloak of ' proletarian dictatorship ' may disguise, it still cannot hide the fact that all these traits of a ' capitalist ' economy are also characteristic of Soviet economy." [25]

This refined demagogy deserves a few words by way of exposure. *Dan consciously confuses the technical category of large-scale production with the social category of capitalism.* A railway or a chemical *combinat*[26] cannot under any conditions be the private property of the immediate producer; only in a small-scale artisan production can the producers be the individual owners of their tools. In the Soviet Union the means of production are the *collective property of the people,* not the property of the bourgeoisie! In large-scale production it is impossible that the " tasks and conditions " of work be individually decided by each worker, as in craft manufacture. Under capitalism the bourgeoisie decides this, but in the Soviet Union the decisions are made by the organs of planned economy, the leaders of Soviet economy or of the individual enterprises, to whom this task has been entrusted by the entire working class. But these social functions, entrusted to them by the working class, in no way makes them a " ruling class." There is no possibility for them to " appropriate surplus value "[27]; their salaries are at most twice the earnings of skilled workers.

The bourgeoisie, the fascists, and the social-fascists combat the revolutionizing influence of the Soviet Union with all sorts of lies, libels and

[25] *Der Kampf,* April, 1932.

[26] An industrial aggregate of several component plants.

[27] Even in the Soviet Union the *individual* worker does not receive the " full product of his labour "; one part of it goes for socialist accumulation, another for the maintenance of the sick, the aged and those unable to work. But the entire product of the labour of all the working population does go either directly for its own benefit or for that of its children; no exploiter, no parasite has any share of it.

slanders : the religious crusade, the dumping campaign, the indictment of " Red imperialism," etc., etc.

But the truth slowly prevails none the less. Bourgeois individuals of all kinds, such as Herriot and the American, Cooper, world-famous writers like Bernard Shaw and Barbusse, and many, many others speak up for the truth. The working class of the capitalist world does not allow itself to be fooled by the Trotskys, Kautskys, Dans and Bauers. Its pressure even forces the Social-Democratic leaders to recognize the truth. Not long ago, for example, the French Social-Democrat Ziromsky said at a united-front mass meeting in Paris :

> "It is undeniable that the Soviet Union represents an element of social progress, where a new civilisation is being built on the basis of love for work. The overthrow of the Soviet Union would be a historical catastrophe." [28]

Truth does prevail!

---

[28] *l'Humanité,* August 25, 1934.

CHAPTER IX
THE SECOND BREACH—SOVIET CHINA

The most important social phenomenon of the last few years, besides the rise of the Soviet Union, is the occurrence of a second breach in the structure of bourgeois society, the emergence and consolidation of Soviet China. Although Soviet China has not been recognized as yet by any capitalist country, although the heroically fighting Chinese Red Army is called a "robber band" by its enemies, and although the frontiers of Soviet China still shift and the individual Soviet regions do not yet form a single connected whole, the significance of Soviet China as a factor in colonial revolution and foreign policy cannot be over-estimated.

The struggle and the success of Soviet China by its deeds concretely point out to the suppressed colonial peoples the road to their liberation. It shows the billion colonial peasants that under the guidance of the bourgeoisie they will never be able to sweep away the landlords and usurers who suck their life-blood, and take possession of the land they cultivate. It shows them that this can be done only through armed struggle under the hegemony of the proletariat. It shows them the betrayal of the "national" bourgeoisie—its alliance with the imperialists against the working people. It shows them the possibility of a material and cultural advance through establishing the democratic dictatorship of the workers and peasants in the form of the Soviet system. It shows them that the capitalist stage of development can be skipped. The revolutionizing example of the Soviet Union is now reinforced by the revolutionizing example of Soviet China which is much closer to the colonial peoples.

From the standpoint of foreign policy: the continued existence of Soviet China is the main obstacle to the final dismemberment of China among the imperialists, and thus constitutes an important factor in the struggle for the Pacific Ocean!

After the bourgeoisie betrayed the movement for the liberation of the Chinese people, Soviet China became the centre of the struggle against imperialist oppression. The proletariat possesses the hegemony in this struggle.

The rise of Soviet China occurred in a very short time. Six years ago, at the time of the Sixth Congress the Chinese revolution had just experienced a severe defeat.

"The first wave of the broad revolutionary movement of workers and peasants, largely marching under the slogans and (to a considerable extent), under the leadership of the Communist Party, is over. In a number of centres of the revolutionary movement, it ended in extremely grave defeats of the workers and peasants, in the physical extermination of a part of the Communist cadres of the workers' and peasants' movement, and of the revolutionary cadres as well, in a sharply expressed development of the extreme camps of the social forces, in the formulation of precise political slogans of

the contending classes, in the complete exposure of the Kuomintang leadership, in the acquisition of tremendously great revolutionary experience by the
toiling masses, and, finally, in the transition of the entire mass revolutionary
movement of China to its new phase : the Soviet phase.

"In connection with the regrouping of classes it is beyond doubt that a
certain consolidation of the reactionary forces is taking place. The bourgeoisie has not only made a definite alliance with the counter-revolutionary
feudal lords and militarists, but actually came to terms with foreign imperialism. . . ." [1]

This was at the time when Trotsky wanted to bury the Chinese revolution and issued the slogan of a "constituent assembly." That was when
several leading Chinese comrades lost courage and became renegades
(Tan Pin-shan, Chen Tu-hsiu), and when others tried to speed up the
revolutionary movement by force, by *putsch* attempts and terror against
the workers. In the resolution mentioned above, the Comintern characterized these events in the following manner :

"... Certain symptoms show that the workers' and peasants' revolution is
on the way to a renewed mighty upsurge." [2]

It demanded that the mass work of the Party among the workers and
peasants be strengthened, that Soviet regions be created, that the guerilla
troops be consolidated and transformed into Red Armies led by Communists.

"The E.C.C.I. believes that the main task of the Party in the Sovietized
peasant districts is to carry out the agrarian revolution and organise Red
Army detachments, with a view to uniting later these detachments gradually
into one common central Chinese Red Army." [3]

The six years since then have fully confirmed the correctness of the
Comintern's line. Soviet power was established in one area after another.
The Chinese workers and peasants in the Red Army, the Red Guards,
etc., organized under the leadership of the Communist Party of China,
have defended Soviet China in heroic battles. Although the Red Army
possesses no arsenal in the central Soviet area [4] and although it is largely
compelled to obtain its arms by capture from the enemy, [5] it succeeded
in victoriously repulsing five major campaigns by Chiang Kai-shek (the
sixth is still under way), and in annihilating armies up to five times its
size, organized by trained European officers (General von Seeckt, etc.),
and equipped by the imperialists with the latest arms.

How was this miraculous success possible? The heroism of the Chinese

[1] Resolution of the Ninth Plenum of the E.C.C.I. on "The Chinese Question," February,
1928.

[2] *Ibid.*

[3] *Ibid.*

[4] Only in the Soviet region in Szechwan are there two arsenals; the Central Soviet Area
merely possesses shops for the production and repair of small arms.

[5] According to Wellington Koo's estimate in the *Memorandum presented to the Lytton
Commission,* New York, 1933, Volume II, page 764, 25 per cent. of the arms were bought in
the foreign concessions, 10 per cent. manufactured in the Soviet areas; the balance, in one
form or another, came from the enemy.

Red Army is unquestionable. But this alone was not enough. The decisive factor is that the Red Army is supported by the entire working population, young and old, men and women, and that most of the soldiers in the Kuomintang armies did not want to fight against the Red Army, but took advantage of the first opportunity to surrender their arms and desert to the Reds. The superiority of the Soviet system to the reactionary Kuomintang regime and the mortal hatred for their oppressors felt by the workers and peasants conscripted into the Kuomintang armies are the underlying reasons for the Red Army's victories.

What Lenin said about the Soviet Union at the Third Congress of the Comintern holds true in even greater measure for the Chinese Soviet Republic:

"Only because the revolution is developing throughout the world is the international bourgeoisie unable to strangle us, although it is a hundred times stronger than we are economically and from a military standpoint." [6]

Only when we compare the conditions of the working population in Kuomintang China and in Soviet China are we able to understand the successes of the Red Army.[7]

During the six years since the victory of the counter-revolution in China the conditions of the working masses rapidly grew worse all along the line. The Kuomintang regime proved itself unable to solve a single problem of the bourgeois revolution. The *dismemberment of the country* still persists. The power of the Nanking government is felt only in the provinces around Shanghai and Nanking, while a hostile government rules in Southern China. The rival government in Fukien was wiped out only with the utmost effort; the North is ruled by a clique in Japan's pay; all sorts of generals rule in Szechwan, etc.

The Kuomintang regime was unable to liberate the land from the imperialists' yoke. On the contrary, it capitulated to the latter completely in order to obtain their support in its struggle against Soviet China. The Japanese imperialists have seized Manchuria; they are pressing onward to Mongolia, are the rulers of Northern China, and are preparing to sever it from Kuomintang China and establish a new puppet government there. Chiang Kai-shek capitulated to the Japanese long ago. He betrayed the battle of the 19th Army and of the Shanghai proletariat against the Japanese; he has *de facto* recognized Manchukuo; and he retreats before the Japanese invasion without offering battle. England and France are pressing forward in the south-west.

The Kuomintang regime has not solved the agrarian problem. On the contrary, conditions have grown appallingly worse. Irrigation works are falling into ruin, while the rivers flood the country year after year. Famine has become a constant phenomenon. The degradation of agriculture is

[6] *Minutes of the Third Congress,* page 748 (German edition).

[7] The following sections are based largely upon the preliminary work of our Chinese Institute, especially of Comrades Kara-Mursa, Grinevitz and Potopalov, as well as the very valuable collection of documents in *Rätechina (Soviet China).* Co-operative Publishing Society of Foreign Workers in the U.S.S.R., Moscow, 1934.

apparent; it is no longer able to feed the population! Importation of food for the cities is assuming ever greater proportions! Although suffering chronic starvation, the great mass of working peasants is no longer able to continue simple reproduction because it has been and still is fleeced on all sides by the landowners, the usurers, the state and the militarists. In many districts the price of land has fallen 50 per cent. Let us cite some data from bourgeois sources.

The burden of ground rent. In Hupei province *rent* formerly ate up 20 per cent. of the crop, in 1928 the figure was 40 per cent., and now 50 per cent. In Kiangsi the tenant must give the landowner 11 *piculs*[8] of the rice crop out of every 17.[9] The landlords, who control the provincial administration, have the tenant farmers who cannot pay rent thrown into jail. " In the district prison of Chansa (Kiangsi) 380 tenant farmers were under arrest in May, 1933." To keep too many peasants from feeling a desire to get their bread in jail " they are compelled to pay for everything : water, bread, and even for using the toilet."

The burden of usury. The peasant must pay at least 12 per cent. interest monthly on money borrowed, 24-36 per cent. on the average, and in many cases *100* per cent., as in Kwantung.[10] The Nanking government has officially sanctioned this usury, issuing a decree early in 1933 with the following provision :

" In view of the fact that usury interest has risen of late to 20-30 per cent. a month, *it is hereby forbidden to charge more than 10 per cent. interest monthly.*" [11]

From now on, of course, nobody lends money at less than 120 per cent. per annum. The usurer dispossesses the peasants of their land; in making a loan a contract is often signed whereby the land becomes the usurer's property if the debt is not paid on time.

The burden of taxation. The taxes weighing down upon the peasants have been raised repeatedly since 1928—not only the land tax, but the various other taxes—to an even greater extent. If the Chinese peasant wants to sell anything in the market, he must pay all sorts of tolls on the way : upon entering the city, for use of the market place, when leaving the city, etc. In some instances, the tax burden is greater than the value of the entire rice crop.

Plundered by the militarists. Looting by the militarists, which knows no limits, has the most devastating effect upon the condition of the peasantry. Preparation for any war, either among the individual generals or against Soviet China, begins with a plunder campaign against the peasants. Here are some instances : in 1929, more than $1,956,690 were extorted as war taxes from nine districts in Northern Honan and Southern Hupei, more than four times the " normal " taxes. In the spring of 1928,

---

[8] One picul = 133.5 pounds.
[9] Report of the Rajchman Commissioner of the League of Nations.
[10] *China Weekly Review*, December 23, 1933.
[11] *Chuanbao*, January 17, 1933.

$29,631,070 were extorted as war taxes in Northern Shansi, *or 226 times the normal taxes*.[12] In many areas the militarists have already extorted taxes from the peasants for *decades in advance*.

Exploitation of the peasantry proceeds in a hundred different ways. Merchants of entire districts set very low purchase prices for silk cocoons, tobacco, cotton, rice, etc., with the connivance of the corrupt administration. Administrative heads " visit " the districts, accompanied by a huge suite; the peasants must feed them and supply them with everything they require, etc., etc. All the various forms of feudal and capitalist exploitation grind down the unfortunate peasants of Kuomintang China. They are often compelled to sell their children, forsake their village, and become bandits.

The condition of the Chinese peasantry is described as follows in an article in the *North China Herald* of January 24, 1934 :

" They [the Chinese peasants] cry for help, but their feeble voices are drowned completely in the deafening clamour of factional disputes and resultant civil wars. The return from their yearly toil, pouring into the Government treasury and the warlord's purse, only brings back more torture instead of relief. Forlorn and desperate, they desert their farms, turn into bandits or Communists. This makes the situation worse and affords the militarists additional excuses for their gladiatorial adventures. . . .

" The figures given by the International Famine Relief Commission indicate that the annual income of 76.6 per cent. of the farm families is below $201 but their average expenditures amount to $228.32. That means that only 23.4 per cent. of them is able to live without going into debt, and this only in a normal year.

" High rent, low wage, exorbitant taxes, usurious interest on credit and unfair exploitation of cereal merchants are responsible for reducing the peasant income to such a deep-sunken level. . . .

" Rural China is now bankrupt. Millions of farmers have perished. Millions are deprived of their homes, land and all means of subsistence. Millions are struggling between life and death. Even the luckiest ones are suffering terribly under their ever-growing burden. . . .

" Facing calamities on all sides, the farmers seem to be compelled to take one of two desperate steps, to desert their farms for other places or to join the ranks of bandits, or Communists. Everywhere the villages have been witnessing a silent but continuous exodus. Everywhere honest and peaceful peasants go ' bad ' or Red." [13]

Under such circumstances it is natural that the secret peasant organizations, such as the " Red Lances," the " Big Knives," the " Black Flag," etc., etc., should grow constantly, that peasant revolts should never cease, that civil war is a chronic phenomenon in China, and that every landowner is compelled to turn his estate into an armed fortress! All this explains why Kuomintang armies, recruited predominantly from the peasantry, disintegrate in battle against the Red Army.

12 *Weekly Statistical Service*, March 27, 1933.

13 *The North China Herald*, January 24, 1934, Yao Hsin-Nung, " Rural China's collapse."

In contrast with this, the revolutionary solution of the agrarian question has improved the conditions of the peasantry in the Soviet territories tremendously. The most important factors in the agrarian revolution are as follows:

1. The land of the landowners (gentry), officials and monasteries was confiscated without compensation and distributed among the poor and middle peasants, agricultural labourers, Red Army men and the workers of the village. The land which the kulaks formerly leased to others, as well as all of their land in excess of the general norm, was taken from them.

2. The landowners' means of production, their cattle and the kulaks' surplus cattle were confiscated and distributed among the poor and middle peasantry. The Soviets publicly fix the price at which the kulaks are obliged to hire out their cattle to the village poor for farming the soil. Committees of the Village Poor supervise the enforcement of the agrarian laws.

3. Usury has been eliminated. All usury contracts were declared null and void. All the peasants' debts have been annulled. All property held in pawn was returned to its owners. Interest on new loans was reduced to one per cent. per month.

4. All rivers and ponds important in irrigation were nationalized (as well as forests and pasture land).

5. All former taxes and military imposts were declared null and void, with a uniform progressive income tax instituted in their place. The village poor owning 3 to 5 mu[14] of land were freed of all taxation. The rest of the peasantry pays 5-20 per cent. of the crop as taxes (in addition to various minor levies for cultural purposes, for the purchase of airplanes and for the Red Army).

The agrarian revolution has made the middle peasant the central figure of the village in Soviet China. The condition of the entire working peasantry, especially of the former village poor and the agricultural labourers, has considerably improved, representing an unattainable ideal under the Kuomintang regime, for the peasantry in Kuomintang China.

It is understandable that the peasants fighting in the ranks of the Chinese Red Army will make every effort to defend their new land and their new life against the landowner armies of Chiang Kai-shek.

Influenced by the agrarian reforms, the cultivated area has already been extended in the Soviet districts, the crop yield has increased, and agricultural productive forces are growing. The Soviets see to it that seed grain is improved, that the fields are regularly fertilized, etc. While millions of peasants in Kuomintang China are starving, there is an abundance of food in Soviet China.[15]

14 One mu = one-sixth of an acre.

15 This is self-evident: all the food that formerly was appropriated by the parasite classes as taxes, rent and interest, etc., in kind (part of which was consumed on the land itself, another part being sold in the cities) is now left with the working population of Soviet China.

The Chinese bourgeoisie, together with the imperialist bourgeoisie, made use of the victory of the counter-revolution to make an unprecedentedly violent attack upon the working class. The revolutionary class trade unions were dissolved; the Communist Party was forced underground, and innumerable courageous comrades have been murdered. The Chinese working class offered heroic resistance in large-scale, stubborn, big strikes and numerous clashes, but the bourgeoisie succeeded in forcing working conditions down considerably, aided as they were by the imperialists, by the influx of millions of peasants driven from their homes, and by the entrance of artisans ruined by the advance of native and foreign manufactured goods into the labour market.

As opposed to this, the living conditions of the rural industrial workers in Soviet China have been basically improved. (There are no big industrial enterprises in the Soviet China districts.) Wages have been greatly increased—doubled and tripled. The ten to seventeen-hour working day has been shortened to from eight to ten hours. The usual system in China of the labour agency concluding a contract with the employer and taking part of the worker's wages for itself has been forbidden, and employment agencies were made a Soviet monopoly. Obligatory social insurance was instituted, and a considerable number of workers were organized into trade unions, which supervise compliance with working conditions. Women's work was placed on the same level as the work of men, provided their output is the same.

Despite the comparatively small number of industrial workers in Soviet Chinese territory, the hegemony of the proletariat is assured. Industrial workers—some of them from Kuomintang China—are at the head of the Party organizations, the Red Army and the Soviet organs. The Communist Party of China is increasingly successful in solving the complicated task of simultaneously governing the Soviet areas as the ruling party and leading the revolutionary movement in Kuomintang China as an illegal, persecuted party.

The cultural revolution now in process in Soviet China is of special importance. In 2,932 villages of the Central Soviet District alone there are 3,052 schools for children and 32,388 schools for eliminating illiteracy among adults. Primitive schools have been established in the vacant rooms of the expropriated landowners' houses. In some areas 92 per cent. of the children go to school, as against 20 per cent. in Kuomintang China. Schools have been politically organized to a considerable extent. Pioneer and youth organizations now exist. Adults are first of all taught the ideographs for the most indispensable concepts; new simple ideographs have been introduced for the new political terms. Classes are held in the afternoon and evening. Several technical schools have been founded in the Central District, as well as its first university. Towards the end of 1933 the Soviet government made an appeal to all the professors of Kuomintang China to support the cultural progress of Soviet China. Clubs, libraries, dramatic circles, sport circles are springing up everywhere. There are 34 newspapers, the official newspaper having 50,000 circulation, and the youth paper 28,000. Pamphlets and schoolbooks are being printed.

Women participate in the cultural revolution with especial zeal. They are in the majority among those taking evening courses. This cultural upsurge forms a trenchant contrast to the cultural decay in Kuomintang China.

The things that Chinese reaction can offer by way of offsetting the achievements of Soviet China in the sphere of improving the material and cultural conditions of the working masses are slander and violence.[16] The slanders are of little use, for the Chinese workers and peasants know quite well that the conditions of the working masses in Soviet China are much better than their own. That is why all attempts at the annihilation of Soviet China by force end in failure.

A White Russian *émigré*, G. Sokolsky, writes as follows in the American magazine *Asia* (December, 1932):

". . . Each spring the Nanking government appeals to the Shanghai bankers to lend hundreds of millions of dollars to save the nation from Communism. Each summer hundreds of millions of dollars are squandered and tens of thousands of lives are destroyed in an effort to wipe out Communism. Then the autumn rains come; the canals are again swollen; rivers are impassable; the roads grow muddy. . . . The anti-Communist campaign is over.

"Five mighty anti-Communist campaigns has Chiang Kai-shek marshaled against them [the Red Armies]. Five times have the best units of the national, German-trained, modernly equipped army, sometimes mounting to as high as half a million men, hurled themselves against the Red Armies. Each campaign has been a failure. Last summer ended with another failure.

"It is practically impossible to suppress the Communists by military prowess; for where does the Red Army end and the peasant population begin in these southern provinces? The national troops find only hungry peasants, ground almost out of existence between the high taxes collected far in advance and the usurious rates of moneylenders and landlords.

"Chiang's army advances: the peasants are an armed body of troops in his rear. His men surrender: the Communists have arms and munitions. . . ."

The story is always and everywhere the same. Communist propaganda demoralizes the armies of Chiang Kai-shek because, as Sokolsky says, "Chiang's officers and men . . . too are peasants or sons of peasants." The Red Army grows in size[17] and becomes better armed as deserters come over from the enemy and volunteers enter its ranks (parents themselves put their sons in the army).[18] Although it is comparatively poorly

---

[16] Neither " Left " manœuvres and phrases, nor the founding of the " Reorganization " Party, was of any avail. At present the Kuomintang resorts more and more to a reactionary, religious, fascist ideology. Chiang-Kai-shek's " new life " propaganda aims at the rehabilitation of the feudal ideology of passive submission to fate.

[17] In China, with its traditional ideology of peace, soldiery is considered a *very inferior* occupation.

[18] APPROXIMATE SIZE OF THE RED ARMY

1928	1929	1930	1931	1932	1933	1934
10,000	22,000	62,000	145,000	170,000	200,000	350,000

(Czan-Shi, *Communist International*, No. 7, 1934, " The Chinese Red Army," p. 273.)

armed, yet wherever it goes it is aided by the entire population, which supplies it with information, furnishes it food, diverts the enemy through false reports, attacks the enemy's rear at night, and so forth. *The Red Army and Soviet China have three hundred million workers and peasants as its adherents in China, in the enemy's territory; that is why they are invincible.*

Chiang Kai-shek can depend only on this small group: the feudal nobility, the big bourgeoisie and the rich peasants, as well as on the aid afforded by the foreign imperialists.[19]

But this support makes the people hate him all the more. The masses realize that the Kuomintang government is a tool of the imperialists, a government of perpetual terror and civil war against the working masses.

Chiang Kai-shek may succeed in defeating certain sections of the Red Army, again subjecting individual Soviet districts to the landowners' rule. But new Soviet districts are in other sections of China; new red Armies are formed. *He cannot prevent the final victory of the revolution in China!*

---

[19] Every time the Red Army menaces or captures a city on the coast or on the Yangtze River, the united imperialist fleets appear and decide a battle in favour of reaction. The American *Foreign Policy Reports,* issue of April 26, 1933, on the Communist movement in China complacently records the gratitude of the *China Weekly Review,* which stated on September 30th, 1932, that the foreign gunboats " in this particular case performed a good service for the Chinese Government by helping to drive the Communists out of Changsha . . . hence there has been no outcry on the part of the Chinese authorities at this most recent activity of foreign gunboats in China.''

CHAPTER X

THE EFFECTS OF THE CRISIS ON FOREIGN AFFAIRS

" With the general instability of relations, the existence of a large number of inner-European antagonisms led to a constant regrouping of states. But one main trend plainly appeared out of all these multifarious and constantly changing groupings, the trend of struggle against the Soviet Union."[1]

The instability of foreign relations, which the Sixth Congress indicated in the case of *Europe*, spread during the subsequent years, *and to-day applies to the whole world*. The crisis has destroyed the foreign policy bases of stabilization and has accentuated the antagonisms between *all* countries. Lenin's phrase of 1915 that: "The old national states have become too cramped for capitalism," is to-day truer than ever. All countries are constantly conflicting with one another in the struggle for markets. The conflicts criss-cross one another in the most complex manner. All bourgeois states are manœuvring uninterruptedly on all sides. All bourgeois states are feverishly arming for a new war, in the hope of solving their own market problem by force at the expense of their competitors. But just this multitude of antagonisms has until now prevented the formation of firm war *blocs* such as existed among the great powers before the first World War. In addition to their fear (increased by the maturing of the revolutionary crisis) that the imperialist war will be turned into a civil war, their fear of the rapidly increasing military strength of the Soviet Union, their fear of entering a war inadequately prepared from the military standpoint (in view of the unusually swift development of the military technique) this is another reason why the outbreak of the second round of the World War has been delayed. This is why the wars still in progress or those that occurred in the last few years (Japan's attack on China, Paraguay-Bolivia, Peru-Chile, Arabia-Yemen, Tibet-China) have not yet ignited the World War. But, with the universal aggravation of all antagonisms and the prevalent armament competition, the world war may break out any day despite these inhibiting factors.

" Again as in 1914 the parties . . . of war and revenge are coming into the foreground. Quite clearly things are moving towards a new war."[2]

The multitude of foreign events and regroupings that have taken place between the Sixth Congress and the Seventh, and the extraordinary complexity of the present situation make it impossible to give a thorough and complete analysis briefly. Our presentation must necessarily be incomplete and schematic.

[1] Theses of the Sixth Congress of the Communist International.

[2] Stalin, Report at the Seventeenth Congress of the C.P.S.U., *Socialism Victorious*, p. 10.

THE SHARPENING OF THE STRUGGLE BETWEEN THE TWO SYSTEMS AND THE
SUCCESSES OF THE PEACE POLICY OF THE SOVIET UNION

In 1925, Comrade Stalin summarized the international situation, as
follows:

> " Then we have two stabilizations: the temporary stabilization of capi-
> talism and the stabilization of the Soviet system. The setting in of a certain
> temporary equilibrium between these two stabilizations—such is the charac-
> teristic feature of the present international situation." [3]

A certain mitigation of the forms of struggle between the two systems
took place in the period of relative stabilization. The bourgeoisie considered the " new economic policy " (N.E.P.) the beginning of a return
to capitalism. They were strengthened in this illusion by the counter-
revolutionary chatter of the Trotskyite opposition regarding the " degeneration " of the Soviet power. In this period of " democratic pacifism "
there took place the *de jure* recognition of the Soviet Union by England
(the first MacDonald Cabinet), France (Herriot) and Italy.

But the situation had already changed considerably at the time of the
Sixth Congress. The " democratic pacifist " episode had reached its in-
glorious end. The illusion that the N.E.P. meant a return to capitalism
had evaporated. The period of " peaceful intercourse of the two systems "
was broken by a period of brutal provocation under the leadership of
England: the Arcos raid, the Zinoviev letter, the break of diplomatic
relations with England; the withdrawal of Rakovsky from Paris; the
murder of Voykov in Warsaw, the attack on the Soviet Embassy in
Peking, etc. Parallel with this went the efforts to draw Germany into
the anti-Soviet front, efforts which met with a friendly reception among a
part of the German bourgeoisie. The " western orientation " began to
outweigh the so-called " eastern orientation." The Theses of the Sixth
Congress state that:

> " The growth of monopolist capitalism in Germany leads on one hand to
> an increasing disintegration of the Versailles system, and on the other to
> Germany's adopting a more definitely ' Western ' (*i.e.,* imperialist and anti-
> Soviet) orientation. While in the days of her economic decline and her
> political and national humiliation Germany sought an agreement with the
> proletarian state, the only state that opposed her imperialist enslavement, the
> matured tendencies of German neo-imperialism are forcing the German
> bourgeoisie more and more towards an anti-Soviet position."

The crisis has brought a new accentuation of the tension between the
capitalist world and the Soviet Union, after a certain temporary abate-
ment during the phase of prosperity.

> " Therefore, every time that capitalist contradictions begin to grow acute
> the bourgeoisie turns its gaze towards the U.S.S.R. as if to say: ' Cannot we
> settle this or that contradiction of capitalism, or all the contradictions taken
> together, at the expense of the U.S.S.R., the land of the Soviets, the citadel
> of the revolution, which, by its very existence is revolutionizing the working

[3] Stalin, *Leninism*, Vol. I, " The Results of the Work of the Fourteenth Conference of the
Russian Communist Party," p. 152.

class and the colonies, preventing us from arranging for a new war, preventing us from dividing the world anew, preventing us from being masters of its extensive internal market, so necessary for capitalists, particularly to-day, owing to the economic crisis? '

" Hence the tendency to adventurist assaults on the U.S.S.R. and to intervention, a tendency which is bound to be strengthened as a result of the developing economic crisis." [4]

The danger of a counter-revolutionary war of aggression against the Soviet Union has been threatening without interruption ever since the outbreak of the economic crisis.

What has prevented this attack until now? The following important factors can be distinguished :

(1) *The increase of the military strength of the Soviet Union by leaps and bounds.* Its basis is the growth of the Soviet Union's economic forces at an unprecedented rate during the successful completion of the First Five-Year Plan and the first year of the second plan. The development of heavy industry and the machinery industry have made it possible to equip the Red Army as well as any capitalist army, independently of the capitalist world. The liquidation of the kulaks as a class on the basis of collectivization, and the coming to the fore of the new type of collective farmer, closely bound up with the workng class, as the central figure in the village have made for an even greater social superiority of the Red Army over the bourgeois armies, which are growing more and more demoralized even in peace-time, owing to the intensification of class antagonisms.[5] Another factor is the thorough replacement of the old bourgeois military specialists by Party comrades, or by new leading military personnel, predominantly of working class origin, and devoted to the Soviet Union through life and death.

This rapid reinforcement of the Soviet Union's military strength and the growing disintegration of the bourgeois armies make any attack against the Soviet Union an extremely dangerous undertaking from the purely military standpoint. This is an important reason why the Japanese war-mongers, for example, have for three years delayed their attack on the Soviet Union time and again, in order to make better preparation for it.

(2) *The thorough-going peace policy of the Soviet Union.* This rapid reinforcement of the Soviet Union's military strength makes the thorough-going peace policy of the Soviet Union more impressive and more successful, because it cannot be regarded as the consequence of military weakness. The Soviet Union makes use of every opportunity to document its readiness for peace; in every country it supports every movement, no

[4] Stalin, *Leninism,* Vol. II, " Political Report of the Central Committee to the Seventeenth Congress of the C.P.S.U.," pp. 260-261.

[5] The mutinies in the British, Dutch, Chilian, and Greek fleets, and in the Japanese army at Shanghai, the mass desertion of Kuomintang troops to the Chinese Red Army in every battle, the desertion of Manchukuo troops to the guerilla bands, etc., are evidence of this process of disintegration.

matter how weak, working for the preservation of peace. The government of the Soviet Union adhered to the Kellogg Pact; at the Disarmament Conference it was the only power which fought (though of course without success) for real disarmament.

This thorough-going policy of peace has resulted in a tremendous strengthening of the Soviet Union's international position. To-day the Soviet Union is the magnetic pole for all the small countries that have nothing to gain in a war, for all countries that are threatened by the danger of dropping to the status of colonies of some imperialist world power during the next world war, and for all countries at present in favour of peace. The external expression of the success of the Soviet Union's peace policy is the creation of a whole network of non-aggression pacts. In evaluating this success, one must avoid two diametrically opposed errors. The significance of the pacts and treaties *must not be overestimated*. By no means would the bourgeoisie of the capitalist countries be afraid to break these treaties at a moment favourable to them. The pre-war Triple Alliance was not concluded with the social enemies of the bourgeoisie, but among capitalist countries on an equal social basis, and it was formally signed by their kings. But this, as we know, did not prevent Italy from entering the War opposed to its allies.

On the other hand, it would be altogether incorrect to underestimate the value of the non-aggression pacts because of this. They form an important obstacle to the ideological preparation for war against the Soviet Union. When the bourgeoisie of the neighbouring countries concludes non-aggression pacts with the Soviet Union, and solemnly declares that it will work together with the Soviet Union for the preservation of peace, it cannot begin a war against the Soviet Union *immediately*. It needs a certain amount of time to prepare public opinion for the change in policy, for war against the Soviet Union. And even if this reorientation would not require a long time, in view of the bourgeoisie's monopoly of the legal press, the pacts do guarantee some gain in time in any case. At the same time they strengthen the movements and forces in every country which are working for the preservation of peace.

This thorough-going peace policy makes it more difficult for the enemies of the Soviet Union to stir up the peoples with the lying tales of " Red Imperialism." Japan's refusal to sign the non-aggression pact repeatedly proposed by the Soviet Union shows the workers of the whole world who is for war and who is for peace.

An important step in the peace policy of the Soviet Union is its entrance into the League of Nations. The exit of Japan and Germany—the two powers whose leading statesmen are not only preparing for a counter-revolutionary war against the Soviet Union at present, but openly advocating it—has placed the League of Nations under the domination of those great powers (France above all) whose bourgeoisie champions the maintenance of the Versailles system. They are therefore in favour of the maintenance of peace in general (even if only for a short time), and hence for peace with the Soviet Union. This makes the entrance of the Soviet

Union into the League of Nations possible and advisable for the maintenance of peace. Wide circles of the petty bourgeoisie and working class in
many countries, who are convinced of the pacifist mission of the League
of Nations, will consider the entrance of the Soviet Union as the most
striking evidence disproving the slanderous charge of " Red Imperialism."

(3) *The effect of imperialist antagonisms.* The economic crisis produced
a pronounced intensification of imperialist conflicts (*cf.* next section for
details), and this has made the relations of some imperialist states with the
Soviet Union more friendly of late, at least temporarily. Japan's attack on
Manchuria led to the recognition of the Soviet Union by the U.S.A., plus
a certain degree of *rapprochement.* The establishment of the Hitler
government produced a sharp turn in France's attitude towards the Soviet
Union. The politicians who only four years ago demanded that France
lead the anti-Soviet front have passed into the background, and a more
friendly policy toward the Soviet Union has won the upper hand. For the
same reason a more peaceable attitude toward the Soviet Union seems to
be arising for the time being among some of the bourgeoisie in England.

(4) *The accentuation of class antagonisms.* One of the most important
factors hindering counter-revolutionary war against the Soviet Union is
the accentuation of class antagonisms in all capitalist countries and the
accelerated maturing of the revolutionary crisis in some countries that
now stand in the forefront of the anti-Soviet front: Germany and Japan.
A war against the Soviet Union would make acute the threat of over-
throwing the power of the ruling classes. As much as nine years ago,
Stalin said : :

> ". . . Our country no longer stands alone, for it has the workers of the
> West and the oppressed peoples of the East for its allies. . . . A war against
> the Soviet Union would also be a war waged by imperialism against its own
> workers and colonies." [6]

*The great increase in the military strength of the Soviet Union, its
thorough-going peace policy and the aggravation of imperialist antagonisms and class antagonisms in the capitalist world are the main causes that
have delayed the daily threatening attack on the Soviet Union.*

THE LIQUIDATION OF THE FOREIGN POLICY FOUNDATIONS OF STABILIZATION

The unsettling of temporary stabilization, which was already under way
at the time of the Sixth Congress, was completed by the crisis in foreign
affairs.

According to Stalin, the stabilization of capitalism was manifested concretely in the following :

> " First, in that America, England and France have temporarily succeeded
> in coming to an understanding as to how and to what extent they will despoil
> Germany. . . .

> " Secondly, the stabilization of capitalism has found expression in the fact

---

[6] Stalin, *Leninism,* Vol. I, " Results of the Work of the Fourteenth Conference of the
R.C.P.," p. 156.

that British, American and Japanese capital has temporarily managed to come to an understanding as to the allotment of spheres of influence in China . . . as to the ways of plundering it. . . .

" Thirdly, the stabilization of capitalism has found expression in the fact that the imperialist groups of the advanced countries have managed for the time being to come to an understanding mutually to refrain from interfering in the plunder and oppression of ' their ' respective colonies. . . ." [7]

Uneven development rapidly unsettled temporary stabilization, as Stalin predicted in the same speech. The crisis brought it to an end. " The world has come close to the second round of revolutions and wars." Only the multiple criss-crossing of imperialist antagonisms, the extraordinarily complex and swiftly changing foreign political situation—still further complicated by the increased international significance of the Soviet Union, the fear of the united strength of the Soviet Union plus the workers fighting to turn the imperialist war into a civil war, as well as of the colonial peoples fighting for their independence, have thus far prevented the " little wars " now in progress from growing into a world war.

(1) The Collapse of the Versailles System is Nearing Its End

Of Versailles' three main pillars : Reparations, disarmament, and territorial provisions, only the last is still in force, and its revision also is imminent. It was only in 1929, in the Young Plan, that the victorious powers " finally " fixed Germany's reparations as lasting 59 years (!), but under the blows of the economic crisis Hoover hastened to declare a moratorium on reparations and inter-allied debts as soon as 1931, by which they were *de facto* ended for ever.

The disarmament of Germany was brought to an end by the German bourgeoisie itself, after fascism came to power. (Hungary and Bulgaria are secretly arming.) In this, Germany correctly depended upon the multitudinous antagonisms among the victorious powers, which prevented a war to stop Germany's rearmament. At this point we can but incompletely sketch these complexities in the roughest outlines.

The Anglo-French antagonism exists on the European continent, as well as outside Europe : in the Near East, South China, Africa, etc. It is the traditional policy of the British bourgeoisie to prevent any one country from gaining hegemony on the European continent if possible. Therefore it supported Germany against France (up to a certain point) throughout the entire post-war period. It manœuvred in Poland and Belgium to weaken French influence, and tried to use Italy against France (most recently in the unsuccessful " Four-Power Agreement " on armaments).

But these anti-French manœuvres of British policy were always kept within very narrow limits by the basic Anglo-American antagonism. The overseas " interests " of the British bourgeoisie, which exploits 500,000,000 people in colonial countries, outweigh its European continental interests. Britain's position as a world power must be constantly

---

[7] *Ibid*, pp. 154-55.

defended against the U.S.A.   War between these two biggest world powers is unavoidable if the proletarian revolution does not forestall it. The centre of the British world empire, however, the British Isles themselves, have strategically lost their island character, because of the development of military technique after the war : long-range guns, submarines, and airplanes, with which France is particularly well equipped.   Britain cannot wage war against any third power if it is not sure of France's benevolent neutrality.   Therefore the English bourgeoisie always abandoned its manœuvres in Germany's favour whenever France demanded this as an ultimatum, uniting with the French bourgeoisie at Germany's expense.

Recently the rearmament of Germany, which is proceeding at a rapid pace, in particular the very rapid growth of its air fleet, has helped the anti-German, pro-French tendency in British politics to gain supremacy, at least temporarily.   At this moment England does not appear to be sufficiently well prepared for war; it is especially backward in air armament.[8]   The British bourgeoisie is afraid that German fascism will seek an escape from the threatening economic catastrophe through a " premature " precipitation of the world war.   Baldwin's statement that the Rhine, and not the Dover cliffs, is England's defence frontier, undoubtedly signifies a warning to Germany not to attempt adventure in the West.

Still more contradictory is the Franco-Italian-German relationship! The French system of alliances in Southeast Europe not only serves to guarantee the traditional provisions of the Versailles system against the vanquished countries (Germany, Austria, Hungary and Bulgaria), but is also an obstacle to the Italian policy of expansion in the Balkans.   The interests of French and Italian imperialism clash in North Africa, in the Near East, and in the question of controlling the Mediterranean.   Hence one line of Italian policy : co-operation with the " vanquished "—Germany, Hungary and Austria—against France, for revising all the provisions of the peace treaties (including the territorial provisions) and support of England's anti-French tendencies, within the framework of a general friendly relationship with England.

But the aggressiveness of Hitler fascism, which has sought to gain one victory in international politics, at least in the Austrian *Anschluss,* has brought Italy into the sharpest conflict with Germany (the demonstrative massing of Italian troops at the Austrian border to prevent *Anschluss* by force if necessary), and has brought it into a common front with France, on *this one* question.   On this basis France now endeavours to reach a further *rapprochement* with Italy through certain concessions in North Africa and in naval armaments, in order to isolate fascist Germany on the South.

The position of *Poland,* which wavers and manœuvres between Ger-

---

[8] Although the English navy is to-day the strongest in the world (the U.S.A. has not built its navy up to parity), the English air fleet stands in the fifth place. That is why England and the British Empire are now building planes very rapidly so as " to have the strongest air fleet in the world."

many, France, England and the Soviet Union, but has veered sharply towards Germany (evidently counting upon Britain's approval), under the influence of traditionally anti-Soviet circles of the bourgeoisie, as a reaction to the *rapprochement* between France and the Soviet Union, is equally contradictory. So is that of Hungary, which maintains " connections " with Germany and France, in order not to fall into wholly one-sided dependence on Italy. Likewise, that of Jugoslavia—which in general is one of France's vassal states, but which is opposed to the Franco-Italian policy on *Anschluss*, because it considers this a factor strengthening its arch-enemy, Italy, etc., etc.

Universal instability has taken the place of the stabilisation founded on the suppression and exploitation of the vanquished states. The *Deutschen Führerbriefe* [*German Letters to Leaders*] correctly stated on April 17, 1934, that:

" What characterizes the latent tension in Europe is that no one is able to say ' Yes ' in order to satisfy one side without all the other partners in the game thinking it is a ' No ' aimed at them."

2. *The Struggle for Domination in the Pacific.*

Japan's attack on Manchuria, and its penetration of North China and Mongolia, constitute a forcible violation of the Washington Nine-Power Treaty on the common exploitation of China, which was an important factor in temporary stabilization.

The centre of gravity of world politics was thereby moved from Europe to the Pacific Ocean, where the redivision of the world by force had already begun, where the four biggest imperialist powers—the U.S.A., England, Japan and France—are competing for their share in the exploitation of China, and thus for the mastery of the Pacific Ocean. This struggle is complicated by the intertwining of imperialist antagonisms with the struggle of the two systems, and by the existence of Soviet China, the second revolutionary breach in the system of bourgeois society!

Why was Japanese imperialism the first to resort to arms for the redivision of the world?

It would be altogether mistaken to explain this as a consequence of Japanese imperialism's strength. On the contrary, in a certain sense it was the economic weakness of Japan that impelled the Japanese ruling classes to this policy of force. Japan is a poor country; the *per capita* income of the population is equal to that of the poorest European countries: Latvia, Lithuania or Rumania. Moreover, inequalities in distribution of income are greater than in all other capitalist countries. In cross-section, Japan has thirty billionaires, three thousand who are rich, and thirty thousand well-to-do. Most of those in the next stratum, the peasants and the urban petty bourgeoisie, are poor, while the workers' living standard approaches that of colonial workers. This inordinate income distribution *limits the population's power of consumption to a minimum, and forces Japanese industry to seek foreign markets for a large part of its production.* But with international competition as bitter as it is at present, sales are certain only in markets under monopoly control. To this must be added the fact that Japan has no raw materials (except silk and copper) in sufficient quantity on its own territory. Iron and steel, cotton and wool, wood and oil, etc.—all must be imported. That is why Japanese imperialism is contrained to try to seize colonial areas rich in raw materials, in order to be able to monopolize the exploitation of raw materials,[9] as well as the sale of industrial goods.

Japan's campaign of conquest has been successful thus far. There were plenty of *paper* protests. The League of Nations condemned the conquest of Manchuria in careful terms. The Japanese puppet-state of Manchukuo was not recognised by a single country, except San Salvador (demonstration against the U.S.A.). America formally declared that it would not recognize the validity of any changes brought about by force. But up to now there has been nothing beyond these paper protests!

The reasons for this are as follows :

By its occupation of Manchuria and its penetration of Mongolia, Japan is erecting a military barrier between the Soviet Union and Soviet China, at the same time preparing a base area for war against the Soviet Union. In this sense it is acting as the vanguard of the world bourgeoisie in the struggle between the two systems. That is why France and England actually supported Japan in the first stages of its plundering campaign (though under the guise of pacific gestures). While fascist Germany placed itself openly on Japan's side.

The motive also played a certain role in the passive behaviour of the U.S.A.[10] But the following factors were the decisive ones :

The fundamental Anglo-American antagonism does not allow the U.S.A. to enter into an open conflict with Japan at the present time without an agreement with England; but all the efforts of the American diplomats to induce England to common action against Japan have remained unsuccessful.

The strategic position of the U.S.A. with regard to Japan is very unfavourable. The U.S.A.'s great naval base, Pearl Harbour, in Hawaii, is far too distant from the Asiatic coast, while the naval bases of Guam and in the Philippines have not been modernized, in accordance with the Washington Naval Treaty. The American navy is supposed to be superior to the Japanese in the ratio of five to three, but Japan has actually

---

[9] Japanese capital has forced its competitors out of Korea completely; more than 90 per cent. of Korea's foreign trade is monopolized by Japan.

[10] It must be emphasized that there is no conflict of interests between the U.S.A. and Japan in the sphere of foreign trade. The U.S.A. is Japan's best customer: it holds first place in Japanese exports, with about 40 per cent. of the total, and first place in Japanese imports, with about 28 per cent. (Japan occupies second place in the U.S.A. imports, and fourth place in the export trade). *Until very recently* there was scarcely any competition in the world market between the two; the U.S.A. exported raw materials and means of production, while Japan exported the products of light industry. American capital is invested in Japanese industry in not insignificant amounts (principally in electric power). Under these circumstances, it is natural that a *pro-Japanese tendency* also exists within the bourgeoisie of the U.S.A.

built its navy up to the limits permitted by the Washington Treaty, while the U.S.A. is only endeavouring this year to make up for lost time by forcing the expansion of its fleet. *Because of the Anglo-American antagonism, the U.S.A. can never use its entire fleet against Japan* (even if England declared its neutrality), while Japan's whole navy can await the attack of the American fleet in its home waters, supported by its numerous naval bases. Under these circumstances, Japan's strategic superiority in Asiatic waters is apparent. In order to gain time for further armament (particularly for the development of a powerful aviation base in the Aleutian Islands), the U.S.A. must, under these conditions, limit itself for the present to peaceful methods of struggle: recognition of the Soviet Union and support of the Nanking Government through loans and through furnishing war material and military instructors, in the hope of creating an army in China capable of fighting Japan, thus gaining a closer base of operations against Japan.

But this hope of the American bourgeoisie has not been realized. The Chinese ruling classes, its generals, and the rotten Chiang Kai-shek government, which also sabotaged the heroic struggle of the Chinese masses against Japan's attack on Shanghai, have surrendered to Japanese imperialism *de facto* in order to be able to concentrate all their energy on the fight against the Red Army of Soviet China. In this fight they enjoy the support of *all* imperialist powers! But the Chinese Kuomintang army cannot be had for a fight against Japan. This gave the Japanese imperialists the courage to claim a protectorate over all China in the notorious declaration of April 17, 1934, by the Foreign Office.[11]

While the American-Japanese antagonism is thus objectively becoming increasingly acute (though not breaking out into war for the present) *a certain change has taken place during recent years in the relationship of England and France toward Japan.*

The Anglo-Japanese relationship is highly complicated and contradictory. Although the British bourgeoisie had no objection to the conquest of Manchuria and Mongolia or to the development of a basis for attack against the Soviet Union, and though it regards Japan as a potential ally in the (sooner or later) inevitable war against the U.S.A., despite the dissolution of the alliance which existed until 1922, it is none the less disturbed by Japan's penetration of North China, which is aimed directly at Britain's interests. Japan's claim to a protectorate over all China cannot be tolerated by England. Japan's propaganda, using such slogans as " China for the yellow race! " " Against all white conquerors! " and " Asia for the Asiatics," in itself constitutes an attack upon the British bourgeoisie's positions throughout Asia. It threatens the heart of English colonial power : India. (This is supplemented by the growing competition of Japanese goods in the world market, particularly the increasing displacement of English cotton goods from all colonial markets.)

[11] This statement was a trial balloon to ascertain the reaction of the U.S.A., and particularly England.

That is why Britain is penetrating further in the direction of Western Szechwan, Tibet and Sinkiang, forcing the establishment of a chain of naval bases from Singapore to Australia (including the Dutch East Indies) to prevent future penetration of the Indian Ocean by Japan, and endeavouring to develop united air defence for the whole empire. Despite all its " friendship," the British bourgeoisie is undoubtedly preparing for a war against Japan in the distant future. At the same time. Britain has taken severe measures against Japanese imports into its colonies[12] (reduction of Japanese imports to the pre-war level by means of the quota system). This has led to a certain estrangement of the two powers which were formerly so friendly. The fighting between English and Japanese troops in North China during the summer of 1934 is symptomatic of this. There are many indications that at the naval disarmament conference in 1935 an Anglo-American front will be directed against Japan—especially on the naval parity problem—rather than an Anglo-Japanese front against the U.S.A.[13] (Although the Anglo-American antagonism is the basic one, it by no means excludes a temporary co-operation between the two powers in individual questions.) It is a matter of course that there are several trends within the British bourgeoisie, with influential circles advocating collaboration with Japan.

The comparative estrangement between France and Japan is founded primarily on Hitler's seizure of power. As we stated above, the French bourgeoisie seeks a guarantee against Hitler in Eastern Europe through a more friendly attitude toward the Soviet Union, while German fascism, with its far-reaching international isolation, looks to Japan as an ally in war against the Soviet Union. Under these conditions, the traditional friendship between France and Japan must cool off to some extent.[14]

Thus, the European antagonisms fit into the more world-wide antagonisms in the Pacific.

The successes of Japanese imperialism in Manchuria have been dearly bought, however. The resistance of the Chinese population engages large Japanese forces in Manchuria. The newly-formed Manchurian army is unreliable : mutinies and desertions to the partisans are regular occurrences. Preparations for war require enormous expenditures. Japan's weak economic foundation is not able to bear these demands for ever. To-day, though the " great war " has not yet begun, unproductive military expenditures are already greater than the excess of pro-

---

[12] In the recent period the relationship of the British dominions to Japan has somewhat changed in that Japan has become an important buyer of Australian wool and wheat. It is also a large buyer of Indian cotton, which enabled it to compel the recent agreement with India regarding the import of textiles. Relationships in the Pacific Ocean are becoming more complex day by day.

[13] Naturally, this by no means excludes the possibility of joint deals. In the summer of 1934 a delegation of the English financial oligarchy, including Lord Barnby, President of the Federation of British Industries, visited Japan and Manchuria to investigate the opportunities for British capital investment in Manchuria. (Japan urgently needs foreign capital to continue arming.)

[14] Japan's intrigues in Siam are also a source of anxiety for the French bourgeoisie.

duction over consumption. The country, which seems to be prospering economically, is in fact becoming poorer and poorer. In order to defray the cost of armaments the Japanese ruling classes are exploiting the workers and peasants, as well as the oppressed colonial peoples, even more intensely, thus creating the objective conditions for the overthrow of their rule. And while the imperialist robbers are contending for the division of their Chinese booty the power of Soviet China is growing, its territory is expanding, and in constant struggles there is being formed that power of the workers and peasants which alone is destined to overthrow the rule of the foreign and native exploiters, to chase the imperialists out of China, and to solve " the problem of the Pacific Ocean " in proletarian fashion!

3. On the Eve of a New World War.

The Sixth Congress had already determined that the course of events

" is inevitably giving rise . . . to a new phase of wars among the imperialist states themselves; wars of the imperialist states against the Soviet Union; wars of national liberation against imperialism." [15]

The economic crisis and the depression greatly intensified the bourgeoisie's urge to solve the market problem by crushing their enemies by force, by the forcible redivision of the world, and by seizing new monopoly-controlled areas. The economics and politics of the capitalist world are being governed more and more by the preparations for war.

(a) Economic preparation for war is in progress all along the line. Rapidly growing sums, constituting an ever greater portion of government expenditures, are devoted to war preparations.

OPEN WAR EXPENDITURES IN THE BUDGET OF MAJOR COUNTRIES [16]
(Per Cent. of Total Budget)

	Germany		Japan		France	
	Million Marks	Per cent.	Million Yen	Per cent.	Million Francs	Per cent.
Expenditures, 1928...	755	10	492	28	9.6	23
„ 1933 ...	674	10	697	35	11.6	23
Estimates, 1934 ...	750	—	852	37	11.4	20
„ 1935 ...	1,354 [17]	21	937	44	11.2	19

	U.S.A.		England		Poland	
	Million Dollars	Per cent.	Million Pounds	Per cent.	Million Zloty	Per cent.
Expenditures 1928 ...	732	20	117	14	824	32
„ 1933 ...	801	15	103	13	761	35
Estimates 1934 ...	716	10 [18]	108	14	762	35
„ 1935 ...	839	19	114	15	762	35

[15] Thesis of the Sixth World Congress on " The International Situation and the Tasks of the C.I."

[16] *Official figures.*

[17] Of this total, 250,000,000 marks for the Storm Troops and police.

[18] The great fall in per cent. is a result of the increase of Civil expenditures under Roosevelt.

It must be emphasized, however, that the open war expenditures, admitted in the budgets as such, are *only a part of the actual war expenditures*! These figures are useful only as indicating the trend of expenditures, not as absolute sums. They show the exceptionally rapid growth of war expenditures in Germany and in Japan; the latter's open war expenditures are officially placed at 44 per cent. of the total estimated budget for 1935.

Besides the open expenditures, entered in the budget of the war ministry, war expenditures are concealed in the budgets of *all* ministries. The ministry of the interior covers the outlays for the police, the frontier guards and the militia; the ministry of transport meets the expenses for civil aviation and for the railway rolling stock intended for military purposes; the ministry of public works finances the construction of largely strategic roads, frontier fortifications, etc.; the ministry of education handles the military education of youngsters in school; the ministry of labour pays for the " voluntary " labour camps, which are disguised military formations, etc., etc. It is therefore quite impossible to determine the actual war expenditures of the capitalist states. As a rough estimate, the actual expenditures for military purposes are at least 50 per cent. higher than the amounts indicated in the budgets.

In judging the significance of the above sums it must also be borne in mind that feeding and clothing soldiers now costs much less than in 1928, owing to the sharp drop in the price of food and agricultural raw materials. Hence expenditures for armament, for the actual instruments of murder, have increased much more than military expenditures in general.

The organizational rearrangement of national economy for war is being carried out systematically. Every nation has " militarized " its industry. The " mobilization plan " for shifting industry to war production is ready everywhere. Most factories already have in hand their orders in the event of mobilization, so that they can put the shift into effect without delay. In the U.S.A. there are regularly recurring trial mobilizations of industry.

Every nation tries its utmost to produce on its own territory the food-stuffs, raw materials and arms most necessary for war. Hence governmental aid for sugar-beet growing in England and for oil-seed planting in Germany; hence the " battle of grain " in Italy. This is the reason behind government subsidies for shipping, for the construction of speedy commercial vessels that can be used as auxiliary cruisers in time of war, for civil aviation, for copper production (in Germany), etc., etc., *ad infinitum*. Every little state endeavours to establish on its own territory a minimum of heavy industry, of armament manufacture and of artificial silk manufacture to avoid being wholly dependent on imports in case of war.

This striving for self-sufficiency, originating in military considerations, coincides with the bourgeoise's effort to monopolize the domestic market in every country as thoroughly as possible and to exclude foreign goods. The result is a tendency to *destroy the division of labour in world economy*: a certain "agrarianization" of the industrial countries and an artificial industrialization of the agrarian countries have taken place during the crisis and the depression of a special kind. The *ideological expression of this trend is the theory of autarky*[19] which has been enunciated most emphatically by the German fascists. (Moreover, "autarky" is always taken to mean *the limitation of imports alone, never a voluntary limitation of exports*.)

The mobilization and militarization of all labour power in the event of war is also provided for (compulsory "labour-service" for the youth in Germany, etc.).

The enlistment of national economy for war has made the greatest advances in Germany and Japan. In Germany the various branches of industry are united in compulsory artels, while raw materials are centrally distributed to the factories under state control. Reserve stocks are being stored for war, and production of all kinds of "substitute goods" has already begun. The transition to "organized starvation" can take place at a moment's notice. As for Japan, its economy largely bears the character of war economy already: absolute precedence of war production, inflation, higher prices, starvation.

(b) *Technical preparation for war* has been carried on at a feverishly accelerated pace ever since the Sixth Congress. Although capitalism is introducing technical innovations only in the rarest instances during the crisis and the present depression, one "improvement" follows on the heels of another in the field of armament. Capitalism's degeneracy is manifested with particular crassness at the present time, in that armaments—the preparations for new mass slaughter—form the principal basis for technological progress.

It goes beyond the confines of our task to describe in detail the perfection of murder instruments since the Sixth Congress. Moreover, the data would rapidly grow obsolete. We shall confine ourselves to a few examples.

Artillery: The range of light guns has been raised from 7.5 to 11 miles, that of 4.1-inch guns from 9 to 16 miles, and that of the giant railway guns (14-inch) from 22 to 40 miles. The longest-range guns have a range of as high as 93 miles. The total weight of the shells that an artillery division can fire at the enemy during a given time has risen some 50 to 100 per cent.

Infantry: Ordinary rifles are being replaced more and more by automatic repeating rifles, while the number and effectiveness of machine-guns have been greatly increased. An American infantry division, which

---

[19] Real "autarky," *i.e.*, a complete isolation from the world market, is out of the question under capitalism. German industry uses 45 to 50 per cent. of foreign raw materials, and its textile industry as much as 90 per cent. The restriction of raw material imports in the summer of 1934, due to the shortage of foreign exchange, has taught the German people a painful lesson on the senselessness of the fascists' autarky demagogy.

formerly could fire 107,000 shots a minute from its machine-guns, can now fire more than 200,000.

The new types of weapons, tanks and airplanes, have undergone enormous development. The speed and the radius of action of all types of tanks have been doubled since the Sixth Congress! Heavy tanks travel on *wheels* at a speed of 60 miles an hour, and cross-country at 30 miles per hour on *caterpillar tread*. Tanks have become enormous moving fortresses as well as irresistible battering rams that " jump " trenches, swim rivers, and know no obstacles. The horse-power of pursuit plane motors increased from 500 to 1,000 h.p. between 1929 and 1933, their speed rose from 175 miles per hour to over 250, and their maximum flying altitude from 27,000 to over 40,000 feet. The number of military airplanes possessed by the major powers is as follows :

		England	U.S.A.	Japan	France	Germany
1929	... ...	1,824	3,129	1,260	5,000	—
1934	... ...	3,000	5,000	2,200	6,000	1,000

The importance of the aerial weapon in the whole system of armaments has increased by giant strides, as is best shown in the war budgets. The radius of action of bombing planes increased from 300 to 750 miles. Thus, almost all the territory of West European countries is exposed to air attacks by neighbouring countries.

Many military specialists consider the airplane the *decisive* weapon of the future world war.

New discoveries and improvements of every sort are being made daily in all types of weapons : Germany's " pocket battleships," electrical gun-aiming at the target, remote control of ships and airplanes, Teslas " death-rays," cutting out a motor's magneto ignition by means of special rays, rockets flying hundreds of miles, giant flame-throwers mounted on tanks and airplanes, and so forth—not to mention the advances in preparation for " prohibited " chemical and bacteriological warfare, regarding which the greatest secrecy is maintained.

The horrors of the coming war will many times exceed those of the past war. The " front " will no longer be a " line " several miles broad, but an area dozens of miles deep. The new frontier fortifications erected at tremendous cost, into which hundreds of thousands of tons of steel have been sunk, will hardly be able to prevent this. On both sides tanks will penetrate far into the enemy's territory; with their bombs airplanes and airships will destroy cities hundreds of miles behind the front; and the entire civil population of the enemy country will be decimated by gas attacks as a potential army. Every factory, and even agricultural land, will be regarded as part of the military, and will be laid waste. The " devastated areas " will embrace entire countries. . . .

(3) *The ideological preparation for war* is what is most difficult for the bourgeoisie. The masses of the people, especially the older generation that experienced the horrors of the first World War, want to have nothing to do with a new war. The masses are undoubtedly filled with

a profound desire for peace. Only the big bourgeoisie, which makes enormous profit in war,[20] and the regular army officers (for whom war means promotion) are interested in war. Under these conditions no government had the courage openly to advocate an ideology of aggressive warfare. Therefore the pacifist phrases mounted on all sides. The feverish preparations for war continue to be masked in pacifist guise as essential for " defence " of the fatherland. In the question of national defence there is a united front of all the bourgeois parties, from the fascist wing on the extreme Right to the Social-Democrats.[21]   But whoever approves of national defence, *whoever is in favour of a " defensive war " is in favour of war in general,* for every war is represented as a defensive war by those who start it.[22]   Whoever is for national defence, is for maintenance of the rule of the bourgeoisie.

The *disarmament conference* that collapsed so ingloriously also served as a pacifist disguise. Its final collapse was due to the aggravation of imperialist antagonisms in general, and to the aggressive policies of Japan and of fascist Germany in particular. Limitations of armaments was conceivable (and was even effected for naval armaments at the Washington and London conferences to a limited extent[23] as long as the main task seemed to be the joint suppression by the victors of the disarmed countries vanquished in the World War, as long as the redivision of the world was not a pressing problem during the period of relative stabilization of capitalism. Any thought of armament limitation became impossible when fascist Germany, demonstratively leaving the disarmament conference, threw off the armament restrictions imposed on it at Versailles, and when Japan started its war for the redivision of the world. Deceiving the toiling masses with talk about " disarmament " could no longer be continued along this line.

The chauvinistic ideology of conquest and revenge now came to the fore more and more strongly (especially in Germany and Japan), disguised and interwoven with agitation against the " inferior " races and against the Soviet Union, but without relinquishing pacifist phrases, with continued emphasis upon the defensive character of armaments. Every effort was made to reawaken the nationalist, chauvinist and militarist spirit, especially among the youth. Youngsters are systematically inoculated with the spirit of chauvinism, from the kindergarten to the university.

[20] It is typical of the bourgeoisie's " patriotism " that the munitions industrialists sell their weapons to any country, friend or foe, for cold cash. They did this even during the World War! They are connected with one another in the most complex fashion. See Fenner Brockway's *The Bloody Traffic,* London, 1933, for many interesting facts and especially the testimony before the U.S. Senate Committee in the summer of 1934.

[21] During recent years the congresses of the legal socialist parties one after another have adopted resolutions for national defence, *e.g.,* the congress of the French party at Tours, the Social-Democratic Parties of Denmark, Holland, Switzerland, etc.

[22] Since all imperialists want war, all aggressors are also on the defensive.

[23] Agreement on limiting the construction of battleships was made easier by the gigantic sums that such ships cost, and by the doubt which has been raised in naval circles, after the experience of the World War, regarding the value of super-dreadnoughts against submarines and comparatively cheap airplanes.

The daily press, the moving-pictures, the radio, the theatre, literature, art and science, are all used for this purpose. Brilliant military parades are supposed to make one forget the horror of war. . . .

The ideological mobilization of the population for the coming war meets an obstacle in the impoverishment of the workers, the toiling peasants and the petty bourgeoisie during the crisis; in the resultant intensification of the class struggle; in the anti-militaristic work of the Communist Parties (insufficient as this still is in many countries); and in the maturing of the revolutionary crisis. Hence, the greatest anxiety of the bourgeoisie is the army's reliability in case of war. That is why special detachments have been established to maintain discipline in the next war. That is the basis of Fuller's proposal to create small armies of reliable class composition, equipped with the latest achievements of military technique. But this concept has turned out to be impossible of execution. The army of the next war will undoubtedly be a mass army. The entire male population will be armed, except for those indispensable for the production of war materials. This means that the more the revolutionary crisis matures in the different countries, the more unreliable will the mass army be for the ruling classes. Moreover, the more complex the whole modern army mechanism becomes, the more complex present-day weapons are as machines, the greater must be the effectiveness of the proletariat's anti-war, class struggle, activity in determining the outcome of the war.

*   *   *   *   *

The new world war is unavoidable if the proletarian revolution does not forestall it. *History places these alternatives before the proletariat: Either to be sacrificed once again in the slaughter-house in the service of the bourgeoisie, or to turn its weapons against its own bourgeoisie under the leadership of the Communist Party, turning the imperialist war into a civil war for the overthrow of the rule of the bourgeoisie!*

CHAPTER XI

THE CHANGES IN METHOD OF THE DICTATORSHIP OF THE BOURGEOISIE

The entire period of the general crisis of capitalism is characterized by an uneven, zigzag process of exposing the democratic-parliamentary disguise of the bourgeoisie's[1] dictatorship. Bourgeois democracy was the given form of the bourgeoisie's rule during the ascending period of capitalism, while the latter was still fulfilling its historical mission of developing the forces of production, while the bourgeoisie could still lay claim to being a progressive class. During the period of the general crisis of capitalism, bourgeois democracy had to be undermined and abolished since the capitalist mode of production has become an obstacle to the further development of social productive forces; since the contradiction between the forces of production and the production relationships are becoming more and more acute; since the number of people interested (or imagining themselves to be interested) in the maintenance of the capitalist system of society is growing less and less as the result of the centralization of capital, the mass ruin of the toiling peasants and the impoverishment of the working class; and since the struggle of the oppressed classes against bourgeois rule grows more and more intense.

Moreover, the struggle among the various groups of the ruling classes for a share in the social profit, which tends to decrease, also grew more acute. This found political expression in splits of the bourgeois parties, in the system of coalition governments, in parliamentary "log-rolling" and in the rapid succession of cabinets. All this undermined the confidence of the masses in bourgeois democracy and parliamentarism, and lessened the prestige of the ruling classes. The bourgeoisie was less and less able to maintain its rule by peaceful, ideological methods. Instead it had to set its machinery of force in motion more and more often, and more and more systematically, in order to protect its rule. This trend was characterized as follows in the Theses of the Sixth Congress:

". . . the imperialist states develop more and more severe methods and weapons for suppressing the revolutionary detachments of the proletariat, particularly the Communist Parties. . . . These measures . . . reflect the general aggravation of class antagonisms, and the intensification of all forms and methods of the class struggle, as expressed in the increasing application of fascist methods of oppression by the bourgeoisie."[2]

The great crisis, which sped up the process of the centralization of

1 As early as 1920 the Theses of the Second Congress of the Comintern declared: "The centre of gravity of political life at present has been completely and finally transferred beyond the limits of parliament." (*The Communist Party and Parliamentarism*, p. 43, "Theses and Statutes of the Second Congress of the Communist International.")

2 Resolution of the Sixth Congress on "The International Situation and the Tasks of the Communist International."

capital tremendously, which ruined millions of hitherto "independent" petty bourgeois and peasants, and rendered half of the working class unemployed, abandoning them to the most frightful misery, accelerated this trend. The fascization of the government machinery is becoming a common phenomenon. Governments are becoming more and more independent of parliaments; government by decree based on "extraordinary powers" is becoming more and more the rule. (Even such traditionally democratic states as the U.S.A. and France are no exception.) In the course of the crisis and depression the bourgeoisie did away with bourgeois democracy even in form in Germany and in several smaller countries, defending its imperilled rule against the revolutionary proletariat by establishing the fascist form of its dictatorship.

"The growth of fascism and its coming into power in Germany and in a number of other capitalist countries means:

"(a) That the revolutionary crisis and the indignation of the broad masses against the rule of capital is growing;

"(b) That the capitalists are no longer able to maintain their dictatorship by the old methods of parliamentarism and of bourgeois democracy in general;

"(c) That, moreover, the methods of parliamentarism and bourgeois democracy in general are becoming a hindrance to the capitalists. . . .

"(d) That in view of this, capital is compelled to pass to open terrorist dictatorship." [3]

THE CRISIS OF SOCIAL-DEMOCRACY

The great crisis, which led to rapid acceleration of the process of fascisization, made the crisis in Social-Democracy apparent. The crisis has seized both the Second International and the Amsterdam Trade Union International, as international organizations as well as the individual Social-Democratic parties. It is manifested in the increasing transfer of the best, most revolutionary Social-Democratic workers to Communism; in the severe internal struggles which lead to splits and defections in practically all the Social-Democratic parties; in the ideological confusion prevailing in the biggest of these parties; in the decline of the influence exercised by Social-Democracy over the working class; and finally in the fact that the bourgeoisie in a number of countries no longer looks upon and treats Social-Democracy as its main social support, but on the contrary abandons it to fascist terror.

This change in the bourgeoisie's attitude to Social-Democracy takes place very unevenly in the various countries, depending upon the extent of economic disintegration and the menace to bourgeois rule occasioned by the maturing of the revolutionary crisis.

From this standpoint the following groups of countries may be differentiated:

(a) Countries where Social-Democracy either participates in the govern-

---

[3] *Theses and Decisions* of the Thirteenth Plenum of the E.C.C.I., p. 6, Modern Books, Ltd., London.

ment, or is considered as the future government party : Sweden, Denmark, England, Czechoslovakia;

(b) Countries where the Social-Democratic parties constitute legal opposition parties, as in the United States, France, Spain, etc.;

(c) Countries where legal and semi-legal Social-Democratic parties exist under a fascist regime, *e.g.*, Hungary and Poland. (Beginnings of collaboration in Italy and Austria as well.);

(d) Countries in which Social-Democracy is suppressed and persecuted as a party, as in Germany and Austria.

This very different situation of the various Social-Democratic parties is the chief cause of the crisis in the Second and Amsterdam Internationals as central organizations.

The differing positions of the individual Social-Democratic parties, which participate in the government in some countries, while they are illegal and persecuted in others, do not allow of even formally unanimous decisions on any problems.

Moreover, the accentuation of imperialist contradictions, more and more sharply divides the various Social-Democratic parties, which side with their respective bourgeoisies. Although the Second International in its decisions before the World War threatened to declare a general strike if war broke out, and although Kautsky's theory that " the International is an instrument of peace " was originated only during the course of the War, to-day we see more and more Social-Democratic parties, even before the outbreak of war, openly advocating national defence.[4]

However, the crisis in the international reformist organizations (which had never exercised much influence on the individual parties) is not important for our struggle, but rather the crises in the individual Social-Democratic parties.

(1) *The social basis of the crisis in Social-Democracy is the impairment of the conditions of the working class in general and of the labour aristocracy in particular* during the period of general crisis and especially during the course of the great crisis and of the depression of a special kind.

" . . . The labour aristocracy . . . is constantly being weakened by the abolition of the privileges of separate groups of the proletariat through the general decay of capitalism, the levelling out of the condition of the working class, and the generalized extent of its need and insecurity." [5]

After the victory of reformism and the transformation of the *ultimate*

[4] It is particularly interesting that not only do the Social-Democratic Parties participating in government or in the legal opposition advocate national defence, but that Otto Bauer (who has since been driven out of Austria) offered the already illegal Social-Democratic Party of Germany the following advice :

" In case of war, German Social-Democracy will have to fight so that a democratic-socialist revolution *tears down those obstacles to the development of the full defensive strength of the German people*. . . . Not defence in the sense of 1914, or even of May, 1933 . . . *but neither the defeatist refusal of any and all national defence.*"—(*Der Kampf,* October, 1933.)

[5] Thesis of the Second Congress of the Communist International on " The Trade Union Movement."

goal into an empty holiday phrase, the basis of Social-Democracy's influence was the belief of a large section of the working class (a belief consistently nurtured by the Social-Democratic leaders in the interests of bourgeois rule) that it is possible to better its conditions within the framework of capitalism by utilizing bourgeois democracy, the peaceable trade union movement and the parliamentary influence of the Social-Democratic parties. This faith was fostered by the fact that certain more or less narrow sections of the working class—*the corrupted labour aristocracy in the imperialist countries and the labour bureaucracy* (members of parliament, officials of the trade unions, the party, and the co-operatives, employees of sick benefit organizations, etc.) actually could better their conditions within the framework of capitalism. The opportunist leadership of the Social-Democratic parties would have been unable to retain control for so long a time if not for this objective basis.

The illusions of the working class regarding bourgeois democracy and the possibility of improving its conditions under capitalism grew considerably immediately after the war, especially in the defeated countries. During the first round of revolutions, the bourgeoisie's rule was acutely threatened in these countries by the revolt of the masses, embittered by their sufferings during the War, and by the collapse of the bourgeois machinery of force as a result of defeat in the War. *Hence the bourgeoisie made far-reaching concessions to the revolutionary masses within the framework of the capitalist social order.* In the defeated countries all the traditional demands of the Social-Democratic workers were met; overthrow of the monarchy; universal, equal and secret suffrage; freedom of assembly and of organization; the eight-hour day; unemployment insurance, etc. At the same time the bourgeoisie handed over the government to the Social-Democratic leaders.

In view of the breakdown of its machinery of force, it was impossible for the bourgeoisie to meet the revolts of the masses with violence at that moment. The bourgeoisie had to mollify the revolt of the masses by offering them concessions, in order to gain time for the restoration of its machinery of force. The fact that the Social-Democratic leaders were in the cabinet created the illusion in the working masses of having already defeated the bourgeoisie. The Social-Democratic leaders nurtured these illusions with such slogans as " Socialism marches on," by instituting commissions for socialization, etc. Under these circumstances, there was a strong influx of workers, officials and petty bourgeois into the Social-Democratic parties immediately after the War. Participation in the government enabled the German and Austrian Social-Democratic parties to extend their base within the bureaucracy by making hundreds of thousands of their followers state and municipal officials.

But with the recovery and strengthening of bourgeois rule and with capital's offensive against working conditions, the illusions of the masses of workers were disappointed more and more. The great crisis, which impaired the condition of the masses of workers to an unprecedented degree, also undermined the privileged position of the labour aristocracy by *re-*

ducing its numbers and its privileged position in comparison to the masses of the workers and by fully extending unemployment to it as well.

Presenting the impairment of the labour aristocracy's condition concretely, in figures, meets with the difficulty of determining what categories and groups of the working class are to be considered as belonging to the labour aristocracy. We cite the following figures from the book by Kuczynski (with all necessary reservations).[6]

INDEX OF REAL WAGES OF THE LABOUR ARISTOCRACY

(1900 = 100)

	Germany	U.S.A.	England
1929	93	143	93
1933	49	115	95

These figures, which are not very accurate owing to the complexity of the calculations, indicate a very severe impairment of the position of the labour aristocracy in Germany and the U.S.A., with slight improvement in England.[7] (This includes losses sustained through unemployment, as well as income from unemployment relief.)

In general we note that the major tendency in the condition of the working class during the crisis is a levelling out on a lower plane. This downward levelling tendency during the crisis is clearly manifested, for instance, in the official statistics of German workers' wages.

INVALID INSURANCE CLASSIFICATION OF GERMAN WORKERS
ACCORDING TO WEEKLY WAGE

(*in per cent.*)

	Up to 6 marks	6-12 marks	12-18 marks	18-24 marks	24.30 marks	30.36 marks	Over 36 marks
1929	3.5	12.3	16.5	13.0	8.8	8.1	37.8
1934 (first quarter)	4.0	25.1	19.4	14.4	10.7	9.5	16.9

Before the crisis, 42 per cent. of the workers earned from 6 to 24 marks;

[6] *Die Entwicklung der Lage der Arbeiter in Europe und Amerika, 1870 bis 1933* [*Evolution of the Condition of the Workers in Europe and America, 1870-1933*], Basle, 1934.

[7] The impairment of the situation of large sections of the labour aristocracy can be demonstrated in England as well, the classical country of corruption of the topmost stratum of the working class. The weekly wage collectively agreed upon for skilled workers is as follows:

	Aug. 4, 1914 s. d.	Dec. 31, 1933 s. d.	Per cent. increase	Per cent. increase in cost of living
Metal Trades ...	41 8	62 4	50	—
Shipbuilding ...	41 7	60 0	43	43
Building ...	39 0	65 5	67	—

These figures indicate that the real wages of the labour aristocracy (when fully employed) improved as compared to the pre-War period. But unemployment has hit just these layers extremely hard in the course of the crisis. As late as May, 1933, unemployment among shipbuilding workers totalled 47.6 per cent., with up to 33 per cent. among metal workers of various categories. Wages above the collective contract level were greatly reduced. The official cost of living index is falsified to a considerable extent. Although certain new sections of better-paid workers develop (motor, radio) the position of the labour aristocracy in England has undoubtedly also been impaired on the whole by the crisis.

at present this group totals 59 per cent. Before the crisis 37.8 per cent. earned more than 36 marks; now 16.9 per cent., or less than half, earn that much. The number of workers with an income of more than 48 marks has been reduced to a minimum. If we take into consideration the tremendous unemployment, the increase in taxes and wage deductions, and the cuts in unemployment relief (which had already commenced while the Social-Democrats were in the cabinet), we can understand why the illusions of the German working class regarding the possibility of advance within the framework of capitalism, through the peaceful methods advocated by Social-Democracy, evaporated during the crisis. The principal basis for the political crisis in the Social-Democratic parties is : disillusionment caused by the failure of democracy and by the futility of the " positions of power " plus the workers' dissatisfaction with the anti-Soviet and war policy of the Social-Democratic leaders.

The Political Crisis of Social-Democracy

Social-Democracy was transformed from an originally revolutionary party into the main social support of the bourgeoisie, by having in practice substituted reformism for revolutionary international Marxism even in the pre-war period; by having openly gone over to the side of its bourgeoisie during the World War, urging the proletarians to murder each other; by splitting the working class and causing the collapse of the revolution in its first round through the use of subtle manœuvres plus armed violence together with the bourgeoisie; by slandering the Soviet Union in every way and seeking to discredit it among the workers.

" The petty bourgeois democracy of the capitalist countries, the most advanced sections of which are the Second and the Two-and-a-Half Internationals, is at the present moment the chief support of capitalism in so far as the majority (or at least a considerable part) of the workers and clerks employed in industry and commerce remain under its influence. In the event of a revolution, the latter fear the loss of their relatively petty-bourgeois standard of living, which is the result of imperialist privileges. But the growing economic crisis is impairing the conditions of the masses everywhere. This circumstance, together with the inevitability of imperialist wars, if capitalism continues to exist (which is becoming more manifest every day), is shattering this mainstay more and more." [8]

The political essence of the crisis of Social-Democracy is the conflict between its function as the main social support of the bourgeoisie and its proletarian (and petty-bourgeois) *mass base,* which conflict grows more and more irreconcilable in the crisis and depression. The bourgeoisie demands that the reformist leaders get the workers to accept the impairment of their working conditions peacefully. The Social-Democratic workers demand that they organize and lead the resistance against the attack of capital.

[8] Thesis of the Third World Congress of the Communist International on " The Tactics of the Russian Communist Party."

The bourgeoisie demands' that the Social-Democratic bureaucracy in government office, such as Severing, Grzesinski, MacDonald and others, defend bourgeois rule against the workers by armed force. The Social-Democratic workers demand that the Social-Democratic leaders take advantage of the government " positions of power " held by them to conduct the struggle against the bourgeoisie.

The bourgeoisie demands of the leadership of Social-Democracy that it perpetuate the split of the working class, isolating the Social-Democratic workers from the influence of the Communists, and assuring the hegemony of the bourgeoisie over the workers. The Social-Democratic workers want to conduct a united struggle with the Communists against the hegemony of the bourgeoisie over the workers. The Social-Democratic workers want to conduct a united struggle with the Communists against the bourgeoisie; they demand the united front, negotiations and reconciliation with the Communist International.

The bourgeoisie demands of the Social-Democratic leaders active participation in preparations for the new imperialist war; the Social-Democratic workers want to have nothing to do with a new imperialist war.

The bourgeoisie demands of the reformist leaders active participation in the ideological and organizational preparation of the counter-revolutionary war against the Soviet Union. The Social-Democratic workers understand that the Soviet Union is realizing the ultimate socialist goal for which the labour movement has been fighting since its beginning; not only do they reject any war against the Soviet Union, but they demand that the latter be defended, in struggle against their own bourgeoisie if necessary.[9]

This conflict, existing on every front, between the function of Social-Democracy as the main social support of the bourgeoisie and its proletarian mass base, and the resultant political crisis of Social-Democracy do not develop evenly in all countries. The crisis of Social-Democracy is less acute in those countries where the conditions of the workers during the crisis have grown worse to a lesser extent, relatively speaking, where the traditions of the revolutionary workers' movement are less and the influence of the Communist Parties weaker, as in England, Sweden, Norway or Denmark. Therefore the Social-Democratic parties in these countries can still participate in their governments or aspire to be the future government parties, and yet retain their mass influence, or in many cases, as in Sweden for instance, even extend their influence during the crisis.

Likewise, the crisis in Social-Democracy is somewhat less acute for the present in those countries where the Social-Democratic parties are in constant " opposition," where they support " Left " governments, it is true (as in France), but their leaders do not participate directly in the cabinet,

---

[9] This is naturally not a complete summary; the conflict develops in every field without exception.

and where the party officialdom is not fused with the state machinery,[10] In such countries the function of the party as the main social support of the bourgeoisie is more easily concealed from the working masses by employing manœuvres and revolutionary phrases.

On the other hand the war question plays a very big role in the crisis of the French party (as well as in several other Social-Democratic parties). While the " Left " and Centrist leaders continue to manœuvre with pacifism, under the pressure of the masses who want to have nothing to do with a new war, the leaders of the Right, under pressure from the bourgeoisie, take an open stand for a new war. This, as we know, has led to the split of the Socialist deputies' group and to the emergence of the neo-fascist Marquet-Déat group.

The crisis of Social-Democracy has gone as far as the complete disintegration of the party in Germany, which was very hard hit by the crisis, where the condition of the proletariat in the post-war period, and especially during the great economic crisis, had grown worse to an exceptional degree, where the leaders of Social-Democracy constantly participated in government,[11] and where the party officialdom had been most extensively interwoven with the bourgeoisie's machinery of force. Hence, Social-Democracy's responsibility for the reduction of wages, for the cuts in social insurance, and for the murder of demonstrating workers could not be hushed up. Hence, a strong Communist Party, rapidly gaining in influence, made it more and more difficult for the Social-Democratic leaders to carry out their anti-working class policies. The inner dialectics of development of the crisis in Social-Democracy is therefore best illustrated in Germany.

The leaders of German Social-Democracy " honestly " endeavoured to meet the demands of the bourgeoisie all along the line. Tarnow frankly declared :

" The crisis must be solved within the framework of the capitalist social order, with the sacrifices by the working class necessary to that end." [12]

The Social-Democratic arbitrators reduced the workers' wages.[13] The Social-Democratic trade union leaders prevented strikes, and expelled the Communists from the trade unions.

The Social-Democratic chiefs of police allowed policemen, members of

[10] However, the fact that the Social-Democratic Party of France controls numerous municipalities has led to a pronounced inter-linking of the Party apparatus with the municipal bureaucracy. This constitutes a strong pillar of opportunism.

[11] Social-Democracy " ruled " uninterruptedly in Prussia from the end of the War until the Braun government was driven out by von Papen in 1932.

[12] *Rote Fahne*, Dec. 10, 1930.

[13] The first wage reduction enforced by the government was based, as we know, on Severing's Oeynhausen arbitration decision.

Social-Democratic organizations, to shoot down demonstrating workers.[14] And so forth.

But this anti-working class policy led to the undermining of Social Democracy's influence among the working masses, and the rapid growth in influence of the Communist Party of Germany (C.P.G.) Election votes showed that the C.P.G. had won the majority of the working class in such important centres as Berlin and the Ruhr area, and was definitely on the road towards winning the majority of the working class in the entire Reich. (Yet, since the majority of the working class continued to follow the leadership of the S.P.G. and it controlled the mass organizations, especially the trade unions and the workers in the big factories, its weakened influence was still sufficiently powerful to hinder a united struggle of the working class in general, and in particular to prevent the general strike proclaimed by the C.P.G. against the fascists' seizure of power.)

The decisive sections of the bourgeoisie reacted to the decrease in influence of the S.P.G. by supporting and extensively financing the fascist movement, in order to subject the workers to intensified pressure and terror and, in view of the probable failure of the Social-Democrats in their role of the bourgeoisie's main social support to have a ready substitute in the fascists. (Although Hitler's agitation was much more " anti-capitalist " than that of the Social-Democratic leaders, the captains of industry: Thyssen, Mutschmann, and the rest, knew quite well that it was no more earnest than the phrases of the Social-Democratic leaders regarding the class struggle and the ultimate revolutionary goal.)

Thus the Social-Democratic leadership was subjected to many-sided pressure. The bourgeoisie demanded that it stifle the economic and political struggles of the proletariat, and threatened to replace it by the fascists; in endeavouring to meet the demands of the bourgeoisie, the leaders of the S.P.G. drove the workers towards the Communists, and the petty bourgeoisie (plus certain tiny sections of the working class) to the fascists. The leadership of the S.P.G. supported every reactionary govern-

---

[14] How very conscious the Social-Democratically organized police officials were of their counter-revolutionary role is shown by the following letter sent by the Brotherhood of Social-Democratic Police Officials to the Leipzig Convention of the Social-Democratic Party of Germany (S.P.G.) in 1931:

" The forthcoming emergency decree provides for another reduction in the salaries of officials. We do not want to repeat the arguments generally valid against such a proviso. But in the justifiable defence of the interests of police officials, to which we are certainly entitled as members of the trade union of government officials, we merely want to protect our members against heavy and unbearable sacrifices and to inform the Party Convention of our political apprehensions, arising from such a reduction. We should like to put the question frankly: *Where in the world has any state, in times of stress and danger, ever reduced and cut the means of livelihood of the protectors of governmental order? When has a state ever alienated the armed forces that protect it in the hours of extreme danger?* It is the duty of the German republic to forestall an agitation among police officials that is counter to the public interest, by assuring them their means of livelihood. Will it really be the fate of the German republic to treat its police officials to a reduction in salary exactly at the moment when it needs them urgently? "

ment, and tried to justify its betrayal to the working class by its " theory of the lesser evil."

" There was only this alternative : the Brüning Cabinet or open fascist dictatorship," according to Sollmann's political report at the Leipzig Party Convention in 1931.

" If we overthrow the Brüning cabinet the scorpions of Hitler and Hugenberg will succeed the whip of Brüning," Dittman said at the same convention.

They also avoided any serious clash with fascism, for they feared that such a struggle would develop into a revolutionary movement against the bourgeoisie. They prepared the way for Hitler's advent to power by suppressing the Red Front Fighters' League, by disarming the workers, by tolerating the organization of the Storm Troops and the Special Guards, by giving the fascists police protection against the workers while the former were still weak, and so forth. They opposed Thälmann's candidacy for the presidency, supporting Hindenburg (who later took Hitler into the cabinet) with the slogan: " A vote for Thälmann is a vote for Hitler." Their struggle against Hitler consisted in trying to convince the bourgeoisie that the latter could find no better support than they themselves were. " We are playing the role of capitalism's physician." But all their manœuvres could not abolish the crisis. *The more they laboured to serve the bourgeoisie, the more their ideological influence upon the working class declined,* the less was their usefulness to the bourgeoisie. The leaders of German Social-Democracy could not break through this vicious circle by any sort of manœuvre. Until Hitler's seizure of power they continued their policy of splitting the working class. They refused the C.P.G.'s offer for common struggle, even when von Papen simply expelled them from the Prussian government. They remained unshakeably faithful to their masters until they were driven out. The German proletariat, however, is paying, under Hitler's whip, for the fact that their traitorous leaders prevented the Social-Democratic workers from carrying on a united struggle together with the Communists against the bourgeoisie.

*   *   *   *   *

The " Left " Austro-Marxists could not bridge the conflict between their role as the main social support of the bourgeoisie and their proletarian mass base any more than could the Right leaders of the S.P.G. Essentially, they pursued the same policy of the lesser evil, although they could easily see whither it led by the fate of the S.P.G. After having played their part they were driven off the scene practically without a struggle, by the weak Austrian bourgeoisie, divided by its own inner conflicts.[15] This is the best proof that the fate of the S.P.G. is no exception due to excep-

[15] The heroic struggle of the Schutzbund, unwanted and unsupported by the leaders, had to collapse because it had no political, revolutionary goal. The purely defensive slogan of defending freedom's rights—not struggle for the overthrow of the bourgeoisie—had to result in defeat: the strategic and tactical errors inevitably followed from this false political approach.

tional circumstances, but *represents the typical fate awaiting all Social-Democratic parties* if the Social-Democratic workers do not realise the united front with the Communists against the menace of fascism, if they do not shatter that baneful influence of their leaders, who serve the bourgeoisie, and do not follow the only practicable revolutionary path, blazed for them by the Russian Bolsheviks. . . .

The crisis in the Amsterdam International is less advanced than that in Social-Democracy. In many countries (especially where each trade union member is automatically a member of the Social-Democratic party, as in Norway, Hungary and Great Britain) Social-Democracy finds support in the free trade unions. In the U.S.A. the A.F. of L. is undoubtedly growing considerably at the present time; hundreds of thousands of workers went on strike in 1934 for the right to organize in unions within the framework of the A.F. of L.

The reasons for the greater stability of the Social-Democratic trade unions compared to the Social-Democratic parties are many and various. The most important are as follows: the individual union-organised workers are directly and materially interested in the existence of the trade unions. The trade unions can adapt themselves to a regime that is going fascist much more easily than the Social-Democratic parties can. Moreover, practically all the Communist Parties have done insufficient work in the trade unions. But the same causes that account for the crisis in the Second International must also aggravate the crisis in the Amsterdam International.

The Ideological Crisis of Social-Democracy

The ideological (and organizational) crisis of Social-Democracy is inter-linked with its political crisis.

The period of relative stabilization enabled Social-Democracy to renew and extend its pre-war revisionist policy, which it had masked with " Left " phrases, during the first revolutionary crisis.

In the field of economics, Hilferding, Kautsky and Tarnow announced that there was no general crisis of capitalism[16]; that capitalism still had a long period of advance before it; that the October Revolution had been a bourgeois revolution, and did not signify the beginning of the overthrow of the capitalist social order (Otto Bauer); that capitalism was developing into a planned state capitalism, free of crisis; and that the transition to socialism had already begun.

As to the theory of the state, their position was as follows: *The state is above classes; parliamentary democracy is the only road to the conquest of state power,* which can proceed only step by step. Until Social-Democracy obtains an absolute majority at the polls it participates in coalition

---

[16] Even as late as Nov. 11, 1930, in the midst of the great economic crisis, Hilferding declared at the Landgemeinde Convention:

" The present economic crisis is much more severe than previous ones, but as a crisis of capitalist economy it is only a cyclic phenomenon that will be overcome. *The basic drive of our economy points upwards."*

governments and occupies "positions of power" in the governmental machinery, but it cannot fully carry out its program of "industrial democracy," socialism (as they understand it), even when governing alone. "The Labour Party is in office, but not in power." Democracy involves the rejection of all use of force, of all dictatorship, even the dictatorship of the proletariat.

This ideology, which temporarily satisfied the bourgeoisie and also kept the majority of Social-Democratic workers from coming over to the revolution, could not withstand the hammer-blows of the crisis. The drop of production to below the pre-war level, the rapid impoverishment of the proletariat, and the ejection of half the workers from the process of production, gave the lie to the theory of the advance of capitalism, and destroyed the illusions that had arisen during the period of stabilisation among some of the Social-Democratic workers regarding the possibility of an existence worthy of a human being within the framework of the capitalist social order. But the fact that in all countries (including those where Social-Democrats were in the cabinet) the offensive of capital was made with the support of the state, and that the workers' resistance was smashed, when necessary, by the most brutal application of the state machinery of force, undermined faith in the state standing above classes. Under the blows of the crisis, the Social-Democratic workers again became receptive to revolutionary Marxism, championed by the Communists. The walls that the Social-Democratic leaders had erected between the Social-Democratic workers and the Communists began to give way.

With unconcealed revisionist ideology the leaders of Social-Democracy could no longer keep the workers firmly under their influence. The political crisis was reflected in the ideological crisis. Some of the leaders again began to develop "Left" theories: Lœbe stated that the crisis of capitalism was general; Otto Bauer demanded that democracy be defended against fascism with armed force; Seydewitz and Co. even demanded the dictatorship of the proletariat. . . .

The ideological crisis grew even greater after the victory of fascism in Germany and Austria. The leaders faced the task of finding a new ideology that would quiet the Social-Democratic workers, embittered over the complete failure of the policy of the lesser evil, but at the same time would not block the way for further collaboration with the bourgeoisie later on.

The ideology of peaceful parliamentary democracy had to be sacrificed for the time being.

"Against *despotism* no parliamentary or constitutional opposition is possible, but only the weapon of revolution," is the phrasing of the first programmatic pamphlet of the S.P.G. leadership from exile.

"In the struggle against the National Socialist dictatorship no compromise is possible, there is no place for reformism or legality," declares the January program of the S.P.G.

But the " revolution " is to be directed only against the fascist form of the bourgeois dictatorship, and not against the rule of the bourgeoisie itself. The revolutionary phrases are intended for the workers, while the bourgeoisie is set at ease by the decisive rejection of Bolshevism.

"The new socialist battlefront . . . must reject the Bolshevik goal programmatically. Replacing the National-Socialist prison by the Bolshevik penitentiary cannot be the goal of the great struggle for freedom against the fascist state." (January Programme.)

"Back to democracy" is Kautsky's slogan. "Through dictatorship to democracy" is the slogan of the exiled Austro-Marxists.

As we see, this clique of leaders, though driven out or locked up in concentration camps, still serves the bourgeoisie, by employing the vestiges of its remaining influence among the working masses against the united front of the proletariat, against the proletarian revolution, and for the re-establishment of a legal dictatorship of the bourgeoisie. But the German and Austrian workers have learned a lesson from the events of the last few years, and see through this double-dealing of their leaders more and more clearly.

The crisis in ideology is a problem for the whole Second International, and not only for the German and Austrian Social-Democratic leaders already driven out by the bourgeoisie. The problem is to create a new ideology, *a new program, that on one hand would satisfy the workers temporarily and keep them with the Party, and, on the other, keep the bourgeoisie from (following the example of the German bourgeoisie) driving out the reformists and making the fascists their main social support.* Or putting it otherwise, to create a program that would enable Social-Democracy to continue successfully playing its role as the main social support of the bourgeoisie, despite the crisis.

The "most successful" attempt in this connection was made by de Man, whose "Program of Labour," which was formally adopted by the Belgian Social-Democratic Party, united "Left" phraseology with a semi-fascist content that is acceptable to the bourgeoisie. The workers are given to understand that the plan constitutes "an attack on the structure of capitalism itself," and that its fulfilment would constitute a step towards realization of the ultimate goal, since the banks, railroads, power production and mining would be "nationalized." The bourgeoisie is reassured that confiscation of its property is out of the question, and that the fulfilment of the plan will take place only by peaceful means, by winning a majority among the people or in parliament. The side of the plan shown the workers is the revolutionary phrases; the side shown the bourgeoisie is an offer of government by coalition on the basis of systematizing state aid to the enterprises of monopoly capital facing bankruptcy.[17]

The crisis programs of the British Labour Party, the Swiss Socialist Party, the French Neo-Socialists, etc., run essentially along the same lines.

[17] See my detailed criticism in the *Communist International*, Nos. 12-13, 1934, "The De Man Plan is a Fraud on the Workers."

That this endeavour to keep the Social-Democratic workers from the United front and revolutionary struggle by means of " Left " phrases[18] did not have the anticipated success is demonstrated by the organizational crisis of the Socialist parties.

THE ORGANIZATIONAL CRISIS OF SOCIAL-DEMOCRACY

The organizational crisis of Social-Democracy is the result of the political crisis, which the leaders attempt to overcome, without success, by changing its ideology and by " Left " manœuvres. This organizational crisis is manifested in defections and splits to the " Right and to the Left," and in transfer to the Communists, not only by individual workers, but whole Social-Democratic organizations.

These defections and splits take place along two main lines. Some of the Social-Democratic leaders want under no circumstances to share the fate of Wels, Heilmann and Otto Bauer. *They want to remain in the favour of the bourgeoisie under all circumstances.* Such are the Mac-Donald-Snowden group in England, the neo-fascist Marquet-Déat group in France, and Noske, Urich, Loebe and Severing in Germany.[19] But through their open desertion to the bourgeoisie they lose their influence over the workers, and with it their value for the bourgeoisie.

Other Social-Democratic leaders attempt to serve the bourgeoisie by placing themselves at the head of the leftward movement of the working class in order to prevent the workers from going over to the Communist Party : the I.L.P. in England, the Socialist Labour Party in Germany, etc. They cannot fulfil their role since the workers are beginning more and more to recognize the difference between the revolutionary struggle of the Communists and the " Left " phrases of these most dangerous representatives. The aggravation of the whole situation prevents the formation of any extensive Centrist groups.

The organizational crisis is also manifested in the fact that the " founder parties " themselves are split into Right and " Left " fractions in the most varied fashion, as was shown most clearly at the last congress of the French Social-Democratic Party.[20]

The organizational crisis is most severe in Germany and Austria, where

---

18 The use of " Left " phrases assumes various forms. De Man speaks of an " attack on the structure of capitalism itself." Otto Bauer, for the time being, proclaims the necessity of armed uprising to overthrow the fascist regime in Austria, etc. All this is for the purpose of keeping the Social-Democratic workers from coming over to the Communist Parties. Only the former extreme Right-wing leader of Spanish Social-Democracy, Caballero, has advanced, under the pressure of the revolting masses, from " Left " slogans to participation in the revolutionary struggles.

19 In Germany the entire Social-Democratic leadership was ready to go over to Hitler had Hitler been willing, as was proved by Wels' speech in the Reichstag on May 17, 1934; the whole technical-bureaucratic staff of the Free Trade Unions has been taken over by the " Labour Front " and is continuing its work under fascist leadership.

20 This organizational chaos is most strikingly evidenced in Switzerland where the Right Social-Democratic chief of police of Zurich had the " Left " Social-Democratic party secretary arrested.

there is no longer any central Social-Democratic Party at all, *but merely loose groups, most of which refuse to have anything to do with the émigré party leaderships.* The case of Germany proves most strikingly how unstable a basis were the labour aristocracy and the Social-Democratic bureaucracy. The huge Social-Democratic bureaucracy in the Reich, in Prussia, in the cities and towns, in the trade unions and co-operatives, have as a body entered the service of the fascists (except for those who were kicked out). For years many had carried the fascist party card in their pocket alongside the Social-Democratic one. As for the highly skilled Social-Democratic workers, most of them, as indispensable to capital, have remained in the factories. But the great majority have become politically " neutral " and are not inclined to jeopardize personal freedom and jobs by engaging in Social-Democratic Party work.[21] The functionary staff of the Party, which had been recruited from these privileged strata, no longer exists as an organizational entity.

The political, ideological and organizational crisis of Social-Democracy, the complete bankruptcy of the policy of the mighty German and Austrian Social-Democratic parties, the blows struck the workers by fascism, and the courage and resoluteness of the German and Austrian Communists in their illegal work, are making more and more Social-Democratic workers begin to lose faith in Social-Democracy. They begin earnestly comparing the policy of the Social-Democrats with that of the Communists, and groups of really sincere, Left Social-Democratic, revolutionary workers are being formed. The road to the united front in struggle against fascism and the bourgeoisie is opening before us.

THE GROWTH OF FASCISM

The growth of fascism—both the fascization of the State machinery and the fascist movement itself—had already begun, prior to the Sixth World Congress, on the basis of the general crisis of capitalism. The great economic crisis and the present depression of a special kind have forced the bourgeoisie to speed up the process of fascization, though unequally in different countries, depending on the degree to which the rule of the bourgeoisie has been weakened and the revolutionary crisis has ripened.

We use the word forced advisedly. It is not merely for pleasure that the bourgeoisie replaces the democratic-parliamentary disguise of its rule by the method of fascist terror. The establishment of the fascist regime, although it does represent a heavy blow to the proletariat, is not the result of the strength, but rather the weakness of the bourgeoisie's position, the loss of its ideological-political hegemony over the majority of the people, which forces it to take refuge in the systematic use of terror.

If the impairment of the position of the proletariat in general, and of the labour aristocracy in particular, is the major basis of the crisis in

---

[21] A certain change has taken place in this respect since the 30th of June, which revealed the internal weaknesses of the Hitler regime as by a lightning flash. The old Social-Democratic functionaries are again beginning to try to do some Party work.

Social-Democracy, the impoverishment of the peasant and petty-bourgeoisie masses constitutes the social base for the growth of the fascist movement.[22]

Intense discontent and a widespread revolt against existing conditions were the political consequences of the mass ruin of the peasantry during the economic crisis. (Demonstrations, boycotting the supply of foodstuffs to the cities, mass refusals to pay taxes, interference by force with sheriff sales, etc.) Throughout the world, the toiling peasantry—hitherto the reserve of the bourgeoisie, but at the same time the great potential reserve of the proletarian revolution—has been stirred to activity. Although this activity, like all petty-bourgeois activity, lacks any clear political goal, it represents a menace to the rule of the bourgeoisie, the danger of which grows with the intensity of the latter's struggle with the proletariat, with the maturing of the revolutionary crisis in a given country. In all capitalist countries the bourgeoisie has always looked to the sections of the peasantry that it led and misled for support in its struggle against the revolutionary proletariat. What they have in common is private property, with the working peasants usually unable to distinguish between peasant property and exploiters' property. As fanatical defenders of peasant property, which to them seems indispensable as the natural basis for the employment of their labour power, they readily permit themselves to be misused for the defence of exploiters' property. Hence, the general revolt of the peasantry against existing conditions, caused by the agrarian crisis, represents a serious threat to bourgeois rule.

The toiling " peasantry " (which in this context we take to include tenant farmers, small farmers and middle farmers, *i.e.,* all the agricultural toilers living wholly or in part by cultivating their own or leased land by their own labour) constitutes the absolute majority of the earth's population and the most numerous single section of the population in most capitalist countries (with the exception of England and Belgium).[23]

The importance of the peasantry for the bourgeoisie is increased by the *special role it plays in the bourgeois state's machinery of force.* It is largely the sons of peasants who form the human material for the bourgeois state's machinery of force : the gendarmes, the militia, the police, the prison guards, are recruited for the most part from the sons of the

---

[22] This is shown most clearly in the votes received by the fascists in Germany. Their vote was as follows (in per cent. of all votes cast in the Reich):

Stabilization period			Crisis period		
1924 May	1924 Dec.	1928 May	1930 Sept.	1932 July	1932 Nov.
0.2	2.5	2.6	18.3	37.4	33.1

[23] According to the latest available census figures, the percentage of persons gainfully employed in agriculture is as follows:

U.S.A.	Germany	France	Czechoslovakia	Italy	Spain	Poland
26.7	30.5	38.4	40.5	55.7	57	76.2

Rich farmers, as well as landless agricultural wage labourers, must be deducted from these totals.

(Data from *Statistiches Jahrbuch für das Deutsches Reich* [*Statistical Yearbook of the German Reich*], 1932, p. 240.)

peasantry. The army, especially the professional cadres of non-commissioned officers, consists very largely of sons of the peasantry, to an extent even higher than the percentage of peasants in the total population. (For class reasons, workers are not readily promoted to positions as non-commissioned officers.) Therefore the general dissatisfaction of the peasantry imperils the reliability of the machinery of force, which is now of such decisive importance in the struggle with the working class.

It follows from all this that the attitude of the toiling peasantry is of decisive importance for the success of the proletarian revolution. This was already emphasized at the Second Congress of the Communist International, which pointed to the necessity of winning the village poor, of neutralizing the middle peasantry, and of decisive struggle against the rich peasants.

Victory of the proletarian revolution is extremely difficult in most countries (and in many countries impossible) so long as the ruling classes succeed in keeping the " peasantry " (in the wider sense of the word) under their moral and political influence, with the help of the rich peasants, " who are the most numerous of the bourgeois strata, the direct and determined enemies of the revolutionary proletariat." That is why the Theses of the Second Congress state that :

" *In the work of the Communist Party in the rural districts chief attention must be given to the struggle against this element, to the liberation of the labouring and exploited majority of the rural population from the moral and political influence of these exploiters.*" [24]

Unfortunately it must be stated that only in a few such countries such as Bulgaria, Greece, China and some other colonial countries, and to some extent in Poland, have the Communist Parties succeeded in using the favourable situation arising from the peasants' revolt to accomplish this task.[25]   In most capitalist countries, especially in Germany, the fascist movement has succeeded, with the help of an unscrupulous hypocritical demagogy (" Breaking interest slavery," " Subdivision of large estates, etc.), in absorbing the revolt of the peasantry and temporarily turning it into a force hostile to the working class. The National-Socialist movement did not confine its demagogy to economic questions. Slogans such as " Blood and Soil," " A People Without Space," and so on, paved the

[24] *Theses and Statutes of the Second Congress of the C.I.*, Theses on the Agrarian Question, p. 78.

[25] The task of the Communists was made more difficult by the traditional agrarian policy of Social-Democracy, which systematically established a barrier between the urban working class and the poor and middle farmers. It pictured the peasants (without class differentiation) merely as producers of foodstuffs in contrast to the industrial workers as *consumers,* as buyers of foodstuffs. Instead of the class distinction between exploiters and exploited in town and country, *the contrast of " urban consumers " and " rural producers " was stressed.* Instead of showing that industrial and agricultural workers, as well as poor and small farmers, are all exploited by the same ruling classes in town and country, Social-Democracy drew a line between the urban and rural districts. Thus there arose a peculiar " united front " between Social-Democracy and the agrarians. Social-Democracy objectively supported the policies of the agrarians who proclaimed the community of interests of all " farmers." This basic line was not changed by the agrarian reformism of David and Herz, and by occasional manœuvres intended to catch peasant votes.

way for demagogy in the race question, and for chauvinism. A huge " scientific " literature was supposed to prove that the peasants represent the pure " *Nordic blood* " in the German people, that the (free) peasants and the nobility were of common descent; they spoke of the " peasant nobility," etc.[26]

In this way the peasantry became a mass base for fascism; as a result the shaky hegemony of the bourgeoisie over them was (with a changed ideology) temporarily restored. The inability of Social-Democracy to influence the peasant movement, and the success of the fascists in demagogically deceiving the peasantry were important factors in the turn of the German ruling classes from Social-Democracy to fascism.

With similar demagogic, chauvinistic, reactionary, " anti-capitalist " slogans, such as " Against greedy capital," " Abolish department stores," etc., the fascist movement succeeded in attracting the urban petty bourgeoisie, which the crisis had abandoned to ruin : artisans, small shopkeepers, intellectuals, as well as the very numerous "new middle classes" : government officials, clerks, office workers, technicians, etc., who comprise almost half the total of actual wage earners in the highly developed capitalist countries.

We cannot give a thorough analysis of fascist demagogy here. Its characteristic features are the unscrupulousness with which absolutely contradictory demands are set up for different groups at the same time, its great flexibility, and its appeals, not so much to the reason, as to the lower instincts of the petty-bourgeois masses.

A constituent of fascist demagogy common to all countries is the cult of nationalism, of jingoism, the presentation of one's own people as the finest, the bravest, the noblest in the world, and of all other peoples as inferior, second-rate. That is why fascism is almost always a movement of the ruling nation in countries with mixed national groups. This demagogy is intended chiefly for the petty bourgeoisie. The peasant, who never leaves his native village as long as he lives, and falls victim to the " idiocy of rural life," the small-town artisan and small shopkeeper, with their narrow outlook, fixed by the limited extent of their economic relationships, and the government official who knows only the room where he works, are especially susceptible to this narrow-minded patriotism and nationalism! (The big bourgeoisie pretends to be patriotic, but is always ready to change its " fatherland," if business so requires; it is always ready to deliver munitions to any enemy of the fatherland, if only he pays a good price!)

Nationalism and patriotism lead to chauvinism, which is indispensable in the ideological preparation for war and as a counterweight to the revolutionary internationalism proclaimed by the proletariat. In many cases (Germany, Japan) nationalism and chauvinism are bound up with a special

---

[26] See, for example, Darre's book, *Das Bauerntum als Lebensquelle der nordischen Rasse* [*The Peasantry as the Vital Source of the Nordic Race*], Third edition, Munich, 1933.

race demagogy[27] or with anti-Semitism. However, anti-Semitism is not a universal method of fascist demagogy: In Italy, for example, Fascism does not use it. In Poland, only one wing of fascism is anti-Semitic, while Pilsudski and his inner circle are friendly to the Jews. In Palestine there is a big Jewish fascist movement, which is directed against the Arabs and the revolutionary Jewish workers.

Everywhere, fascist demagogy makes use of the existing, historically determined ideology of the petty-bourgeois masses. In Japan, fascist demagogy ties itself to the traditional veneration of the monarch and the military virtues: in Austria, to Catholic fanaticism on one hand, and to German nationalism on the other, etc.

Despite the elasticity of its demagogy, the *fascist movement has nowhere succeeded in penetrating the proletariat of the major industries;* at most it has been able to win over agricultural workers, domestic workers, youths and unemployed (partly because of the material advantages of membership in the Storm Troops). The National-Socialists even tried to call a few strikes, taking part in the Berlin transport strike, but they could make no headway in the industrial working class.

This petty-bourgeois mass basis is fascism's principal weakness. Irresolute vacillations are characteristic of the petty bourgeoisie. Lenin said in this regard:

" . . . the small proprietor, the small master (a social type that is very widely represented in many European countries), who, under capitalism, suffers constant oppression and, very often an incredibly sharp and rapid worsening of conditions of life and even impoverishment, easily becomes extremely revolutionary, but is incapable of displaying perseverance, ability to organize, discipline and firmness. The petty bourgeois, in a "frenzy" over the horrors of capitalism, is a social phenomenon which, like anarchism, is characteristic of all capitalist countries. The instability of such revolutionariness, its barrenness, its liability to become swiftly transformed into submission, apathy, phantasy, and even into a 'mad' infatuation with one or another bourgeois 'fad'—all this is a matter of common knowledge."[28]

And, in fact, the petty-bourgeois following of the National-Socialists in Germany began to waver in the fall of 1932, even before the seizure of power, as the drop in the National-Socialist vote showed. This, and the lack of any influence among the industrial proletariat proper, is the reason why the German big bourgeoisie hesitated so long before handing the government over to Hitler; and why in England, for example, only a few

---

[27] The concept of the "race" is handled according to political circumstances. At one time it is the entire "Aryan" race, which is set aside from all others, especially the "Semites"; at another time it is the "Teutons" who are superior to the Slavs. But since the French are largely descended from the Germanic race of Franks, the Germans are "racially" subdivided in turn, and the "Nordic race" is placed above all the other peoples in the world. For the German fascists the Japanese are a "*noble race*" in contrast to the Chinese, while the Japanese themselves contrast the "yellow race" with the white, the Asiatics with the Europeans, etc.

[28] Lenin, "*Left-Wing*" *Communism, an Infantile Disorder.*

big capitalists support the fascist movement up to the present time. For the very reason that fascism everywhere has its mass basis in the constantly vacillating petty bourgeoisie, and not in the industrial proletariat, *it can never completely replace Social-Democracy as the main social support of the bourgeoisie.* The greater the relative importance of the proletariat of the major industries in a given country, the more is this true.

This explains the efforts of the bourgeoisie, even after it has placed the fascists in the government, to call upon the collaboration of the Social-Democrats at difficult moments, above all upon the reformist leaders of the trade unions. (The P.P.S. in Poland, d'Aragona and Co. in Italy, the negotiations between the Schuschnigg government in Austria and the Social-Democratic leaders, and between the Hitler agents and Wels after the great fascist slaughter of June 30, 1934.)

The fact that the rural and urban petty bourgeoisie serves as the mass basis for fascism, and that fascism makes use of anti-capitalist demagogy in its fight to win the masses, has in some cases led even Communists, as we know, to fail to recognize its character as a tool of finance capital against the proletariat! Fascism was mistaken for an independent class movement of the petty bourgeoisie (the Right wing of the Communist Party of Poland—C.P.P.), and even as a movement of the declassed intellectual *lumpen*-proletariat (Remmele). Inadequate insight into the nature of fascism led to such serious errors as active support of Pilsudski's seizure of power by sections of the C.P.P. Such facts show how successful fascist demagogy is, and how essential it is to have a correct understanding of the class character of fascism in order to fight it successfully. Failure to recognize the real nature of fascism necessarily results in weakening the struggle against it. On the other hand, since the fascization of the bourgeois regime and of the bourgeois parties is a general phenomenon, and the rule of the bourgeoisie often takes on fascist characteristics step by step, the Communist Parties also made the error in many cases (C.P.G.) of stating that a fascist dictatorship already existed, when only an increased fascization of the bourgeois regime was taking place. This, too, necessarily led to a weakening of the struggle against fascism, because the workers said to themselves that this fascism was not so very terrible, so that the struggle was diverted from the real fascist danger.[29]

To sum up : the mass ruin of the petty bourgeoisie in town and country, and the mass unemployment of the intellectuals, employees and the youth, provide the base for the fascist *mass movement.* An unscrupulous and elastic nationalist, chauvinist, and anti-capitalist demagogy, adapted to the separate strata of the population, serves to win the masses. Financial support by a few groups of the ruling classes makes it possible to organise a huge paid machine for propaganda, agitation and terror. Open or dis-

---

[29] The renegades Trotsky and Thalheimer did everything they could to confuse the workers, by calling fascism " Bonapartism " : the rule of a clique which, based on the petty bourgeoisie and the *lumpen*-proletariat, governs against the bourgeoisie!

guised co-operation with the state machinery of force[30] facilitates the terror campaign against the proletariat in general, and against the Communists in particular, even before the seizure of power. The split of the working class by Social-Democracy, the latter's policy of step-by-step surrender, of avoiding every revolutionary class struggle (the theory of the "lesser evil"), the terror employed against the Communists by Social-Democratic cabinets and government officials, in short, the fascization of Social-Democracy (which is most glaringly manifested in defections and desertions to fascism), all pave the way for fascism. The mistakes of the Communist Parties, especially the inadequate or incorrect use of the united front tactic for mobilization of the working masses against the danger of fascism, makes the victory of fascism easier.

But it would be the most fatal error if the counter-revolutionary theory that the victory of fascism is inevitable were to spread through all countries: the theory of a whole "epoch of fascism." This theory is equivalent to denying the general crisis of capitalism and the ripening of the revolutionary crisis. It declares that the struggle against fascism is hopeless, and it demoralises the masses. Therefore it must be combated most resolutely.

Fascism in Power

"In periods of acute crisis for the bourgeoisie," the *Programme of the Communist International* states, "fascism resorts to anti-capitalist phraseology, but after it has established itself at the helm of state, it casts aside its anti-capitalist rattle and discloses itself as a terrorist dictatorship of big capital."[31]

The reader is already familiar with this process of discarding the anti-capitalist trappings, from the history of Italian and German fascism. With Hitler, the toning down of his anti-capitalist phrases began to some extent even *before* the seizure of power. (Hitler's 1928 interpretation of Par. 17 of the National-Socialist party program, according to which only "land *that had been acquired unlawfully*" could (not must!) be subject to confiscation.) On the other hand, it would be quite incorrect to interpret this point in the program of the Comintern as meaning that fascism would discard the "anti-capitalist rattle" *immediately after the seizure of power*. The seizure of power does not yet mean the "consolidation of power." Therefore fascism continues its anti-capitalist demagogy to some extent, even after the seizure of power.

Two opposed processes begin with the fascist seizure of power. On one hand, the swift elaboration and ideological-organizational consolidation of

---

[30] The kind of co-operation with the state machinery of force differs depending on the country. Japanese fascism is very closely connected and interlocked with military circles; we therefore speak of "military fascism" in Japan. In other countries, such as Latvia, it is the conservative, governing parties which are fascisizing the governmental machinery and themselves. This took a special turn in Austria, where the struggle between the two fascist camps —the pro-German, fighting for *Anschluss*, and the pro-Italian, fighting for an "independent" Austria—to some extent undermined the state machinery of force itself!

[31] *Program of the Communist International*, p. 13.

the state machinery of force, which is cleansed of all "unreliable" elements and fused with the fascist party machinery. At the same time, the regime's ability to manœuvre increases as a result of the abolition of the parliamentary system (which had become a fetter) and it becomes more suitable for the thorough-going execution of finance capital's policies. On the other hand, with the seizure of power there begins the disillusionment of the urban and rural petty-bourgeois masses who had been deceived by fascist demagogy, and wait in vain, after fascism's seizure of power, for the fulfilment of its demagogic promises. Fascism's mass base begins to weaken. The big bourgeoisie therefore faces the danger that the disillusioned petty bourgeoisie may swing toward the side of the revolutionary proletariat and take part under the latter's leadership in the revolutionary struggle for the overthrow of the bourgeoisie.

The weakening of fascism's mass base after its seizure of power makes it more difficult to carry out its principal aim, "the destruction of the revolutionary labour vanguard, *i.e.*, the Communist sections and leading units of the proletariat."[32] Fascism is therefore forced to do considerable manœuvring, even after seizure of power, in order to retard the process of its followers' disillusionment, and if possible to isolate the Communist vanguard from the great mass of workers. Here we can mention only the most important forms of these manœuvres:

Providing jobs for their "old" supporters in the state machinery, especially in the machinery of force; favouring their followers in the free professions by displacing the Jews (the *numerus clausus* in Hungary and Germany); preferential employment of unemployed fascist workers and clerks in the factories, and guaranteeing their jobs;[33]

Expanding its mass base by favouring the rich peasants and the richer *middle peasants* at the expense of the great masses of middle and small peasants and the agricultural workers: the hereditary farmstead law, Mussolini's "battle of grain," assigning unpaid farm hands tax concessions, etc.;

Certain concessions to its urban petty-bourgeois followers, at the expense of Jewish shopkeepers and artisans.

As for the proletariat, fascism, once in power, must limit itself, except for high-sounding phrases like "restoration of the honour of labour" and the like, to minor manœuvres (the demonstrative arrest of a few unpopular directors) and petty gifts: lengthening vacations and the period of giving notice for a few categories of workers, cheaper margarine for the unemployed, "winter relief" and "Hitler relief," cheaper moving-picture tickets, etc.—petty gifts, which of course can effect no change in the enor-

---

[32] *Ibid.*

[33] In this way a new type of "labour aristocracy" develops, on the basis of chronic mass unemployment. This consists of workers who in general do not get any higher wage—like the real labour aristocracy—but who have the assurance that they will be the last to lose their jobs, and who therefore betray the working class to the bourgeoisie, serve as strike-breakers, denounce Communists, etc. In contrast to the real labour aristocracy, however, they are very largely isolated from the working masses in the shops, because their role as betrayers of the working class is rather obvious.

mously worsened position of the working class, and which for this very reason can have only a very transitory influence at most on those receiving them.

Once in power fascism immediately sets up a *monopoly of legal ideological influencing of the population*. Schools, the press, radio, movingpictures, the theatre and literature are placed completely in the service of fascist ideology, *i.e.*, in the service of finance capital. All anti-fascist activity, and much more so, all Communist activity, is forbidden; all nonfascist organizations and parties are dissolved. Undoubtedly this monopoly of ideological influence must have a certain effect, especially upon the youth, when it lasts for a long time as in Italy, and is not counteracted by sufficiently strong illegal Communist work among the masses.

This process of setting up the fascist party's monopoly of the government machinery and of all legal political, organizational and ideological activity develops very unequally in different countries, according to the concrete historical conditions. In Italy, where fascism's mass base at the time of the seizure of power was very narrow, this process lasted a very long time. In Poland and Hungary, only the Communist Party is illegal; the bourgeois parties and Social-Democracy adapted themselves to the fascist regime,[34] and are legal, even though often persecuted. In Bulgaria, after various modifications in the regime, the other bourgeois parties were prohibited only this year! The National-Socialist Party's monopoly in Germany of all legal activity was carried out at a very rapid rate by the liquidation of all bourgeois and Social-Democratic organizations.

Needless to say, the prohibition of parties does not destroy the classes they represent nor the latter's struggles, however much the fascists may shriek about the abolition of the class struggle and of " Marxism." The working class continues its class struggle illegally, as well as by using all legal possibilities, predominantly under the leadership of the Communist Parties. The conflict within the ruling classes and the disillusionment of the petty-bourgeois masses—who have been deprived of the opportunity for open expression—appear as the struggles of tendencies and cliques within the fascist party, in many cases—as in Germany on June 30, 1934— turning into a mass murder of their own supporters.[35]

The race between the disillusionment and revolutionizing of the masses, and the elaboration on a party basis of a secure fascist state machinery of force for the suppression of the revolution, is characteristic of fascist dictatorship. The more severe the crisis of capitalism, the less are the possibilities for manœuvring against the working class in general and against fascism's own supporters in particular, and the less willing is the big bour-

[34] The S.P. of Hungary co-operates with fascism by supporting the foreign policies of the fascists, by not organizing the agricultural workers and poor peasants, by leading the trade unions in a strictly reformist spirit and by combating the Communists and delivering them into the hands of the police.

[35] Hitler's mass murders of his own followers, as well as of prominent bourgeois persons such as Schleicher, Klausener, etc., on June 30, 1934, has thrown a severe scare into the petty-bourgeois masses abroad and temporarily deterred sections of the bourgeoisie in other countries (as in England, for instance) from further support of the fascist movement.

geoisie to tolerate " Left " manœuvres. So much more clearly does the character of fascism appear as an unveiled terrorist dictatorship of finance capital, the more does the fascist party take on the character of a " party of order," chiefly supported by the armed forces, and the greater does the role of the Communist Parties become (provided their policies are correct) as the leader of the masses in struggle for the overthrow not only of the fascist form of bourgeois dictatorship, but of bourgeois rule in general.

The fascist form of bourgeois dictatorship is historically the last form of bourgeois rule. A lasting return to the democratic form is made impossible by the increasedly monopolist character of capitalism, by the accentuation of class antagonisms during the period of general crisis (especially conditioned by the end of capitalist stabilization), and by the nearness of war. This does not at all exclude the possibility that in some countries the open fascist dictatorship may be temporarily replaced by a somewhat " more democratic " form of monopoly capital's dictatorship. This is primarily what the Social-Democratic leaders in exile are aiming at. Even after their exile from the country they still try to serve the bourgeoisie as a reserve by nourishing democratic illusions in the working class, and offering it the prospect of automatic " *ruin* " of fascism as a result of the inner contradictions in the camp of the bourgeoisie. They thus endeavour to hold the working class back from revolutionary struggle against fascism, against bourgeois rule. The *émigré* Social-Democratic leaders tell the bourgeoisie rather frankly : " We are always ready to resume our role as a bulwark against the proletarian revolution within the country itself, whenever you offer us the opportunity of doing so."

The Communist Parties in the countries of open fascist dictatorship must therefore continue to wage a struggle on two fronts : against the fascists and against those Social-Democratic leaders who sabotage the revolutionary struggle against the bourgeoisie. With good Bolshevik organization and leadership, this struggle must be victorious, and finance capital's fascist rule of force must be replaced by the dictatorship of the proletariat. The victorious proletarian revolution, under the leadership of the only revolutionary world party, the Comintern, will overthrow the rule of the bourgeoisie, and will free the proletariat simultaneously from the yoke of capital and from the terror of the fascists.

CHAPTER XII

THE FIGHT FOR THE UNITED FRONT
AND VICTORY

Since 1921, in numerous resolutions, the Communist International has stressed the necessity for creating a united front of the proletariat in struggle against the bourgeoisie, instructing the Communist Parties to conduct the struggle for its realization. (The earliest detailed document in this regard is the resolution of the Executive Committee of the Communist International adopted December 18, 1921.[1]) The bases for this were the strivings of the working masses themselves towards unity for struggle, because they correctly ascribed their defeat in the first cycle of revolutions chiefly to the division of the working class, and they wanted to fight unitedly against the new attack by capital.

The resolution referred to above states that

"under the influence of the increasing attacks of capital . . . there has awakened among the workers a spontaneous, literally irresistible striving for unity, which goes hand in hand with the gradual growth of confidence in the Communists among the masses of workers."

It is not our task to give a history of the Communists' struggle for realization of the unity of the working class, and of the tactical errors committed therein. We shall confine ourselves to the most important factors that make the struggle for unity more favourable at present, and are of importance for the prospects of revolutionary victory in the coming second round of revolutions.

The primary difficulty encountered by the struggle for unity of the working class in the first period was that most of the Communist Parties had just been founded, and therefore faced the necessity of demarcating themselves sharply from the reformists, primarily in order to make the workers understand why a new revolutionary party of the proletariat was absolutely essential. This sharp demarcation from the Social-Democrats—the precise formulation of the fundamental conflict between the Communists, as the party of the revolution, and the Social-Democrats, as the party of reform, between the party of struggle for the overthrow of capitalism and the party for the defence of capitalism—was all the more necessary, since remnants of Social-Democratic ideology were still very strong within the Communist Parties themselves, and many former leaders of Social-Democracy had come over to Communism only under the masses' pressure, against their inner conviction.

The Social-Democratic leaders fought the Communist Parties by paint-

[1] " Theses on the united front of the workers and on relations with the workers belonging to the Second, the Two-and-a-Half and the Amsterdam Internationals, as well as with the workers supporting the anarcho-syndicalist organizations."

ing them as splitters, demanding organizational unity as opposed to unity for struggle. They used the correct principle of unity and proletarian discipline as a pretext for demanding that the Communists reunite with the Social-Democrats or at least refrain from all criticism before the broad working-class public, as a pre-requisite for fighting unity—conditions which the Communists could not possibly accept and can never accept.

In the countries where a small Communist Party confronted a large Social-Democratic party (e.g., England, Austria and the Scandinavian countries), the argument was repeatedly advanced that the unity of the working class was already realized in the Social-Democratic party and that the necessary premises for a united front did not exist.[2]

In the period of relative stabilization, the pressure of the workers for unity relaxed somewhat. Exploiting the tactical errors of the Communists, the Social-Democratic leaders had succeeded in strengthening their own ranks and building a wall between the Communist Party and the Social-Democratic workers, by excluding the active Communist workers from the trade unions and expelling many revolutionary workers from their party. The Social-Democratic leaders were aided in their fight against the Communists and against the united front by the Communist Parties' tactical errors : putting the Social-Democratic leaders on a plane with the Social-Democratic workers; calling all the Social-Democrats social-fascists; and slogans such as those issued by Comrade Neumann—" Smash the trade unions," " Smash the A.D.G.B." (German General Trade Union Federation).

Such tactical errors by the Communist Parties originated in a sectarian attitude toward the masses of workers. In many cases the difficulties of work in the trade unions led in practice to the organization in some cases —as a substitute for this work rather than an extension of it—of special revolutionary trade unions, which for the most part did not attain a mass character and made struggle for trade union unity more difficult.

The third period, the great economic crisis, the end of the relative stabilization of capitalism, and more particularly the victory of fascism in Germany and Austria, brought a new sudden intensification of the working masses' drive for unity in the struggle against fascism, and against the rule of the bourgeoisie in general. In 1933, the Social-Democratic leaders already had to initiate new manœuvres because of the mass pressure, although in July, 1932, when the Braun-Severing government of Prussia was expelled by von Papen, and this much-touted " commanding height " of German Social-Democracy was razed by the bourgeoisie with-

[2] As recently as the 1932 convention of the Social-Democratic Party of Austria, Otto Bauer declared (Arbeiter Zeitung, Nov. 15, 1932):

" As far as the united front of the proletariat is realizable at all, it is in Austria already realized in Austrian Social-Democracy. Those who have set about destroying the actually existing unity of the Austrian proletariat in order to negotiate regarding the united front later on . . . are simply swindlers."

Bauer held that only international negotiations, between Moscow and Zurich, were of any use!

out song or ceremony, the S.P.G. refused the C.P.G. proposal for a general strike.

Even now the essence of its manœuvres is the same: *organizational unity instead of unity for struggle,*[3] with renunciation of criticism by the Communists as a preliminary condition for common struggle. Stampfer (as well as Léon Blum) demanded a " non-aggression pact " between the Communists and the Social-Democrats.[4] At the beginning of February, 1933, the Centrist Parties (I.L.P., the Norwegian Workers' Party, the Dutch Independent Labour Party, the German Socialist Labour Party, the French Proletarian Unity Party and the Polish Independent Labour Party) submitted a proposal to the Second International and the Communist International that negotiations be undertaken between the international organizations.

The Communist International, as is known, answered in a manifesto calling on all our parties to make proposals to the Central Committees of the parties affiliated to the Second International for joint, definite actions against fascism and against the offensive of capitalism.[5]

The Second International, in its answer (March 31, 1933), on the contrary, " urgently recommended " its affiliated parties to refrain from all separate negotiations with the Communist Parties in their countries, " because only negotiations between the two Internationals as such can lead to an understanding." In accordance with these instructions the Central Committees of all the Social-Democratic parties rejected the offer of joint struggle, some politely, some rudely.

The meaning of this attitude is clear. The leaders of the Second International are afraid of negotiations in the several countries on concrete issues of struggle, because the Social-Democratic workers, with their in-

[3] Some members of our parties, such as Doriot, Guttmann (both expelled since then) and Merker, acting on this basis, committed Right opportunist mistakes.

[4] This was connected with a veiled attack on the Soviet Union, in that the statement was made that the Social-Democrats were no worse than the governments of capitalist countries with which the Soviet Union concludes " non-aggression pacts."

[5] The E.C.C.I. proposed the following points as a basis:

" (a) The Communists and Social-Democrats are to commence at once to organize and carry out defensive action against the attacks of fascism and reaction on the political, trade union, co-operative and other workers' organizations, on the workers' press, on the freedom of meetings, demonstrations and strikes. They are to organize common defence against the armed attacks of the fascist bands by carrying out mass protests, street demonstrations and political mass strikes; they are to proceed to organize committees of action in the factories, the labour exchanges and the workers' quarters, as well as to organize self-defence groups.

" (b) The Communists and Social-Democrats are to commence at once to organize the protest of the workers, with the aid of meetings, demonstrations and strikes, against any wage reductions, against attacks on the working conditions, against reduction of social insurance, against the cutting down of unemployment benefit, against dismissals from the factories.

" (c) In the adoption and practical carrying out of these two conditions the E.C.C.I. considers it possible to recommend the Communist Parties during the time of common fight against capital and fascism to refrain from making attacks on Social-Democratic organizations. The most ruthless struggle must be conducted against all those who violate the conditions of the agreement in carrying out the united front, as strike-breakers who disrupt the united front of the workers." (*International Press Correspondence*, March 9, 1933, " For the United Front Against Fascism," p. 262.)

tense urge towards unity and struggle, would exercise pressure on their leaders to this end. The gentlemen of the Second International would prefer to negotiate far away from the masses of workers, in genteel bureaucratic seclusion, in order to make an agreement impossible. . . .

In 1934, the crisis of Social-Democracy (which we discussed in the foregoing chapter) led to a break in the Second International's anti-unity front; the French Social-Democratic party was forced, much against the wishes of the Second International's leadership, to conclude the well-known united front agreement with the C.P.F. This was soon followed by the Italian S.P. (which is of little importance in view of the very slight following it possesses in Italy), and by the united front of the Communist Party of Poland with the " Bund." All the other parties, however, stubbornly persist in their refusal, and those participating in bourgeois governments or on the verge of such participation do so with special emphasis.

The most important reasons for the acceptance of the offer of common struggle in France were as follows: the ominous charge of the French fascists on February 6, 1934, which led to the fall of the Daladier cabinet; the French Social-Democrats' fear of sharing the fate of the German and Austrian Social-Democratic parties; the strength of the Paris organization of the C.P.F., and the energy with which our French Party immediately mobilized the workers for a counter-attack against the fascist bands, thus drawing along with them a considerable section of the Social-Democratic workers. *Actually the united front from below had already been established to a considerable extent before the leadership of the French Social-Democratic Party finally decided to accept the offer of our Party for a united front*,[6] placing the leaders of the Second International in an extremely uncomfortable position.[7]

The French example clearly shows that in the present severe political, ideological and organizational crisis of Social-Democracy, the Communist Parties—by placing themselves boldly and decisively at the head of the

[6] The difficult position in which the leadership of French Social-Democracy had been placed is apparent from the report of the *Populaire* on the meeting of the National Party Council on July 15, 1934.

[7] On July 22, the Brussels *Peuple* published an article by Vandervelde (reprinted verbatim by the *Information Bulletin* of the Second International) which clearly reflects the difficult position in which the leaders of the Second International found themselves. Vandervelde writes:

" Let it be understood at the start that I am in complete agreement with Leon Blum, Paul Faure and Lebas *that it would have been morally impossible to decline this proposal flatly* . . . because the initiative for joint action, which was started in Paris after the February days, obviously satisfies the strongest feelings of the masses of workers, at least in the capital . . . but not only must the decision or recommendation of the National Party Council in favour of the united front—which stands ' at the edge of the International '—be immediately justified before the International, but the Socialist and Labour International must at once concern itself with the entire problem. And here one must not be deceived—the matter will doubtless not run so smoothly in the Executive of the L.S.I. as in the National Party Council of the French Socialists."

The remainder of the article is an effort to present the action of our French Party for unity as if it were action, not in the interest of the French proletariat, but of the foreign policy of the Soviet Union. Parenthetically, at the request of the French, discussion of the French question was tabled at the meeting of the Executive of the Second International.

struggle, and by setting up demands and slogans whose correctness is apparent to the working masses—can establish a united front of the working masses from below in the struggle against fascism, in order to realize the slogan of " Class Against Class " *and to compel the Social-Democratic leaders either to join in this united front or under the Communists' criticism to lose the remainder of their authority among the Social Democratic workers.* It is obvious that unity of the proletariat in struggle can and must be established not merely on a political basis but also in trade union struggles which under present-day conditions always tend to turn into political struggles.

The formation of the united front is taking place in a different way in Austria. The defeat suffered by the Austrian proletariat, despite the heroic struggle of the Schutzbundlers and the Communists, finally showed the Social-Democratic workers how incorrect and traitorous was the policy of the " lesser evil " which Renner, Seitz and Bauer continued even after Hitler's victory. The leadership has lost all authority. The Austrian Social-Democratic Party no longer exists as an organizational unit! Its very name is scorned by the workers. The best and most active Social-Democratic workers have joined together in a new illegal party, under the name " Revolutionary Socialists." The disillusionment of these revolutionary workers with their former leaders and their readiness to fight together with the Communists is evidenced in their well-known letter to the leadership of the Second International :

" The fascist dictatorship has smashed all the democratic and reformist illusions of the proletarian masses here. To-day the workers know that the fascists' might can be broken only by the might of the proletariat. . . . The goal of this revolution (for the overthrow of fascism) cannot be other than the conquest of state power, the dictatorship of the proletariat. . . . In the struggle against the fascist dictatorship there is no difference between the socialist workers and their Communist-organized class comrades. They have to endure the same persecutions and sufferings, and, as they have always aimed at the same goal, now, under the fascist dictatorship, there are no longer any antagonisms in the tactics of struggle."

This is the voice of *genuine Left Social-Democratic workers,* who, organized together with their functionaries, are on the road to Communism, who have lost faith in their own leaders but still have illusions with respect to the Second International—illusions that will also disappear rapidly.[8]

[8] The answer that Friedrich Adler " as a private individual " gave the Revolutionary Socialists is in essence a defence of the " policy of the lesser evil."

" One must understand that the labour movement uses two methods side by side, that of revolution and that of reform. One method or the other stands in the foreground, depending on the historic-economic conditions of a country. In fascist countries it is revolution, in democratic countries it is reform. . . . If we undertake a rational division of labour, it will be found that the two methods do not conflict, but complement each other. And thus the unity of action will be realized for each of the two methods."

Instead of calling for the unity of all proletarian forces in struggle against fascism, Adler incites against the Communists libelling us in the most shameless manner, by accusing us of sabotaging the fight against fascism.

" It is not at all surprising that to-day, just as in 1919, many readily wavering elements,

Favoured by the severe crisis in Social-Democracy, the united front of the proletariat against fascism and against the rule of the bourgeoisie is being achieved in unrelenting struggle against those leaders of the Second International who are indissolubly linked with the bourgeoisie, and in the interests of capital *either strive to perpetuate the split of the working class or to realize unity in the form of organizational liquidation of the Communist Parties.* (Otto Bauer's article for another Hainfeld![9].) Initial successes have been obtained but the struggle for a united front must be continued for a long time to come, with great patience, persistence and elasticity. With the Communist vanguard alone, without the united front of the proletariat, *without mobilizing the great masses of Social-Democratic and non-party workers for the struggle to overthrow bourgeois rule, victory in the second round of revolutions now beginning is impossible!* The unity of the working class in struggle is not merely the premise for successful defence against fascism, but also for the victory of the proletarian revolution as a whole!

If the fight against the bourgeoisie is to be successful, the unity of the working class in struggle must be established not only in the political sphere, but in the trade union field as well. It was never the aim of the Communists to establish special revolutionary trade unions. This was forced upon them by the trade union bureaucracy which had formed a united front with the bourgeoisie and was systematically expelling the revolutionary workers from the trade unions with utter disregard for trade union democracy. In this field, therefore, it would be possible to overcome the split at once through organizational reunion, provided the class struggle character of the trade unions is insured! Although the Communist Parties' relinquishing of their independence is out of the question of course, we have no objection in principle to an organizational merger of the trade unions, because the trade unions are fighting organizations of the whole working class, irrespective of the political views of the individual workers. . . .

*   *   *   *   *

The bourgeoisie and the proletariat are both preparing for the second round of revolutions on the basis of their experiences in the first. The factor of surprise (in the historical meaning of the word), which played a part in the first round, is now excluded. The seventeen-year history of the Soviet Union has eliminated faith in the invincibility of bourgeois

stunned by the events, go over to the Communists. If they were then motivated by the fantastic hope of the impending world revolution, now it is the boundless despair over the defeat we have suffered which is driving them into the arms of the Bolshevik belief in miracles. I can only say that, just as in 1919 I considered the Bolshevik perspective false, to-day I am convinced that it is a dreadful misfortune for the international labour movement *that the Bolsheviks still do not understand the conditions of struggle in the democratic countries,* and that, trapped by the delusion that fascism must be victorious everywhere, they themselves contribute to its advance by making the defensive struggle of the workers' parties more difficult—yes, and by sabotaging it.''

The revolutionary Austrian Social-Democratic workers did not succumb to the blandishments of this slanderer.

[9] The 1892 unity convention of the Austrian workers' parties.

rule, the belief that the capitalist order of society is the only possible one, the belief that the proletariat is not able to govern a country. To-day the bourgeoisie in all countries knows that in the second round of revolutions it must fight for its life.

The first round of revolutions developed out of the World War. (The Russian Revolution, which was rapidly maturing even before the outbreak of the World War, is perhaps an exception.) Without the World War, the crisis in the ruling classes and the loss of their authority, especially in the defeated countries, would not have occurred at that time. Without the terrible suffering of the War the mass revolt in Europe would not have taken place at that time—and both of these are necessary conditions for a revolution.

" The revolution," Lenin writes, " was imminent in 1914-16, concealed in the womb of war, growing out of the war.[10]

The main and decisive historic difference between the first round of revolutions and the maturing second round is that now the revolutionary crisis is maturing before the second round of wars. It is possible, of course, that the second round of revolutions will coincide with the new world war and be interwoven with it. This is even probable. If the beginning of the world war or of a counter-revolutionary war against the Soviet Union precedes the revolution, undoubtedly the outbreak of the latter will be greatly accelerated. *But war is by no means an essential condition for the beginning of the second round of revolutions,* as it was in the first round. The circumstance that the revolutionary crisis is now maturing before the war, without war, is a consequence of the accentuation of antagonisms in the period of the general crisis of capitalism, a consequence of the extraordinarily severe economic crisis of the last five years. Viewed historically, the conditions for a victory of the proletarian revolution in the coming second round are therefore much more favourable than they were in the first round, even though there are a few unfavourable factors. Let us first consider the latter.

The factor of surprise (as stated above) is eliminated! The bourgeoisie is very consciously preparing for defence against the danger threatening it.

The bourgeois machinery of force, which at the beginning of the first round of revolutions had completely collapsed in the defeated countries and was considerably demoralised in the victor countries as well, is now considerably stronger. Fascization makes it possible to concentrate the power of government in a few hands. Special reliable civil-war formations (secret police, armed fascist bands, etc.) serve in the struggle against the proletariat. This is not true of the armies as a whole (although there are also special civil-war detachments within the armies), which have already lost much of their reliability for the bourgeoisie because of the intensification of class antagonisms, and which in the event of general mobilization would be largely permeated by revolutionary elements. The

10 Lenin, *Collected Works*, Russian edition, " On the Junius Pamphlet," Volume XIX, p. 188.

proletariat itself is disarmed to a great extent, whereas in the first round it still possessed many weapons from the imperialist war.

Finally, the influence that fascism temporarily exercises over large sections of the rural and urban petty bourgeoisie, instilling a counter-revolutionary spirit in them and mobilizing them on the side of the bourgeoisie against the proletariat, is also an unfavourable factor.

But these unfavourable factors are outweighed by much more favourable factors.

The Revolutionary Role of the Soviet Union

The decisive factor among the favourable prerequisites for the victory of the proletarian revolution in the second round is the greatly increased revolutionizing role of the Soviet Union.

During the first round of revolutions the Soviet Union had to cope with the greatest economic difficulties, partly because of the War and the Civil War, and partly because of the inevitable " overhead costs of the revolution." That was the time when the world proletariat was called on for famine relief for the Soviet Union. Although the world proletariat energetically supported the Soviet Union in its struggle against intervention, the bourgeoisie and the Social-Democrats were able, none the less, to take advantage of the Soviet Union's serious economic situation. The slogans of the bourgeoisie : " It is impossible to keep production going without the bourgeoisie! " " The dictatorship of the proletariat means hunger and suffering! " did not remain without effect on the less class-conscious workers, checking the development of the prerequisite subjective conditions for a revolutionary crisis.

Now the situation has fundamentally changed. *The Soviet system has proved its superiority in the struggle of the two systems.* In the capitalist world, crisis and serious depression, the decline of production below the pre-war level; in the Soviet Union, the increase of production at the most rapid rate. In the capitalist world, chronic mass unemployment; in the Soviet Union, shortage of workers. In the capitalist world, mass ruin of the peasantry and degradation of agriculture; in the Soviet Union, the rise of the working peasantry on the basis of collectivization and the rapid development of agriculture. Under capitalism, cultural decay everywhere; in the Soviet Union, mighty cultural progress. Under capitalism, the inescapable impoverishment of the masses; in the Soviet Union, joyous work on the clearly outlined road towards a classless society!

Under these conditions, the example of the Soviet Union has an incomparably greater revolutionizing influence than during the first round of revolutions, on the industrial workers, as well as on the exploited sections of the peasantry throughout the entire world.

The Crisis in Social-Democracy

The second decisive factor is the crisis in Social-Democracy. Without the latter's aid it would have been impossible for the bourgeoisie (outside of Russia) to overcome the revolt of the masses during the first round. By soothing the masses of workers with fine phrases about socialization, and by taking over the government, promising (and in part carrying out) various social reforms, it gave the bourgeoisie the respite it needed to re-organize its machinery of force. By splitting the working class and isolat-ing the revolutionary Communist vanguard from the great masses of the workers, it enabled the bourgeoisie to repress the revolution by force.

Owing to the severe crisis in Social-Democracy (see the preceding chapter) its influence is to-day much less than it was, with the exception of a few North European countries, and it is generally on the down-grade. In the next round it will by no means be able to play its counter-revolutionary role as the support of the bourgeoisie with the same success as in the first round. The more successful the Communist Parties are in their struggle for the united front, the less successfully will it be able to play this role.

The Change in the Nature of the Revolutionary Movement in the Colonies

During the first round of revolutions, the colonial revolutions deve-loped almost exclusively under the hegemony of the bourgeoisie (Kemal-ism, Gandhi-ism, the Kuomintang under the leadership of Sun Yat-sen). In the colonial revolutions during the first round on the whole the pro-letariat played the role of a force subordinated to the bourgeoisie. Now the situation has fundamentally changed. The revolutionary struggles of the colonial peoples for emancipation are developing on the widest front, in South and Central America, as well as in Asia, taking on more and more the character of class struggles not only against the imperialists, but also against the national exploiters—the feudal landlords and the bour-geoisie—who for their part turn more and more to the imperialists for protection against the revolting peasant masses.

Hegemony in the struggle for national liberation is shifting to the prole-tariat more and more. Communist Parties, trying to assure the hegemony of the proletariat in the movement, have arisen in almost all the colonies. Although the development of the subjective factor still lags far behind that of the objective factors of revolution, this change in the nature of the colonial liberation movement is nevertheless one of the most important factors making the outlook for a victory of the proletarian revolution in the coming second round more favourable than it was in the first.

This change in the character of the colonial liberation movement is re-inforced by the successes of Soviet China in repulsing all the attacks of the better-armed Kuomintang troops, supported by the imperialists, and in improving the condition of the working masses. (See Chapter IX.)

The Revolt of the Peasantry in the Capitalist Countries

The agrarian crisis, which was scarcely mitigated by the transition to the depression of a special kind, led to a widespread revolt of the peasant masses. With the help of the fascist movement, the bourgeoisie has suc-ceeded for the time being in diverting this revolt, which is really directed against capitalism, into a counter-revolutionary channel. But since the bourgeoisie and its fascist tools can in no way prevent the mass ruin of the toiling peasantry, it is primarily up to the correct work of the Communist Parties to turn these peasant masses, now in motion, into a revolutionary force, as the Russian Bolsheviks did. That the peasantry has entered into such tremendous activity is a favourable circumstance to the revolution.

THE PROGRESS OF THE SUBJECTIVE FACTOR OF THE REVOLUTION

The main reason for the defeat of the proletariat outside of the Soviet Union during the first round of revolutions was the weakness of the Communist Parties, which in part were sects without any mass influence, or (in some countries) mass parties with strong Social-Democratic vestiges. In many cases they were headed by persons who had come over to Communism temporarily, under the proletariat's pressure, and who returned to the camp of the proletarian revolution's enemies when the first wave of the revolution subsided. The Communist Parties did gain in experience during the first round itself, making advances towards Bolshevization. But the progress in the development of the subjective factor during the revolution itself could not catch up with the impairment of the objective conditions for revolution. This was the principal reason for the defeat of the proletarian revolution in the first round.

One of the decisive factors for the better prospects of victory in the impending second round of revolutions is the process of Bolshevization that has taken place in the Communist Parties during the last ten years. Although in many countries the Communist Parties still are very weak, and although there are still many inadequacies in several fields, particularly in work in the trade unions, in winning over the middle sections and in carrying out the struggle for unity, *it nevertheless cannot be doubted that the Communist Parties of to-day are somewhat different qualitatively from the Communist Parties in the first round.*

But even to-day, despite this progress of the Communist Parties in Bolshevization, the development of the subjective factor still lags behind the development of the objective prerequisites. This is the reason why the proletariat has not succeeded in fighting through to the revolutionary way out of the economic crisis.

The revolutionary crisis is continuing to mature. But victory, the prerequisite conditions for which are much more favourable objectively than in the first round, depends primarily on the Communist Parties. *Victory must be fought for!* That is why we want to call Stalin's words to mind:

> " Some comrades think that as soon as a revolutionary crisis occurs the bourgeoisie must drop into a hopeless position, that its end is predetermined, that the victory of the revolution is assured, that all they have to do is to wait for the bourgeoisie to fall and to draw up victorious resolutions. This is a profound mistake! The victory of revolution never comes by itself. It has to be prepared for and won. And only a strong proletarian revolutionary party can prepare for and win victory. Moments occur when the situation is revolutionary, when the rule of the bourgeoisie is shaken to its very foundations and yet the victory of the revolution does not come, because there is no

revolutionary party of the proletariat sufficiently strong and authoritative to lead the masses and take power. It would be unwise to believe that such 'cases' cannot occur." [11]

It is probable that in many countries the struggle for power during the next imperialist war will be very closely interwoven with it, in the form of changing the imperialist war into a civil war. The tasks of the Communist Parties will be tremendous and complicated. But the most important task is *to overcome the split in the working class, to establish the united front against the bourgeoisie. If this succeeds, the victory of the proletariat during the coming second round of revolutions and wars seems assured in a number of countries!*

[11] Stalin, Report to the Seventeenth Congress of the C.P.S.U., *Socialism Victorious*, p. 16.

SUPPLEMENT

Computation of Surplus Value in American Industry

The data of the periodic census afford the opportunity of approximately computing the rate of surplus value in American industry. The following are available as elements in this computation:

Total wages paid $= v$.
Cost of raw material $=$ circulating c.
Cost of wear and tear of machinery $=$ fixed c
Value of products $= w$.

For exact computation the following are lacking:

1. The value of wear and tear of that part of fixed capital invested in buildings; but this part is so comparatively slight that it can be neglected in this necessarily rough computation.

2. One very important element is missing, however, *i.e.*, the total commercial profit, which constitutes a split-off part of the surplus value produced in industry. For according to the Marxian theory of value, industrial capital does not turn commodities over to commercial capital at the full production price, but below it, at a price enabling commercial capital to realize the average rate of profit on its own capital by selling the commodities at their production price. Hence, the profit of commercial capital is therefore contained in the surplus value produced in industry, and, therefore, if one is to find the actual rate of surplus value, it must be added to the surplus value produced in industry. But the data necessary for that purpose are not available.

The rate of surplus value computed in the table below is therefore considerably lower than it actually is in reality.

With these reservations in mind the following table can be computed:

	I Total Wages ($= v$)	II Cost of raw material ($=$ circulating c)	III Wear and tear of machinery ($=$ fixed c)	IV ($= I + II +$ $III + V$) Value of products ($= w$)	V Total Surplus Value ($= m$)	VI ($= \frac{V}{I}$) Rate of Sur- plus Value (per cent.)
1899 ...	2,008	6,576	250	11,407	2,573	128
1904 ...	2,610	8,439	330	14,618	3,239	124
1909 ...	·3,427	12,065	500	20,450	4,458	130
1914 ...	4,068	14,278	600	23,988	5,042	124
1919 ...	10,462	37,233	1,600	62,042	12,747	122
1921 ...	8,202	25,321	1,400	43,653	8,730	106
1923 ...	11,009	34,706	1,800	60,556	13,041	118
1925 ...	10,750	35,936	2,300	62,714	13,748	128
1927 ...	10,849	35,133	2,300	62,718	14,436	133
1929 ...	11,621	38,550	2,600	70,435	17,664	158
1931 ...	7,226	21,420	2,100 [12]	41,333	10,587	147

[12] The decrease in the amounts set aside for amortization of machinery reflects (as in 1921) the decrease in prices of machinery as well as reduced actual amortization as a result of the standstill of large parts of the production apparatus.

Data expressing the total value of the machinery utilized in industry were available for computing the depreciation of machinery[13]:

(Millions of dollars)

1900	1904	1912	1922
2,541	3,298	6,091	15,783

In accordance with commercial usage we have assumed a yearly depreciation of 10 per cent. of the value, extending the data by interpolation to the years not given, under the basic assumption that the value of machinery rises more rapidly than the value of production, corresponding to the rise in the organic composition of capital.

In studying this table, the major fact deduced is that the 100 per cent. rate of surplus value accepted by Marx (which was generally declared to be quite exaggerated) is exceeded in American industry. At the same time it must be emphasized again and again that this rate of surplus value is lower than it actually is, since commercial capital's share in profits, which is also produced in industry, is not expressed here.

We expressly emphasize that *this is merely a very rough attempt at an approximate determination of the rate of surplus value on the basis of inadequate data, doubtless deviating considerably from actual reality.* We can only say that this deviation tends towards too low a figure for the actual rate of surplus value.

13 Taken from the government publication, *Wealth, Public Debt, and Taxation*, p. 18, 1922.